IMAGES
of America

STURGIS
SOUTH DAKOTA

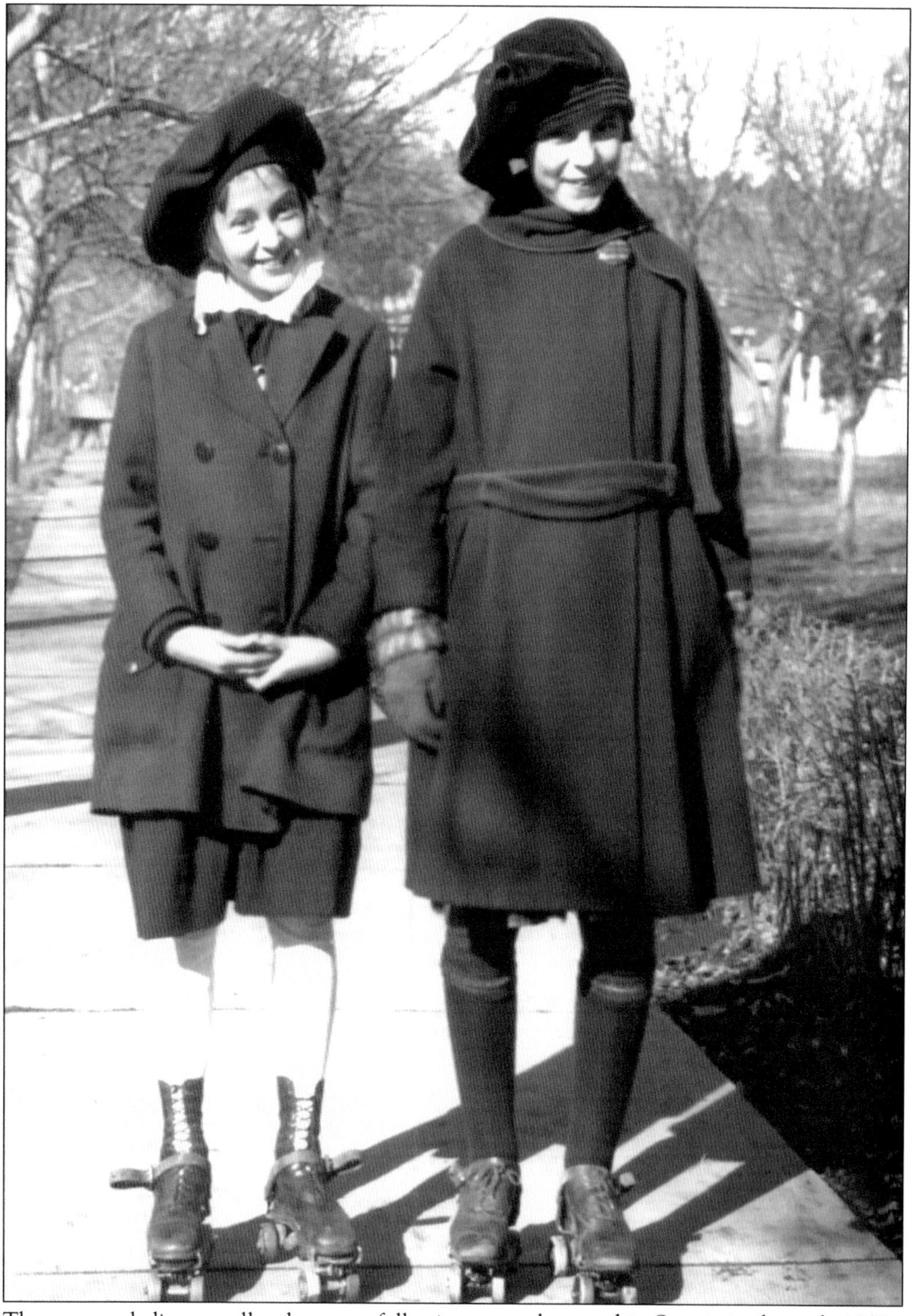

These young ladies on roller skates are following a popular trend in Sturgis in the early 1900s. Sturgis had a roller rink for many years that provided hours of entertainment for city residents and also for soldiers and their families from nearby Fort Meade. In the background is the Junction Avenue neighborhood.

IMAGES
of America

STURGIS
SOUTH DAKOTA

Bev Pechan
for the Sturgis Area Arts Council

ARCADIA
PUBLISHING

ISBN 978-0-7385-3171-7

Published by Arcadia Publishing
Charleston, South Carolina

Printed in the United States of America

Library of Congress Catalog Card Number: 2003109371

For all general information contact Arcadia Publishing at:
Telephone 843-853-2070
Fax 843-853-0044
E-mail sales@arcadiapublishing.com
For customer service and orders:
Toll-Free 1-888-313-2665

Visit us on the Internet at www.arcadiapublishing.com

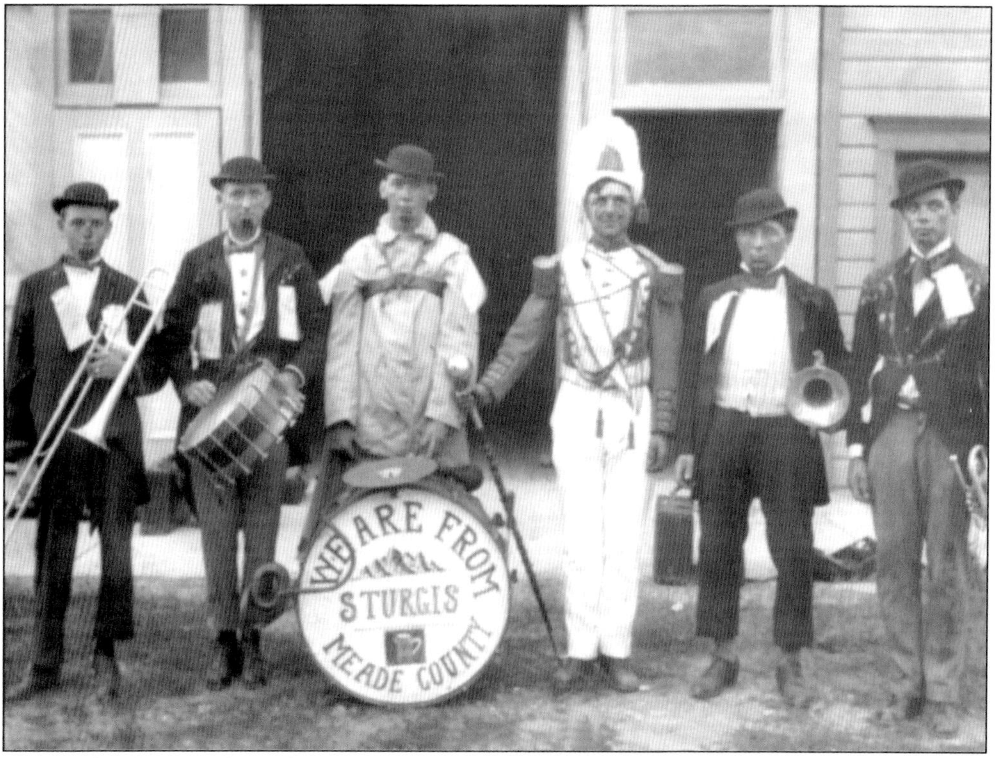

Not much is known about this German band, but it's quite certain they were an "entertaining" group. Sturgis boasted of several fine musical organizations, beginning with its earliest days, and the trend continues today.

Contents

Acknowledgments		6
Introduction		7
1.	The Early Days	9
2.	Fort Meade	17
3.	Main Street and More	31
4.	Taking Care of Business	51
5.	Around the Town	61
6.	Familiar Faces	79
7.	A Day at the Races	95
8.	What's a Fella to Do?	103
9.	Back at the Ranch	115

ACKNOWLEDGMENTS

Putting together a compilation of photos and local history is always a fascinating challenge. The trick is often to make the finished product pleasing, palatable, and interesting while staying within an allotted word count. As the reader would expect, such an undertaking requires lots of effort by a lot of people: research, requests, interviews, correspondence, coordinating, and so much more is involved in gathering, selecting, and finally presenting the end result.

Sturgis is 125 years old this year (2003), and generations following those first settlers remain here. Many have generously shared special photos and memories from their family albums with us for this book, and the author, book staff, and members of the Sturgis Area Arts Council—sponsors of this volume—would like to thank the following contributors: Old Fort Meade Museum; Mary Lou Davis; PEO; Ernie Miller; Kathy Grant; Edna Long; Vivian and Leonard Herbst; Leona Bruch; Dale and Mary Ann Stroschein; Bob Lee; Bob Williams; Doris Sparks Clarke; Pearl Hoel; First United Methodist Church archives; Ramona and Walt Saubers; Dorothy Allison; Janice Feaney; Grace Lutheran Church; Rita Schwartz; Diana Hayes; Doris Forbes; Angie Schemmel; Thelma "Toots" Mayer; Jeanne Bachand; Jeannie Blair; Kay Snyder; Alva and Irene Roberdeau; Sarah Murray; Ernest Conway; Anna Hendrickson; Louise Rogers; John Kenoyer; Bob and LaVonne Holland; Marvell Means; Gunner Earley; Masonic Olive Branch Lodge #47 AF and AM; Sturgis Women's Literary Club; Dorothy Short; Chuck Tribby; Babe Pelkey; Bob Grams; Community Memorial Hospital Auxiliary; Dorothy Hamm; Margie Jones; Mark Lee; Black Hills Health Care System (part of VAMC); VAMC Community Affairs; First Western Bank—Greater Sturgis Foundation; Bob Regan; Sylvia and Joe DesJarlais; Marget McNenny; Bob Murphy; Barb Lutz; Ross Lamphere; Carol Walker; Twyla Hefner; Connie Gray; Erwin Hartmann; Francie Ruebel Alberts; Dorothy Getsgo; Deloris Koch; Gertrude Hutter; Delayne Kinney; and special thanks to pioneering photographer Bill Groethe for the motorcycle rally shots; Maurie LaRue, who tirelessly scanned all of the photos used in this book; and to Dorothy Pulscher and Dode Lee of the arts council who gathered and catalogued the hundreds of images we finally selected from.

Bev Pechan

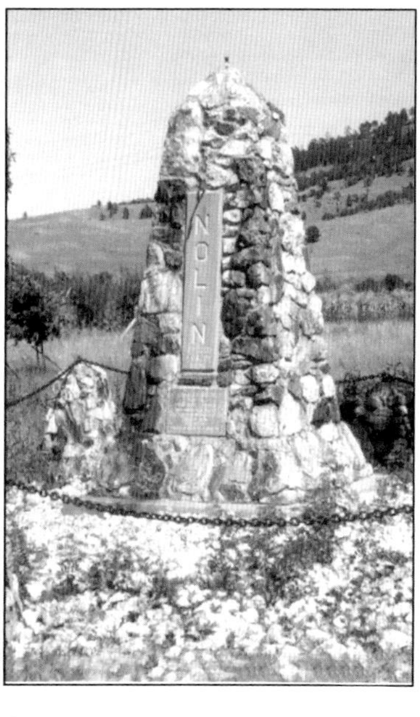

INTRODUCTION

Welcome to Sturgis! Each Black Hills community has its own special identity, and though the region was settled almost overnight with the discovery of gold, some towns fared better than others. Sturgis is one of those success stories.

When Fort Meade was located—actually, it was the third military presence in the region in about as many months—it was only natural that a town would spring up nearby to provide goods and services to the soldiers and also to provide their entertainment. In July 1878, Camp J.G. Sturgis was located in the shadow of Bear Butte by the remaining troopers of George Armstrong Custer's Seventh Cavalry, following the battle at the Little Big Horn on June 25, 1876. The placement of a fort at the edge of the Black Hills was to protect settlers and miners in the vicinity and to guard the bull trains that passed regularly on the trail from the Missouri River at Fort Pierre with supplies headed for the gold camps. The Sioux Indians had relinquished the Black Hills the year before. The tent encampment soon moved south and west to a supply camp named Camp Ruhlen, and it was from this location that materials were supplied for the permanent post named for Civil War General George Gordon Meade.

The first known occupant of the area was George Bosworth, who arrived in the summer of 1877 and claimed a section referred to as the Bosworth Addition. A Mrs. Beck also was reported to have claimed a piece of ground prior to the location of the townsite; later selling it to William McMillan, and there is mention of a Henry Schulz and Frank and Louise Meyers who arrived that summer. On October 25, 1878, the town of Sturgis was laid out with the formation of a townsite company under the direction of Jeremiah C. Wilcox, related by marriage to Gen. Samuel D. Sturgis, for whom the new venture was named. Wilcox came by the land through dealings with an attorney named Caulfield and some shares of scrip (Valentine scrip) that originated with an old California land grant transaction. General Sturgis was said to have invested a 20-dollar gold piece in the deal. Sturgis city was officially incorporated in 1886.

In 1880, Sturgis and Fort Meade were a part of Lawrence County. That year, Sturgis had a population of 60; while Fort Meade's residential status was 525 souls, mostly of foreign birth. By 1900, Sturgis had grown to 1,100 in population, and Fort Meade had outlived its purpose.

However, the fort became active again with the onset of World War I and played a vital role in World War II, besides serving as a Civilian Conservation Corps headquarters, a German prisoner-of-war camp, and later and currently, as a Veterans' Administration medical center and South Dakota National Guard training installation.

But early Sturgis was bawdy by all reports. Gambling dens, prostitutes, shootings, and hangings were common enough. Soldiers had paydays with nowhere to spend it and black entrepreneur Abe Hill went head-to-head with fort commander Joseph Green Tilford in litigation that went all the way to Washington as Tilford attempted to clean up the area for law-abiding citizens. Hill lost, but others would take his place—including the odd "Grasshopper Jim" and notorious Poker Alice.

Charles Nolin, a volunteer who carried the first mail by horseback from Sidney, Nebraska via the Spotted Tail Indian Agency and Crook City, Dakota Territory to Deadwood, didn't complete the journey. On August 19, 1876, Nolin was en route to Crook City, when he stopped to visit with Jesse Brown and company, who were camped at Alkali Creek near the Enos Blair property, and was warned not to continue on. Nolin waved, saying the "mail must go through," and rode off. Shots were heard, and later Nolin's arrow-riddled body was found. Strewn around him were the precious letters from home he was so anxious to deliver to the men in the mining camps. Horse thief Curley Grimes likewise met his fate while trying to escape the law along Alkali Creek a few years later.

Sturgis soon prospered, however, as a rich agricultural community, and as a part of present day Meade County, it is the county seat. A rock quarry, sawmills, ice-harvesting operations, and related industry served the needs of early residents for many years. In 1938, a backyard get-together for motorcycle enthusiasts unknowingly began one of the world's largest and most eye-popping spectacles of our time—the Sturgis Rally.

North to south and east to west, Sturgis has had an interesting past. Climb aboard the old wagon and ride along with us for a ways, won't you? You'll be glad you did!

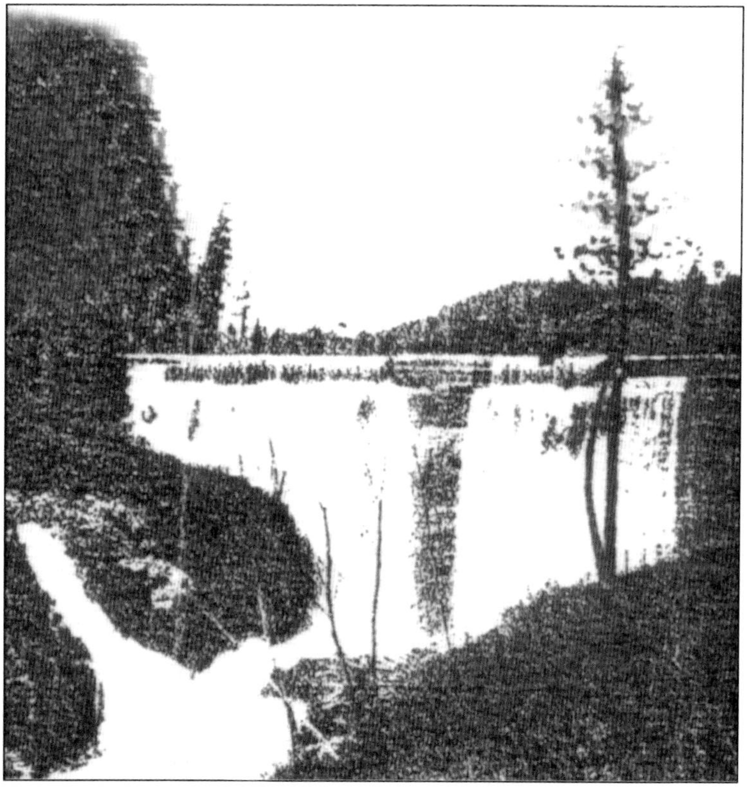

Sturgis Water Works dam, c. 1912.

One

The Early Days

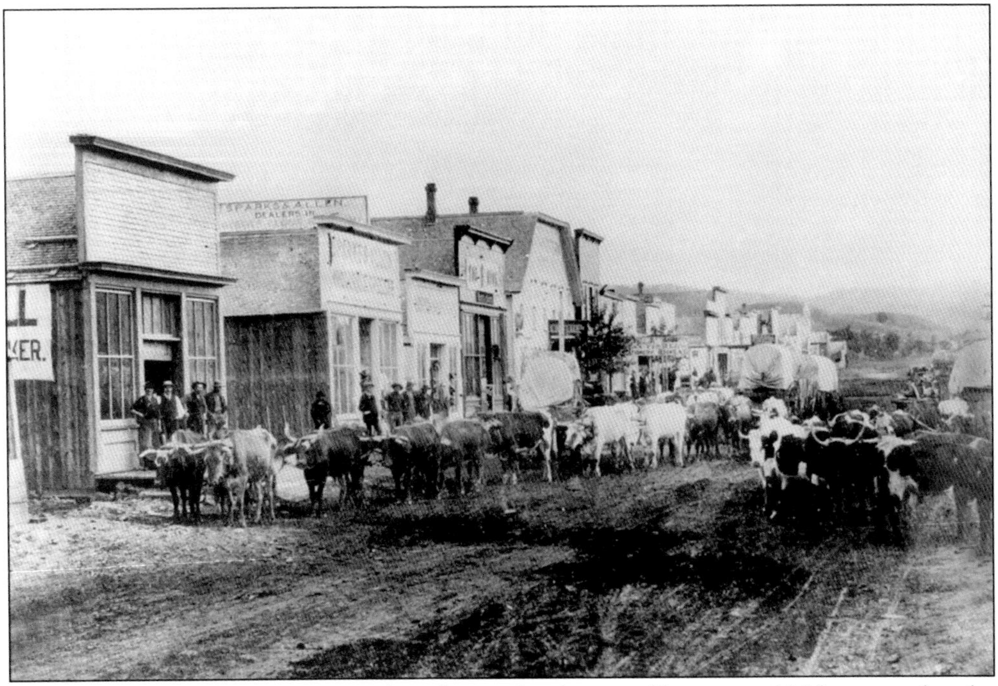

"You ought to see what a town was here last night, 4 trains, 51 wagons, 104 horses and mules and 110 bulls and if you had been listening you might have thought that there was a camp meeting over the way,"—James J. Brown, November 28, 1879.

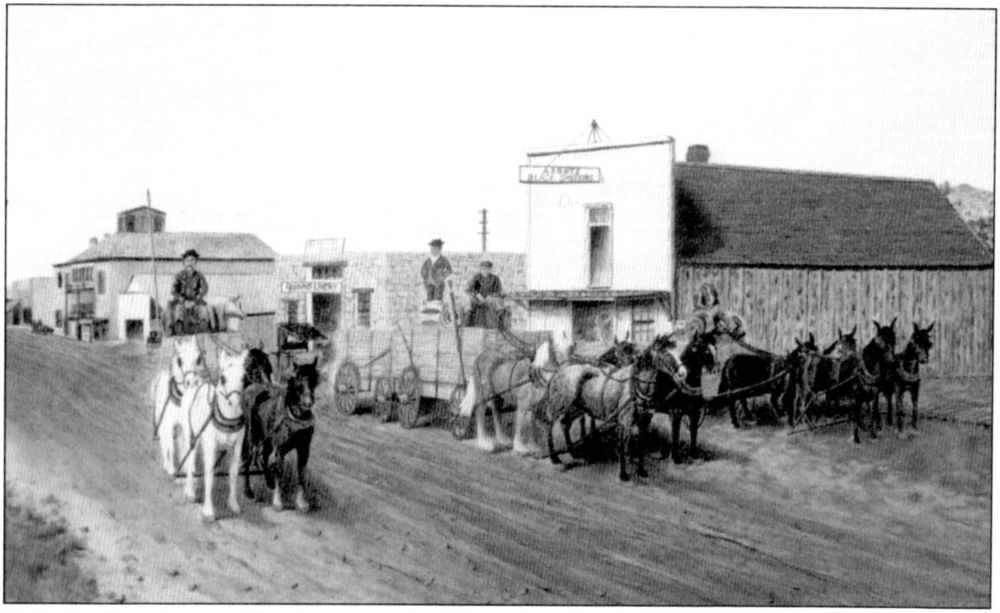

Early day Sturgis was said to have more buildings than Deadwood—or perhaps they didn't have as many fires. "The immense immigration into the valleys to the north of us has made great demand for agricultural implements." *Sturgis Weekly Record*, July 27, 1883.

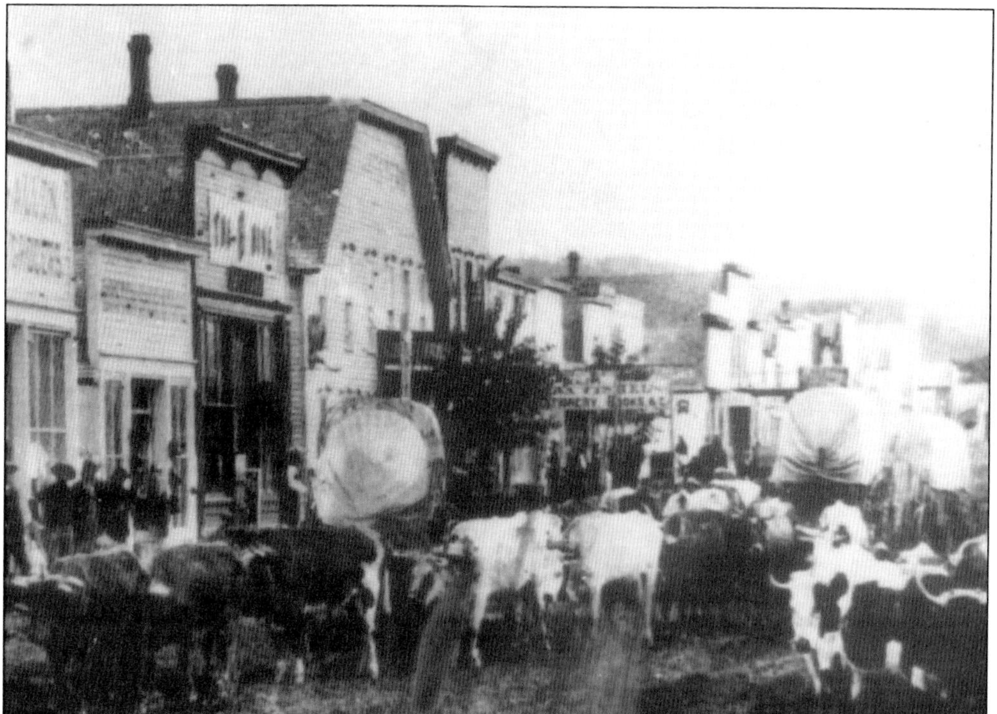

"All the week, the musky bull trains have been coming to town, loaded to the poop decks with machinery and other stuff. . . . It is estimated that 500,000 pounds of freight will be moving toward the hills in a short time." *Sturgis Weekly Record*, July 27, 1883.

This photograph shows one of Sturgis's unique cut stone buildings from rock quarried nearby. In use today as a barber shop at the southwest corner of Junction and Main, businessmen, ranchers, and one of the gentler sex pose for this photo in the late 1800s. The windows reflect hills to the north and a billboard for "The Wizard of . . . "—perhaps a play or show.

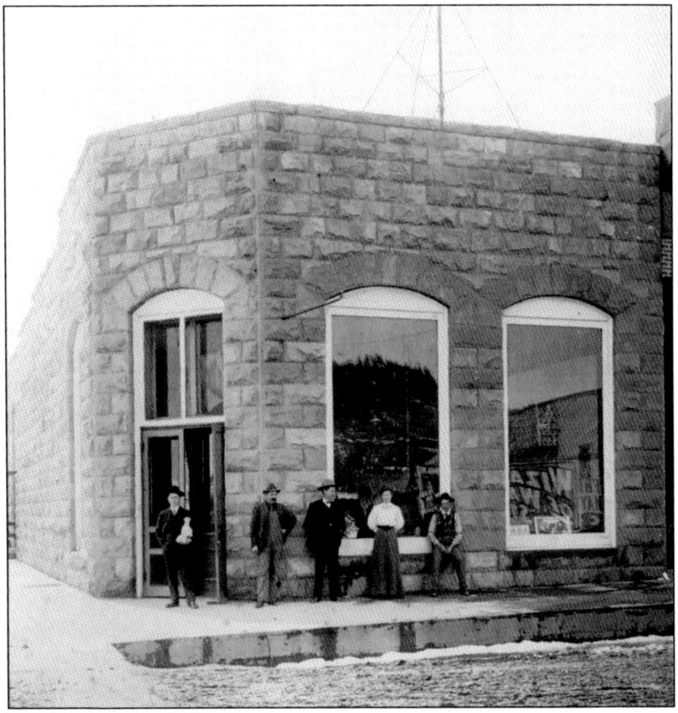

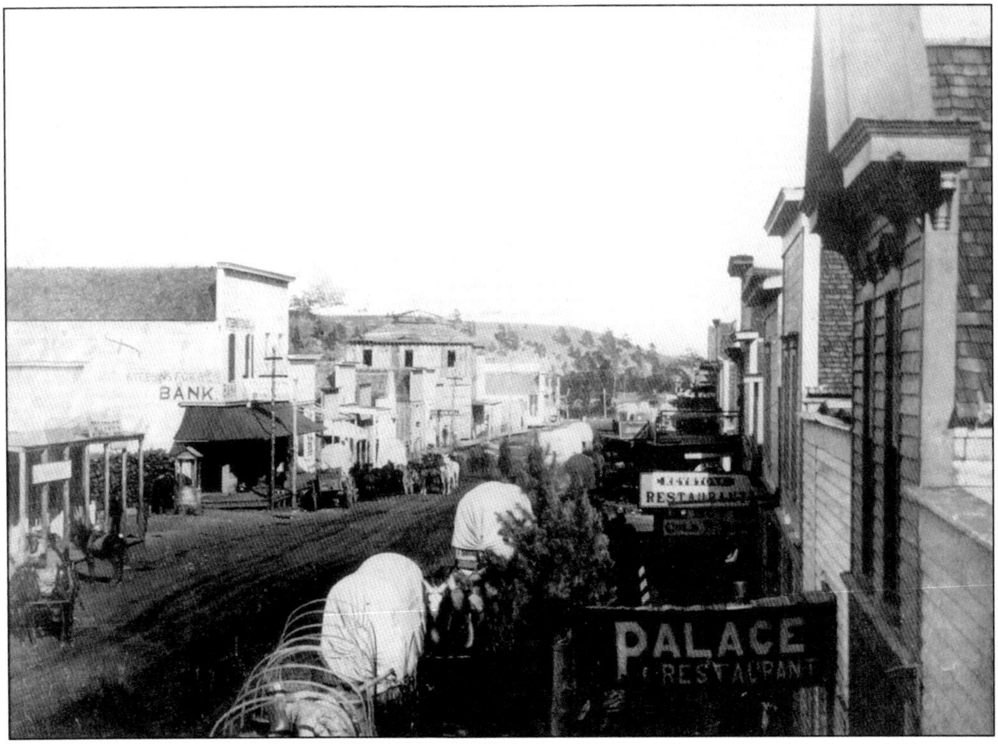

Main Street in 1885 is pictured here. This Ole A. Vik photo shows the Palace and Keystone restaurants in close proximity. Note the interesting kiosk or booth next to the bank on the left and freight wagons on the well-traveled thoroughfare.

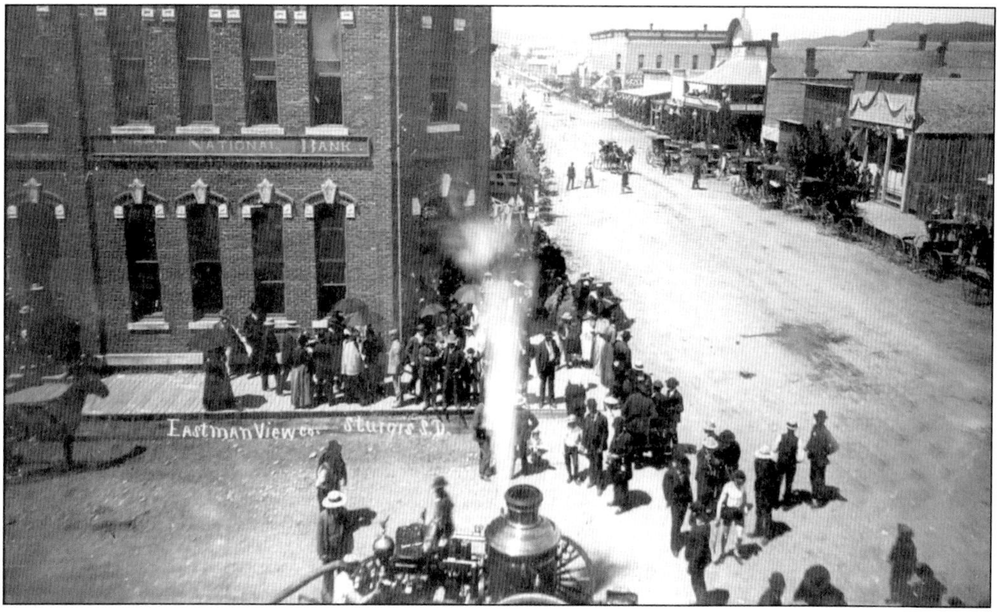

West Main, probably on the Fourth of July, is shown here *c*. 1890. The fire engine has a full head of steam and the half-naked man in the foreground appears to be a race participant. One of the year's biggest events, Fourth of July contests, picnics, fireworks, and concerts drew families from many miles distance—like those seen here arriving from the west. New sidewalks are visible to the far right. The Hooper family band was a popular attraction.

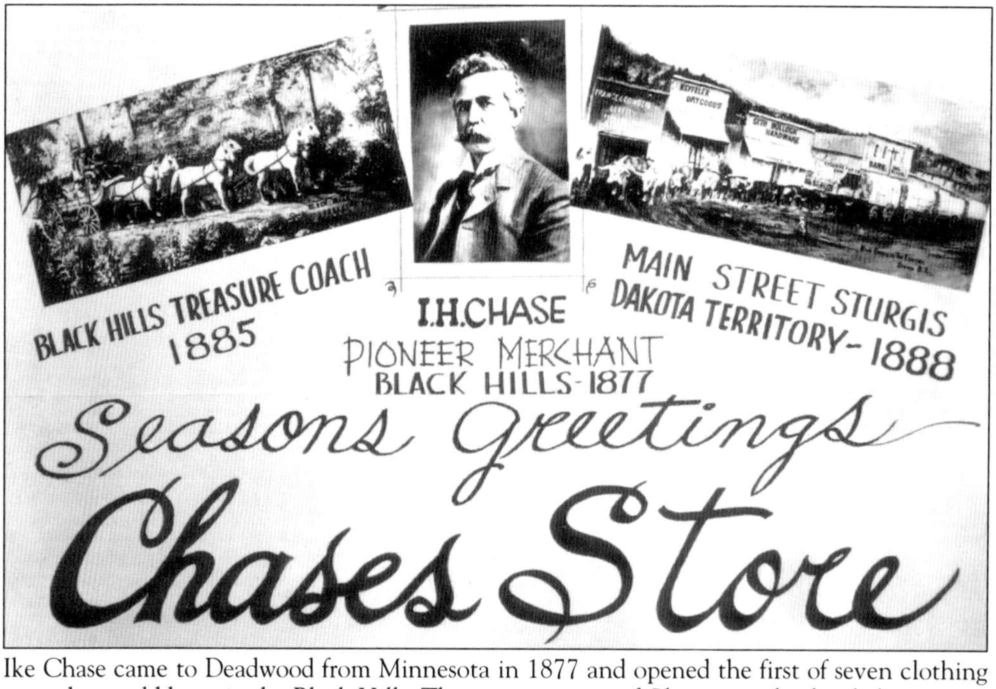

Ike Chase came to Deadwood from Minnesota in 1877 and opened the first of seven clothing stores he would have in the Black Hills. Three generations of Chases ran the family businesses. Ike Sr. moved to Rapid City in 1897 and branched into horse and cattle raising. An early capitalist, he was involved in community affairs.

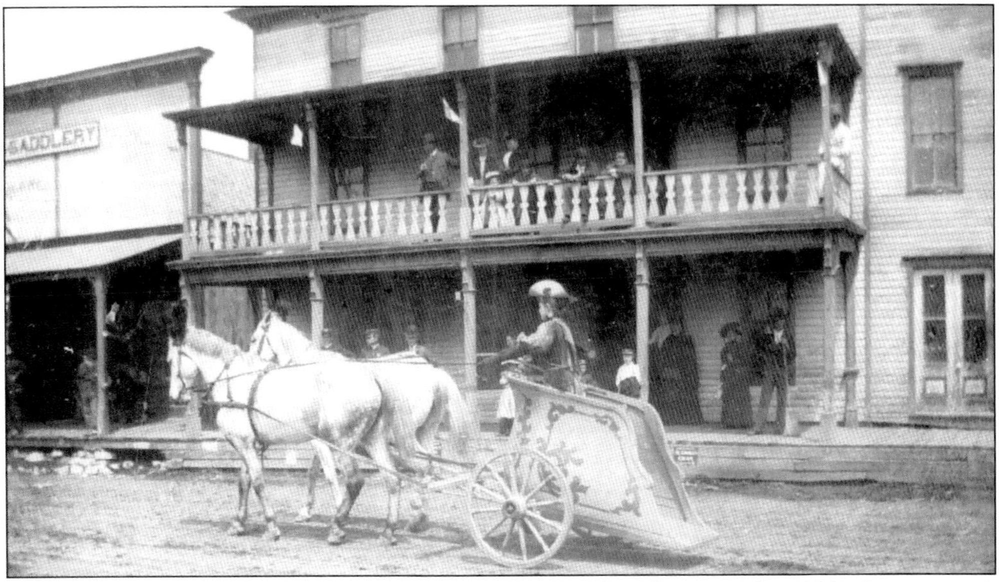

The Commercial Hotel, also known as the Pierson Hotel, is shown in the 1880s. It is anyone's guess what the costumed driver of the Roman chariot may be doing out here in the Wild West. It looks like a speedy trio and may be part of a circus act.

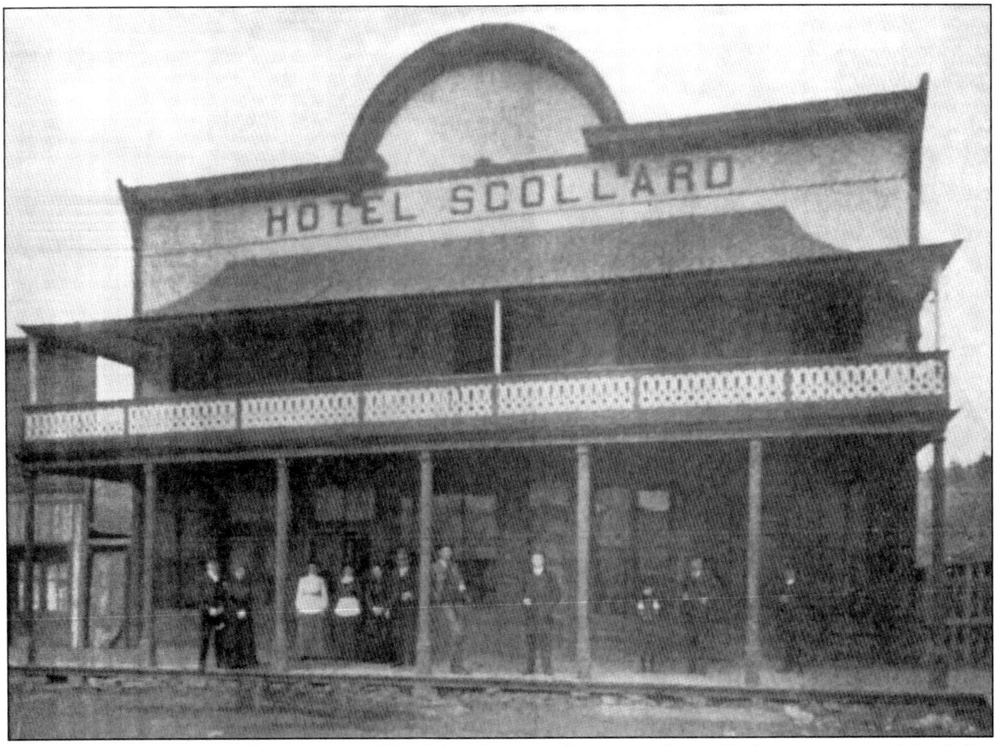

The Scollard Hotel with its noticeable false front is the second establishment opened by John Scollard. One enterprise, called the Northwestern Hotel, was in partnership with Calvin Duke. The building was renamed The Sheridan House and officially opened on January 21, 1879.

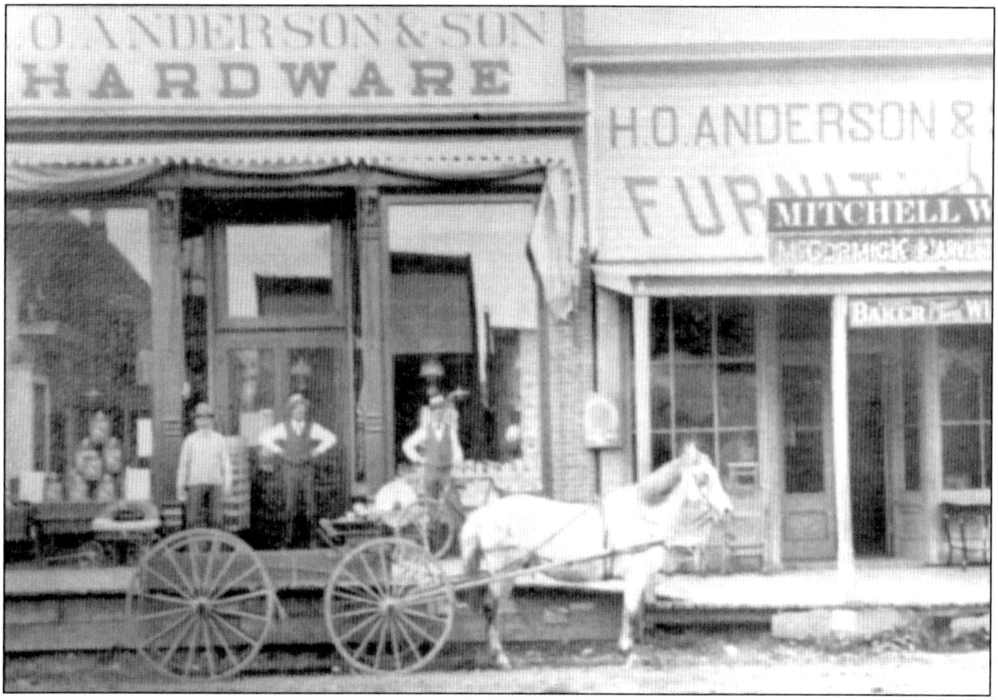

In 1890, the H.O. Anderson & Son Hardware store looked like this. Anderson came to the Black Hills as a miner in 1876, but soon realized that it was the businessman—not the prospector—who would "strike it rich." Traveling to Yankton by wagon, he bought windows, doors, and sashes, and began a millwork plant. He bought Wenke Hardware and expanded many times. In 1905 and 1907, he added a tin shop and a mortuary.

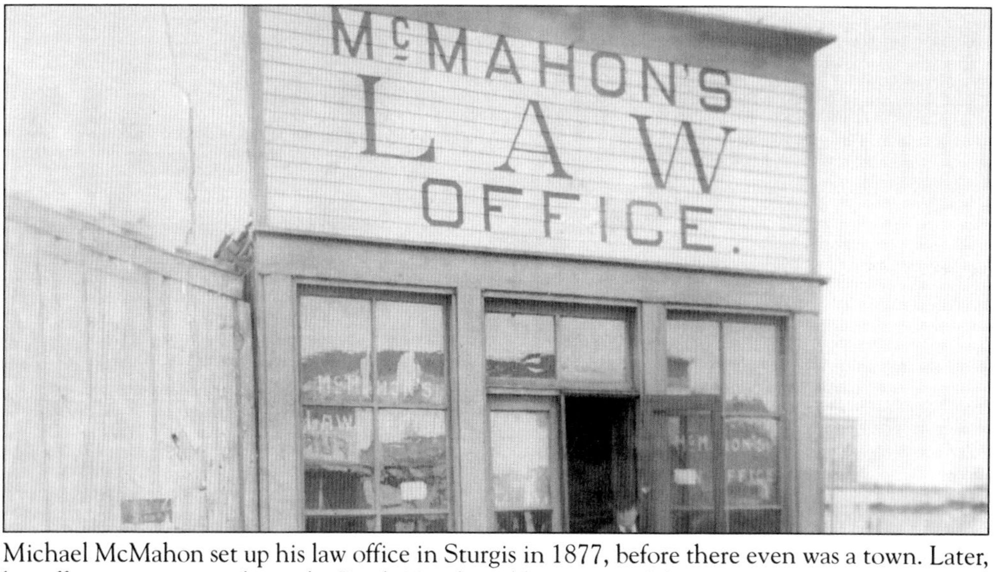

Michael McMahon set up his law office in Sturgis in 1877, before there even was a town. Later, his office was upstairs above the Fruth Hotel, and he practiced for a time in Tilford. McMahon married widow Nellie McPherson and became a law partner with controversial David Thomas. Michael McMahon died suddenly, leaving Nellie emotionally unstable. On July 10, 1910, Nellie borrowed a gun and killed Thomas, suspecting him of mismanagement of affairs.

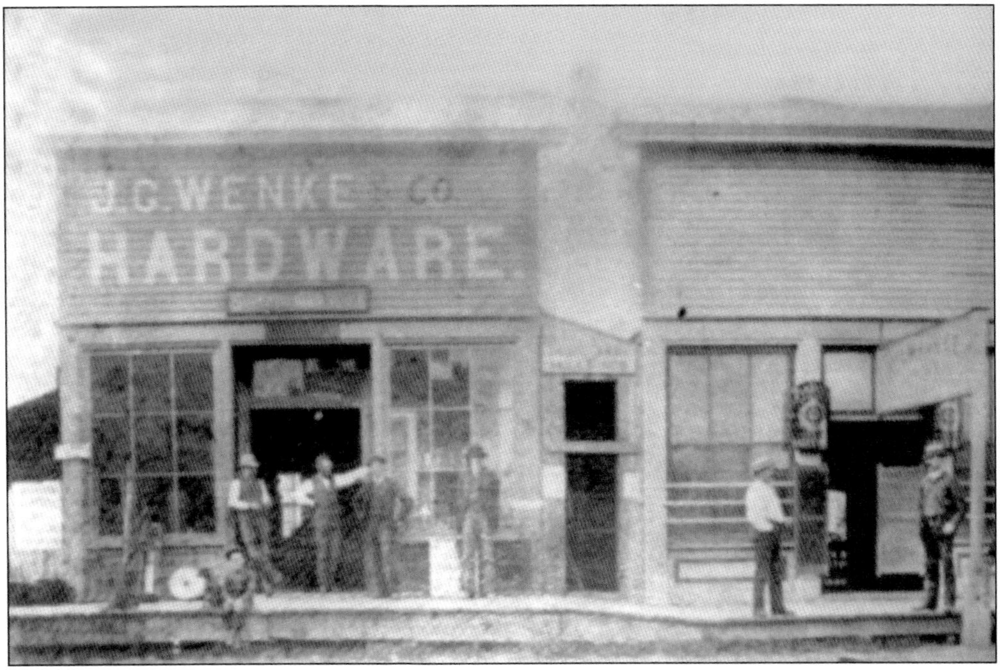

J.G. Wenke came to the Black Hills in 1877 and opened the first hardware store in Deadwood, adding a branch store in Central City that fall. In 1884, Wenke opened another store in Sturgis, managed by H.O. Anderson. He sold the Central City business 10 years later and took over the Sturgis enterprise, selling out to Anderson in 1890. The photo dates to about 1884.

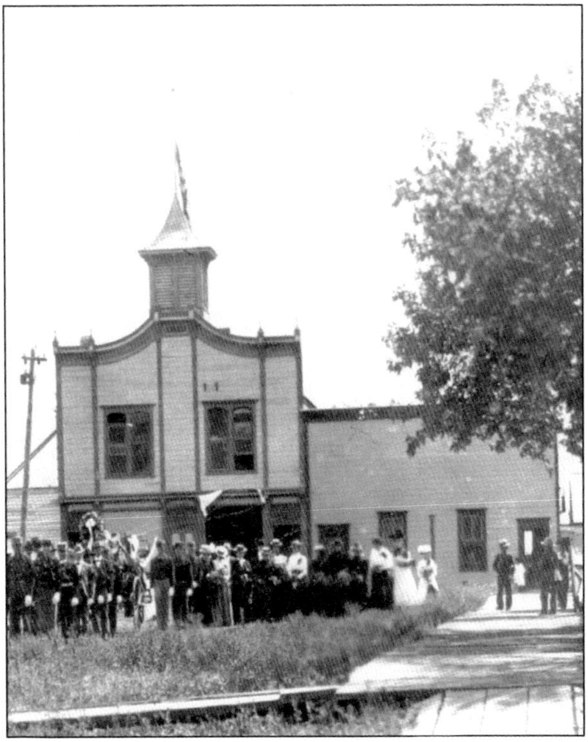

The city hall and boardwalk are seen here on a festive occasion. The ladies are wearing straw sailor hats—a fad of the Victorian era. Firemen and their wheeled apparatus are bedecked in special finery (note the white gloves). Grace Lutheran Church used the hall for services at a later time.

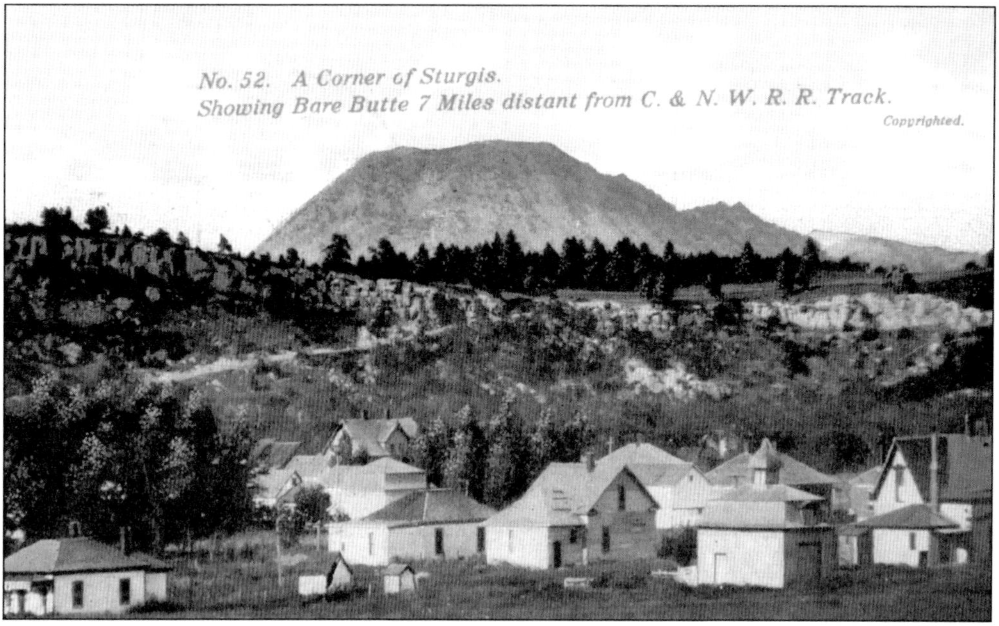

Railroads entering a town most always assured its future. While Sturgis never became a major shipping point, the presence of the Chicago and Northwestern railway, formerly the Fremont, Elkhorn, and Missouri Valley Railroad, brought ranchers to town for supplies. Bear Butte looms in the distance. This postcard from the early 1900s spells it "Bare Butte."

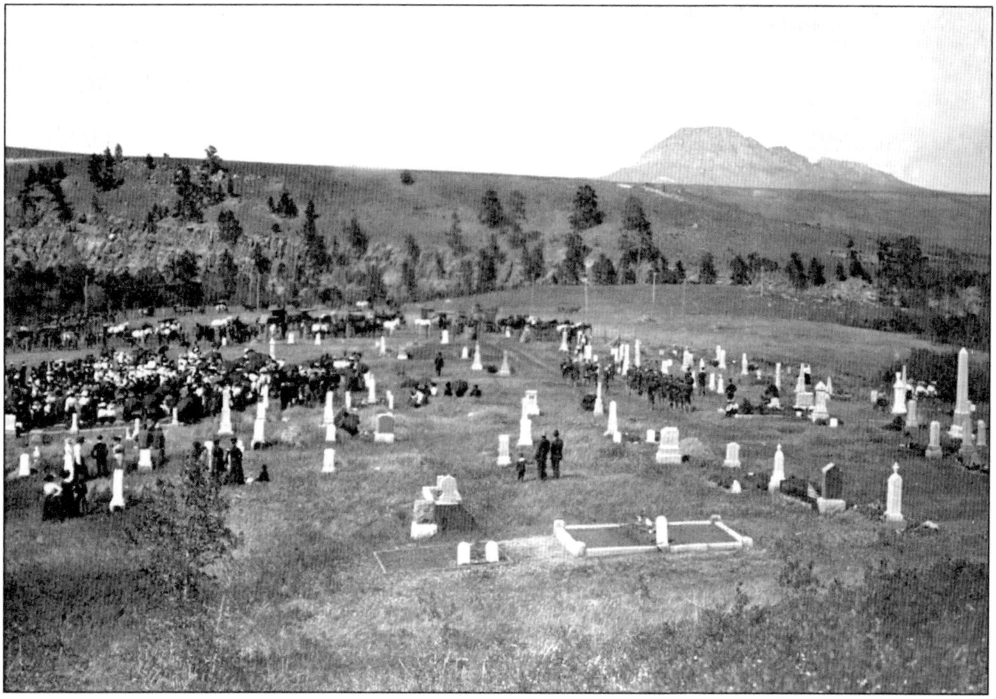

Bear Butte cemetery sits high on a bluff just west of Fort Meade and is the final resting place of many Black Hills pioneers and their families. In recent years, some of the hillside began to erode away, prompting major reconstruction in the area of the center shown in this photo.

Two

FORT MEADE

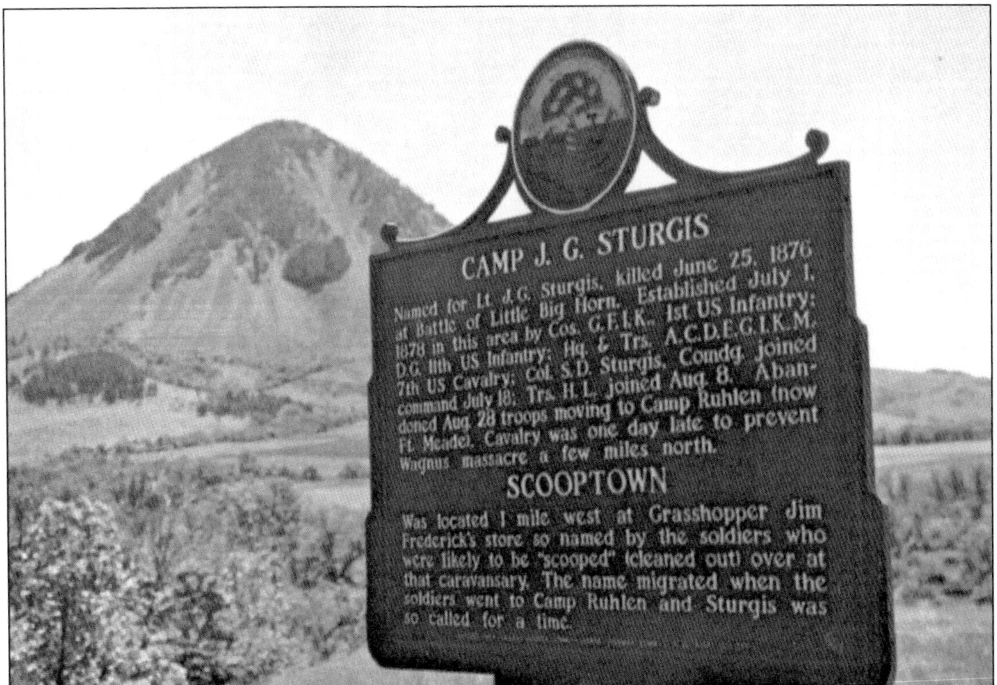

The State of South Dakota placed this metal sign marking the location of Camp J.G. Sturgis in the shadow of Bear Butte. Lt. James Garland Sturgis was killed at the Little Big Horn. Surviving Seventh Cavalry troops arrived here in the summer of 1878 with two companies of infantry to build a cantonment. The sign states that the cavalry arrived a day late, as they helped to prevent the massacre of the Wagnus party along the trail. Mentioned also is "Scooptown"—a miserable collection of illicit operations established for the sole purpose of parting the population from their money.

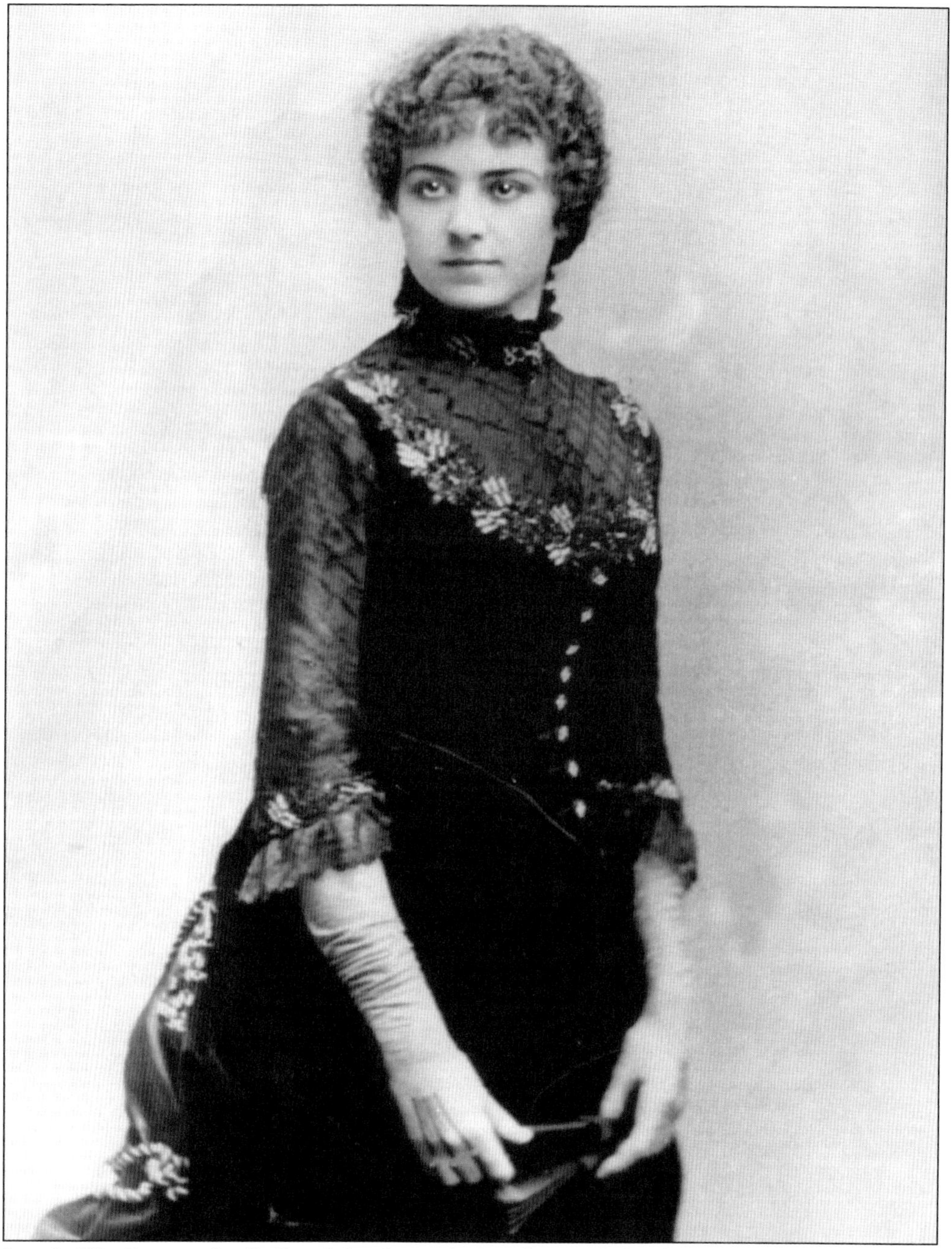

Lovely Ella Sturgis, the "belle of the Seventh Cavalry," and the daughter of Col. Samuel D. Sturgis, caused her father much consternation at Fort Abraham Lincoln when she pouted that other ladies of the fort were also being allowed to ride Comanche, the horse who survived Custer's defeat at the Little Big Horn. The colonel then issued an official order honorably retiring the gallant warhorse, which stipulated that he was never to be ridden again by anyone. Miss Ella turned her aspirations to the stage, and her beauty gained the favor of many male admirers—including the unfortunate Maj. Marcus A. Reno, whose military career ended at Fort Meade when he was accused by the elder Sturgis of "window peeping" at his home.

Col. Samuel Davis Sturgis, Civil War and Indian Wars veteran and commander at Fort Meade, succeeded Major Reno in 1880. Colonel Sturgis reportedly contributed a $20 gold piece as an investor to the townsite company for the new city of Sturgis that was being promoted by Jeremiah Wilcox.

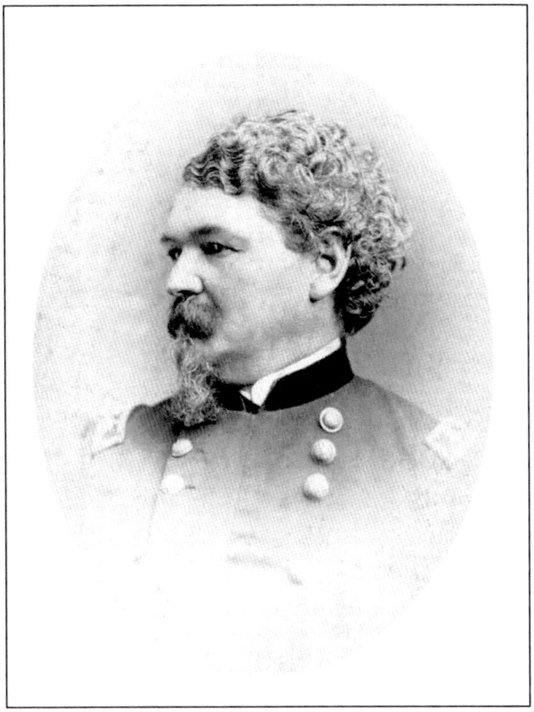

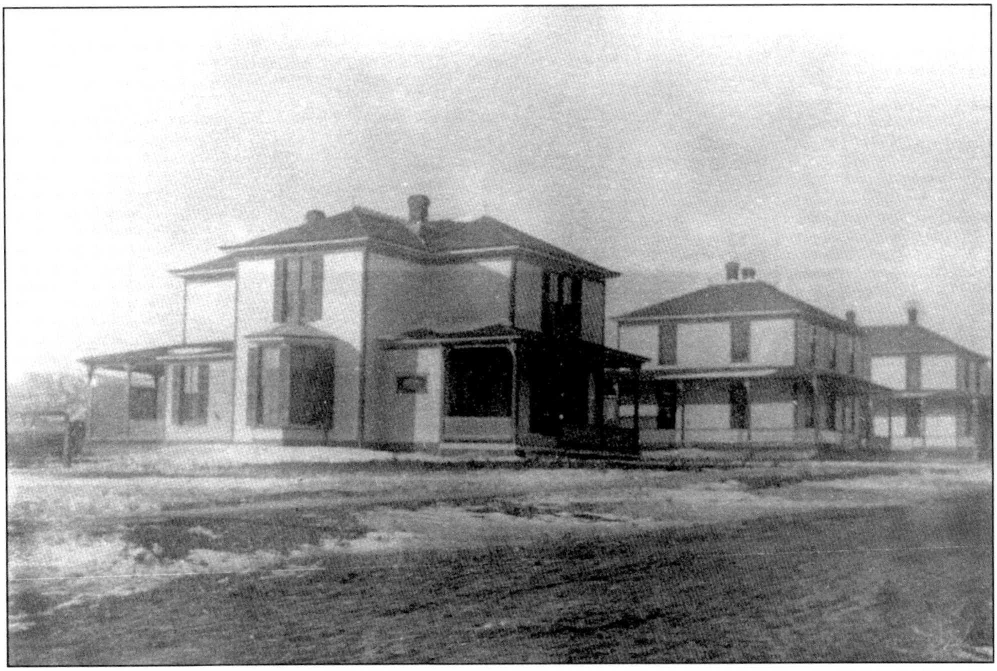

These homes from officer's row were moved to Sherman Street in Sturgis by Henry Bruch. Declared surplus, they sold for about $165 each. While at the fort, the residences were painted a drab green with red trim. Bruch dismantled the homes before moving them, completely rebuilding them at their new site, shown here.

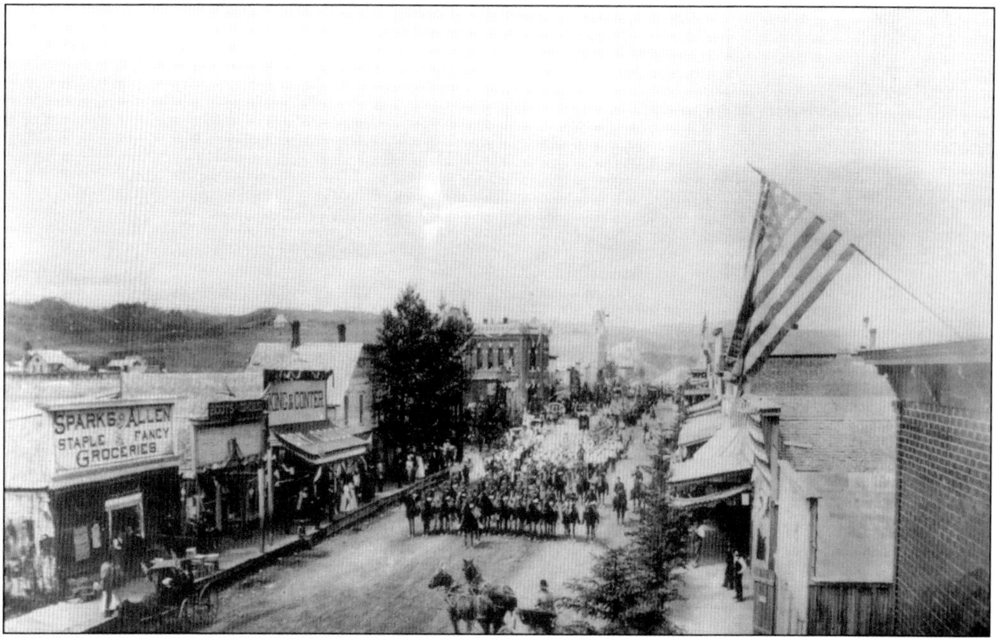

Mounted Fort Meade soldiers lead a parade down Main Street *c.* 1890, and were probably companies of the Eighth US Cavalry under the command of Col. Caleb Carlton. Flags and decorated buildings indicate a patriotic observance—probably Fourth of July.

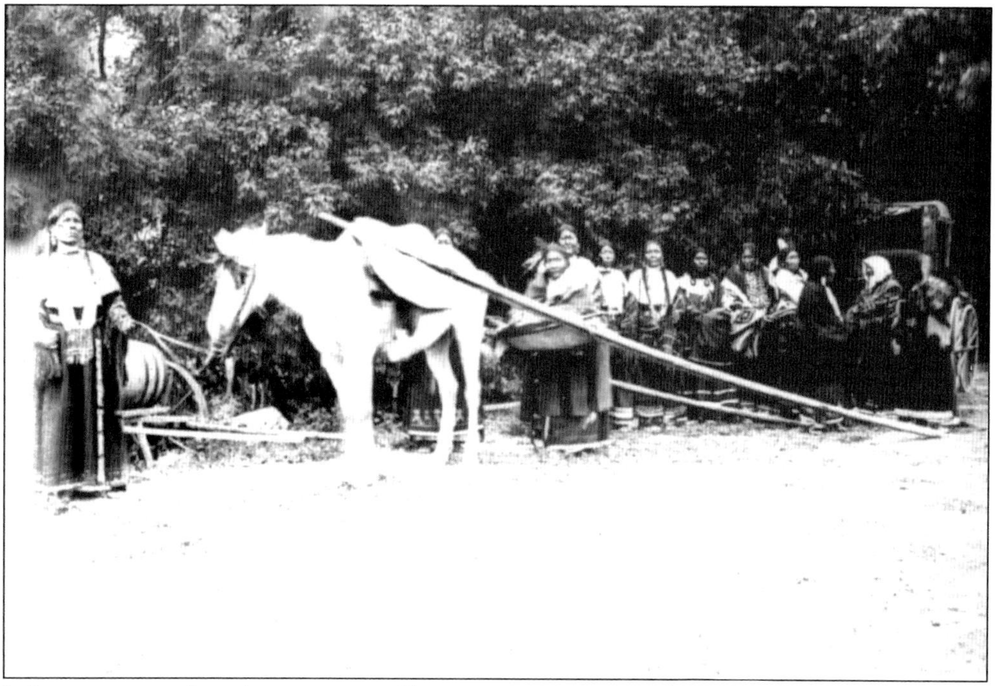

Indian travois, such as the one pictured here, were a common sight on Sturgis streets, as families came to town or traveled through. A well-used trail passed near Fort Meade, which led to the government Indian school in Rapid City, and a camp existed for some time on the banks of Bear Butte Creek. A "knife rock," where the Indians sharpened their tools, remains in the area.

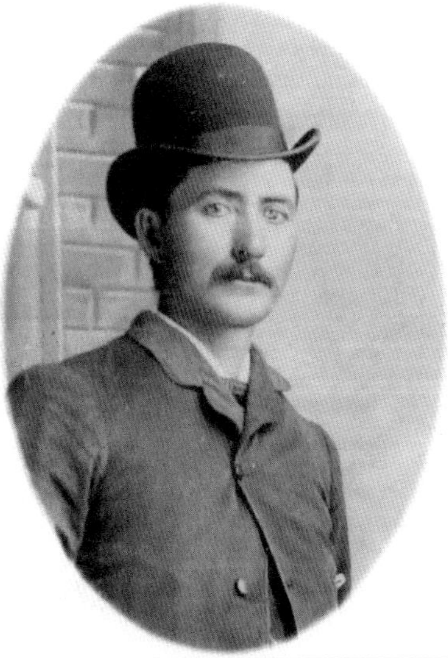

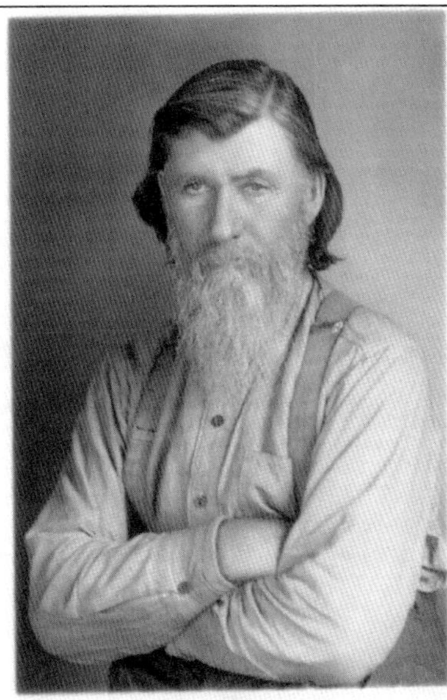

A dapper young James Frederick (Fredrick) is shown on the left. As a youth, Frederick spent his time working on steamboats, learning to gamble, and trapping. At Fort Sully, he became a prisoner in leg irons for disobedience on the 1873 Stanley Expedition. Gold brought him to the Black Hills in 1874—it was said he lived in a dugout and ate grasshoppers to survive. "Grasshopper Jim" carried papers claiming European nobility, but he became a lawless and wild-eyed character (right) on the frontier.

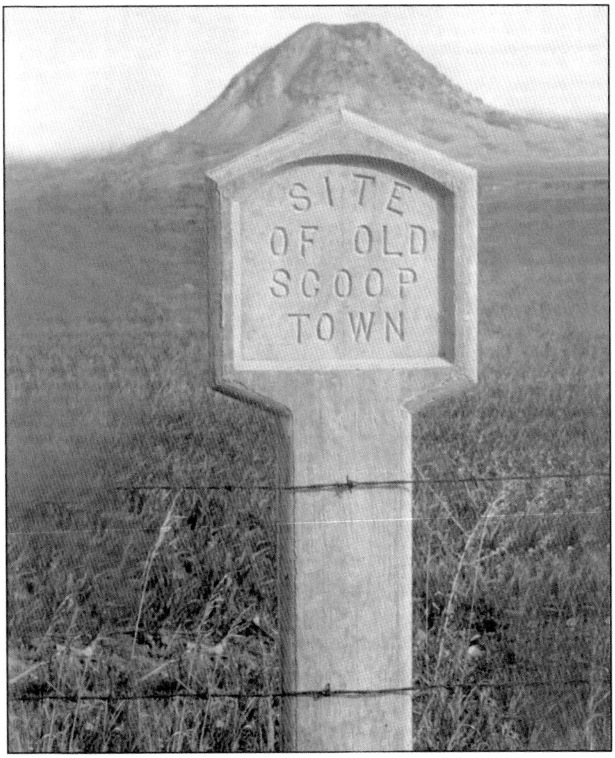

All that remained of Grasshopper Jim's neighborhood of Scooptown was this concrete post at the original site. Besides his unsavory businesses, he was a successful farmer, raising crops and livestock that he also provided to the surrounding community. Today's athletic teams at Sturgis High School are known as "the Scoopers."

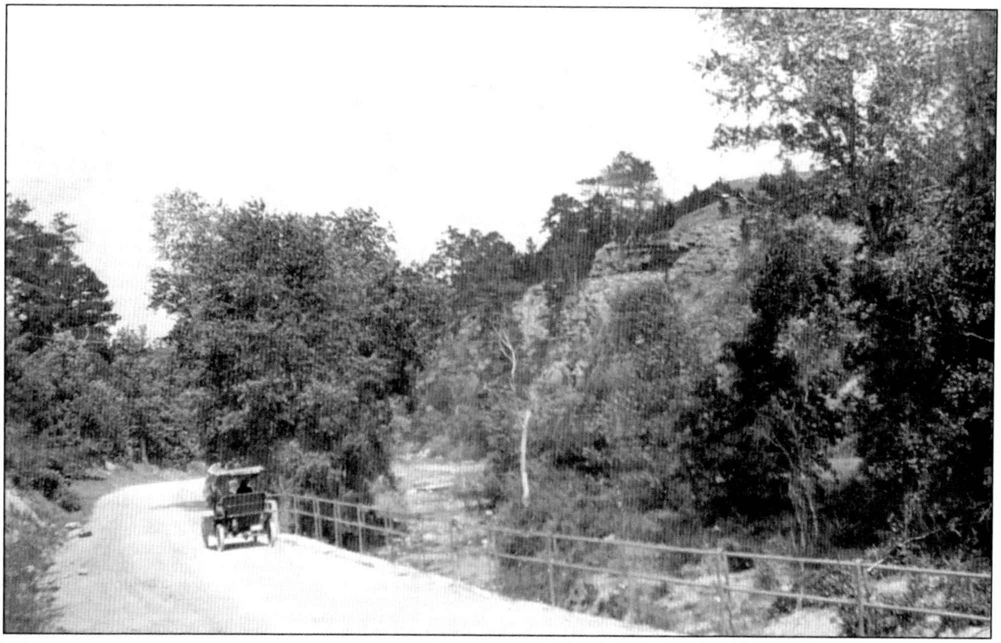

This lovely winding road is leading west from Fort Meade toward Sturgis—two miles distant. Bear Butte Creek follows the road to the right. Now State Highway 34, the road is paved and is the main route to reach the Fort Meade Veterans' medical complex, the BLM scenic byway, Old Fort Meade Museum, and Bear Butte State Park.

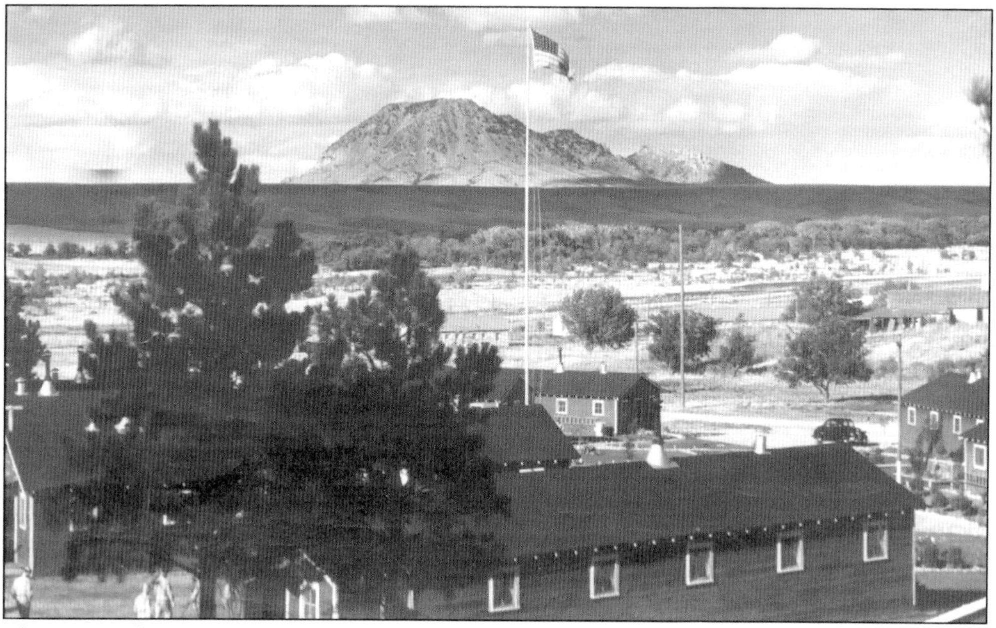

The Stars and Stripes fly over a portion of the Fort Meade Military Reservation with Bear Butte in the distance. In 1891, Col. Caleb Carlton ordered that "The Star Spangled Banner" be played at the fort every evening for retreat and at special occasions. The practice caught on at other military installations across the country, and in 1931, an act of Congress officially made the stirring number our national anthem, but the idea really began here on the South Dakota plains.

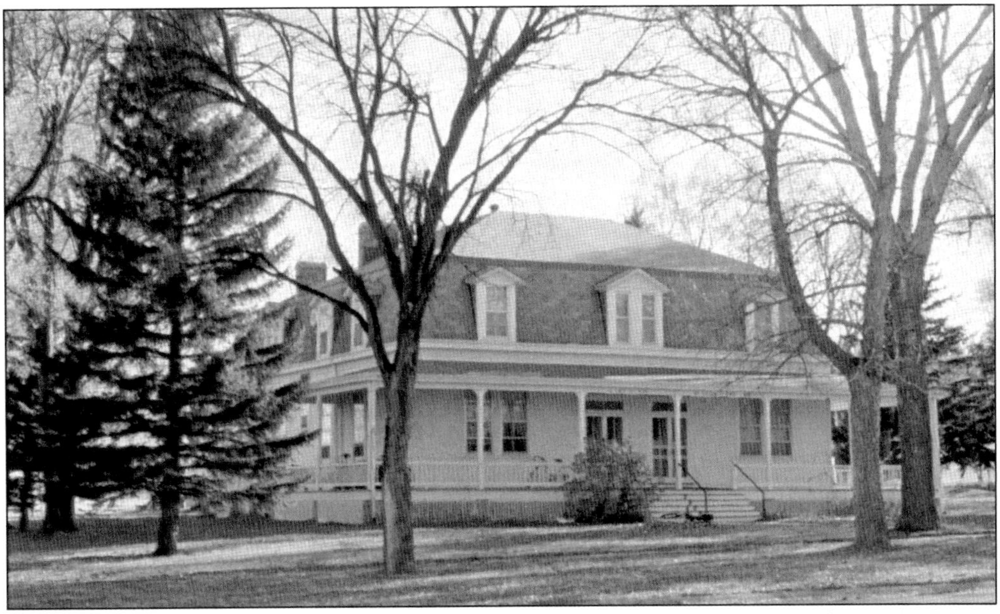

This frame officer's residence with mansard roof and Italianate styling dates to the 1880s. Facing north, it is approximately a half mile walk across the parade grounds to the administration building and barracks on the other side. This home is in pristine condition and is still in use as a home at Fort Meade.

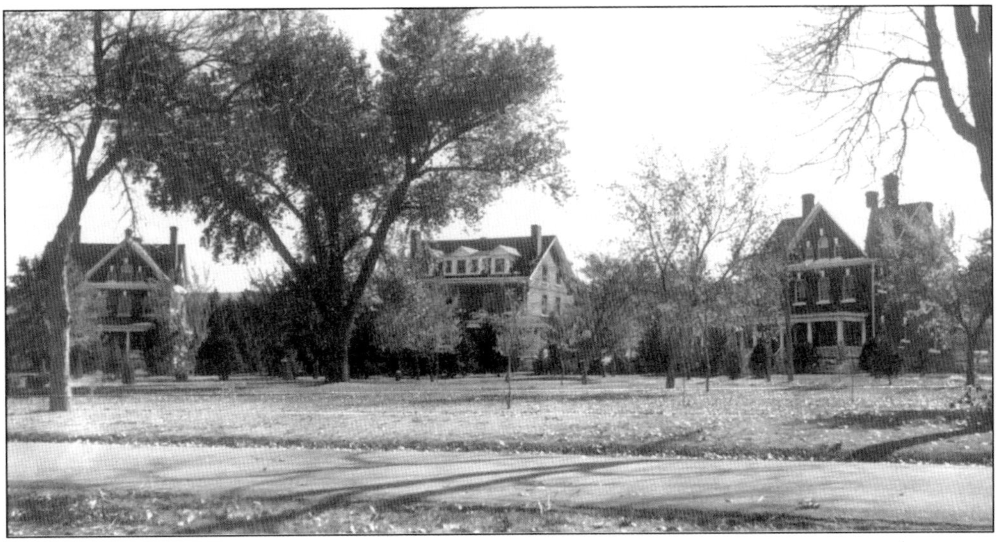

Also, facing the Fort Meade parade grounds are these brick mansions from the early 1900s. In restored condition, the elegant homes are living quarters for executive personnel and their families serving the Veterans' Administration hospital and programs.

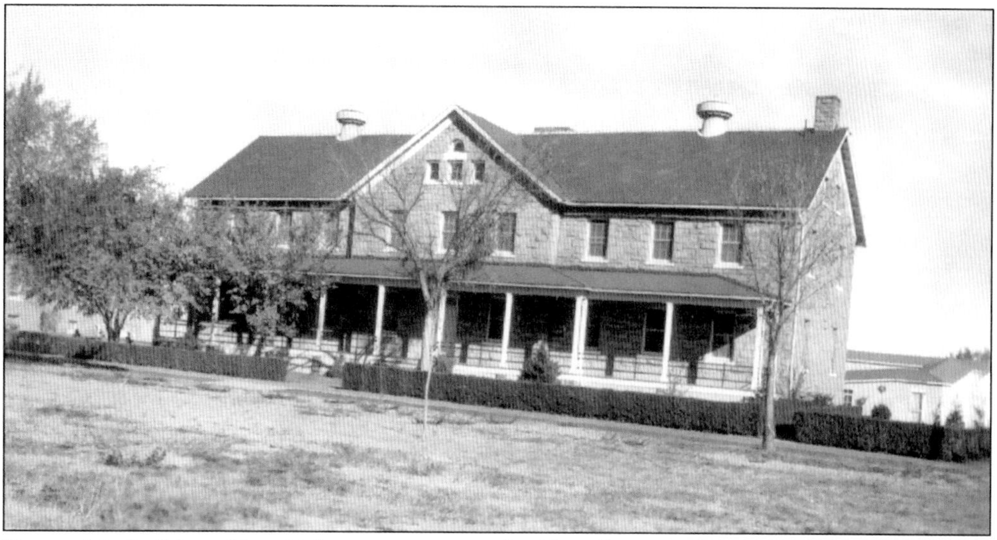

Pictured is Building 53, which was constructed of locally quarried stone during the second building phase and dating to the pre-1890s. The original buildings were of frame construction in the fall of 1878. One of those—the commissary store—remains today. In recent years, the South Dakota National Guard has used many of the buildings for their training programs.

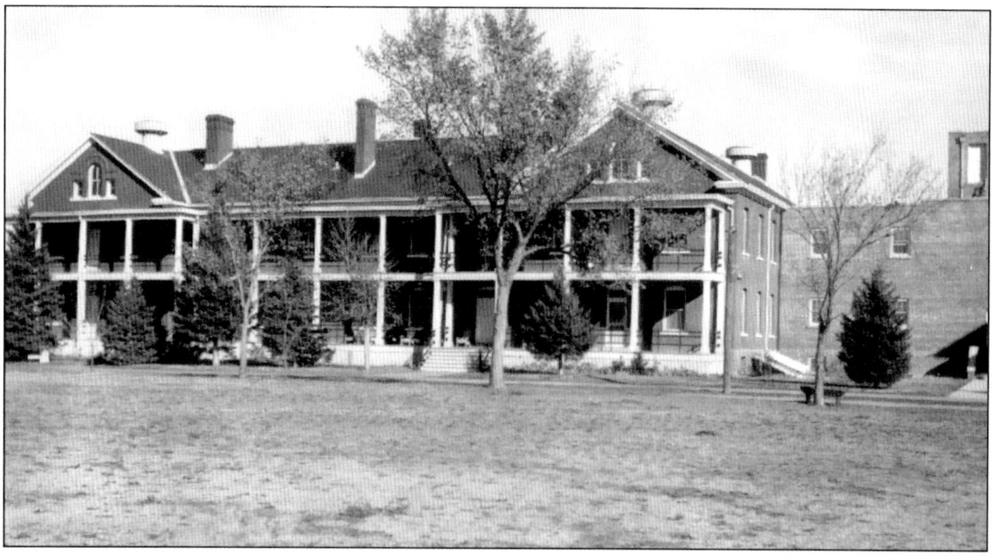

Brick facing was applied to several buildings prior to World War I. A former Fourth Cavalry man recalled a prank played in one of the barracks in the 1920s when a horse was coaxed up the stairs to the top floor. He didn't seem to mind the climb to the top, but coming down was another matter that caused quite a ruckus, and disciplinary action was taken against the soldiers. The Veterans' Administration (VAMC) hospital can be seen in the background.

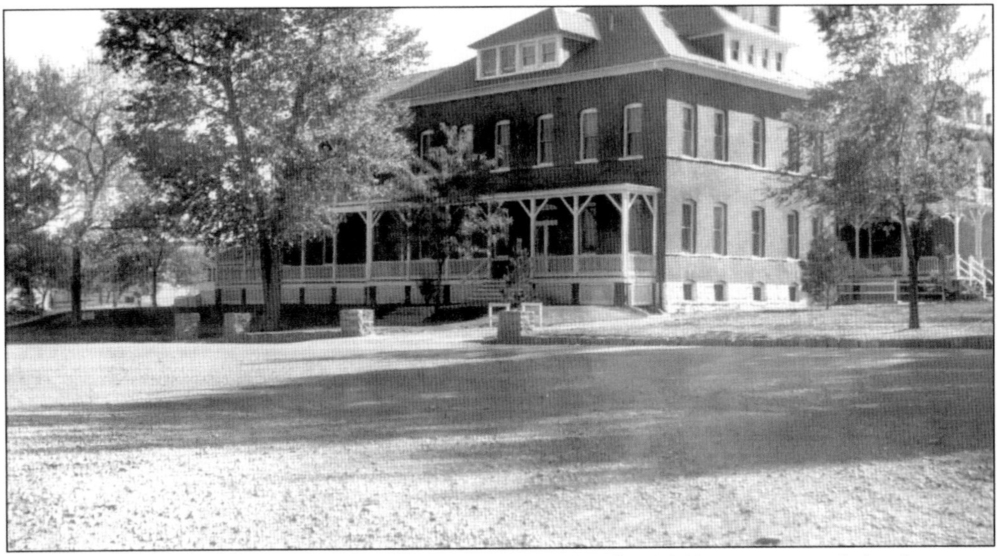

Today, Old Fort Meade is a National Historic Site. In the 1960s, portions of the fort were dismantled—local residents were responsible for saving the remainder, and a fine museum in the administration building shows this history from the early days through World War II. Shown above is the post's second hospital.

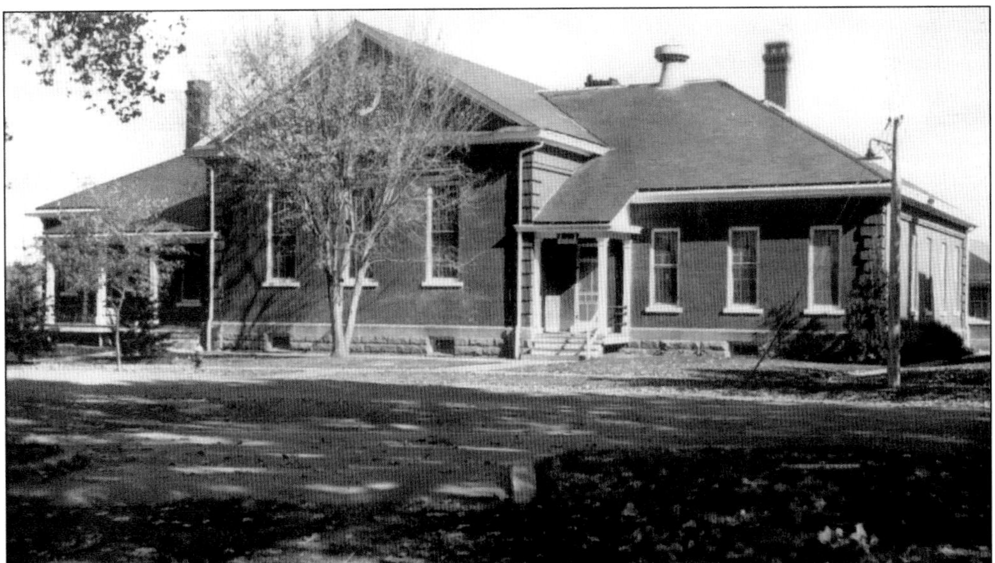

Building 63 at the eastern edge of the parade grounds has seen a number of uses over its lifetime. Today, it is the chapel for interdenominational services, but it has also been a library and quartermaster's depot. A bowling alley was located to the rear of the building.

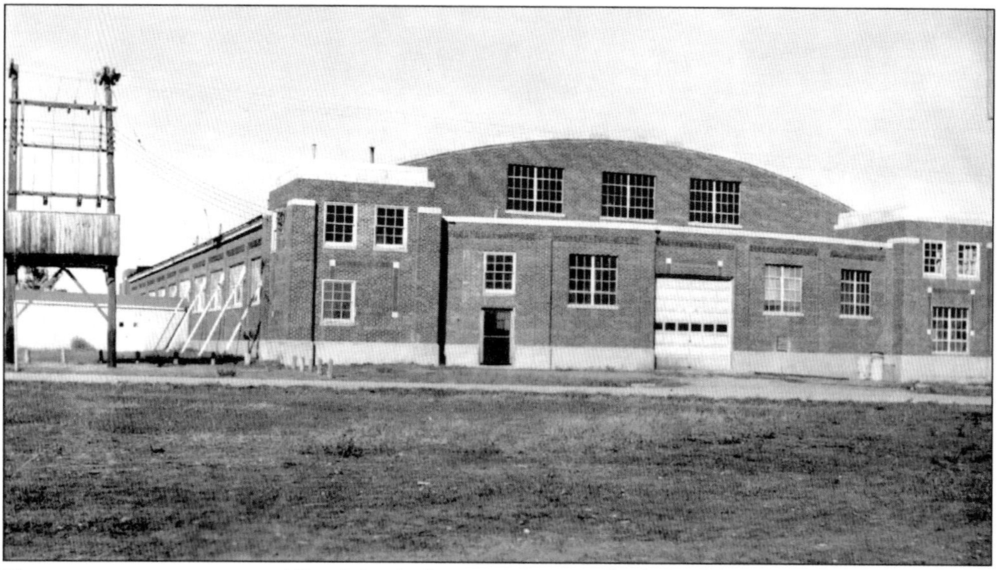

Horses were a major part of Fort Meade for many years—the last of them were mustered out of service in 1942. This indoor arena was an all-weather training facility and the site of numerous horse shows. In the summertime, Fort Meade had a polo team and fox hunting club, and also held outdoor competitions in Barry Stadium. A favorite show jumper, Indian Lament, is buried in a standing position overlooking the arena ampitheatre.

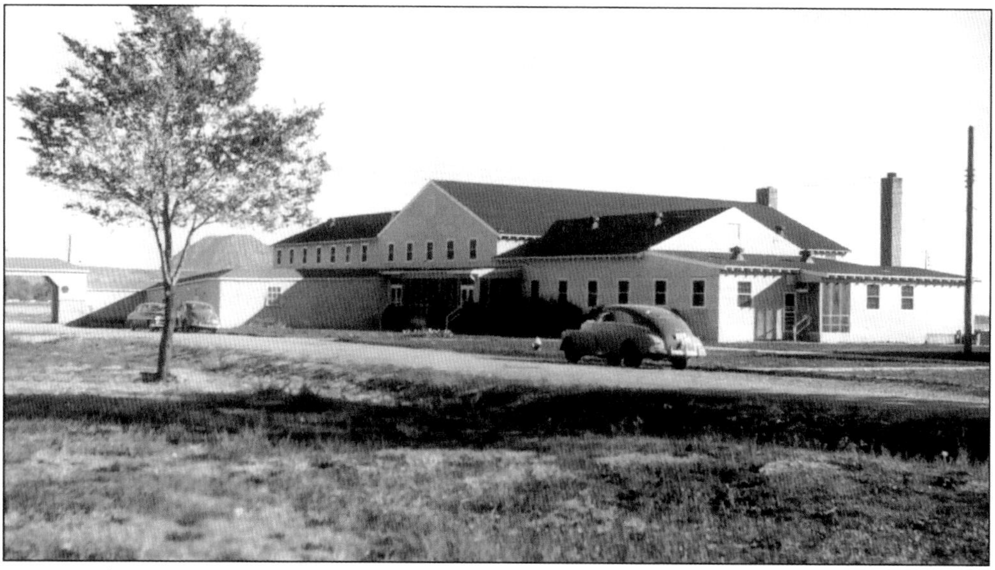

Fort Meade's recreation building has been and continues to be a community gathering place. Nearby, there is a laundry and even a greenhouse. Indoors, colorful murals remain that were painted by servicemen stationed here.

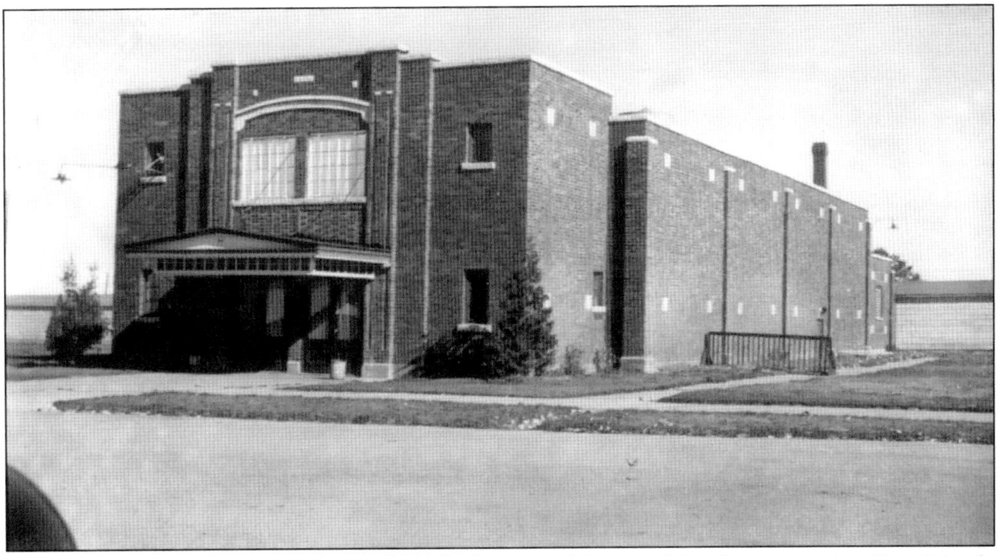

The Art Deco-styled theater housed USO shows and featured the latest movies. Fort Meade had its own theatrical group, a boxing and baseball team, and of course, musicians, who were always in demand. Costume parties and fancy dress balls were a part of the entertainment during Victorian times.

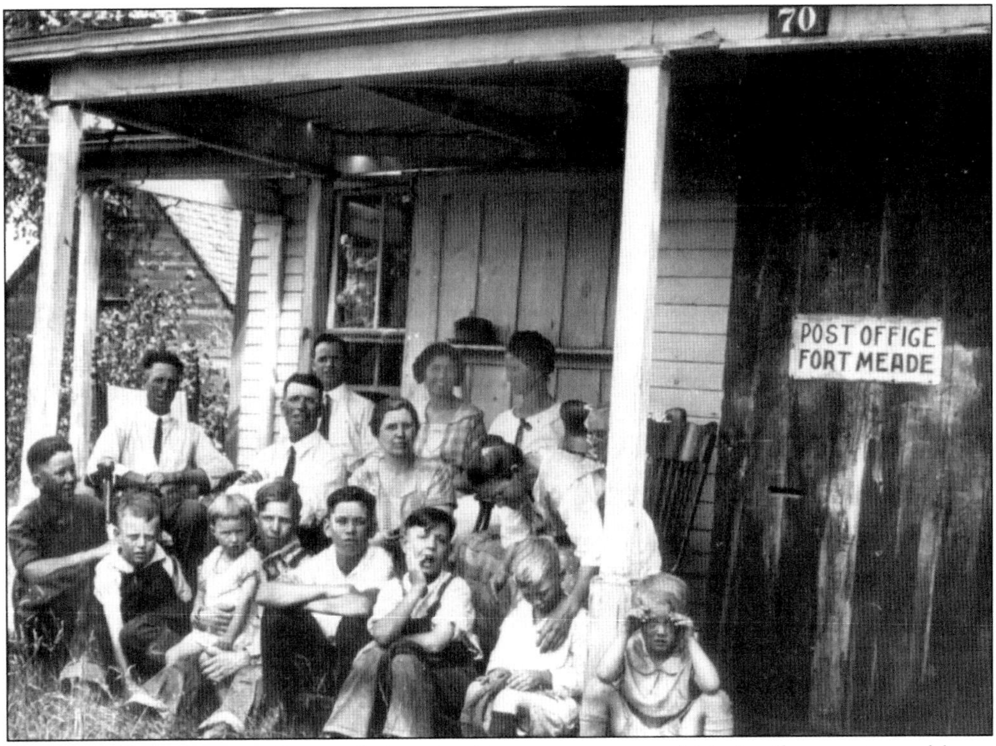

Fort Meade's early post office and, (we think) a postmaster and his family are pictured here. In more recent years, the sandstone guard house has become the post office, and many persons who have come and gone—including German prisoners-of-war—carved their names or initials near the doorway and window sills.

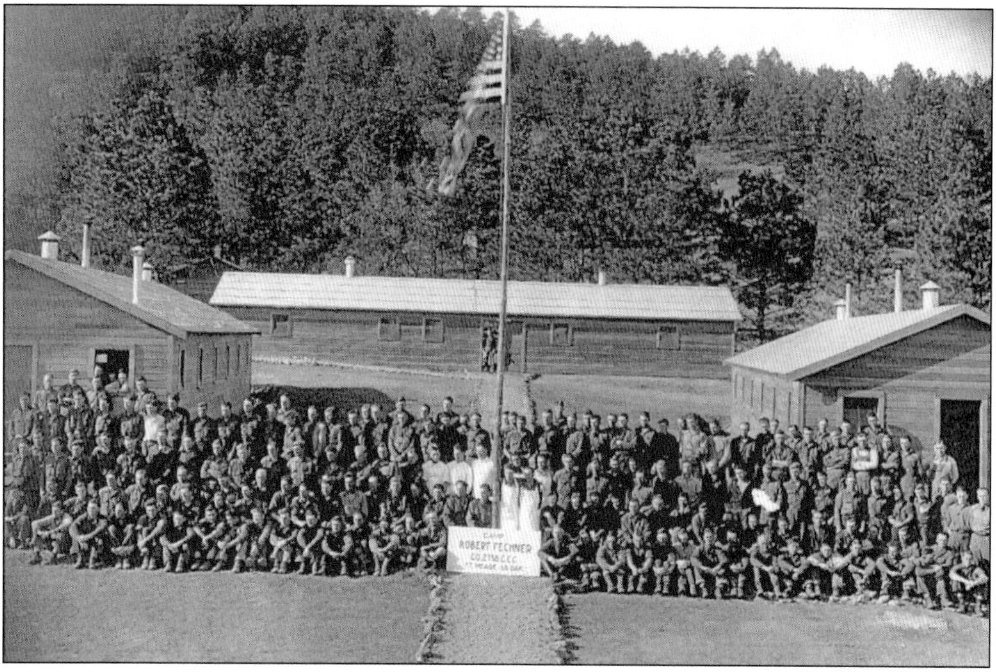

Young men enrolled in the Civilian Conservation Corps (CCC) during the Great Depression years pose for this photo at Camp Robert Fechner, located just west of the Fort Meade complex. One of the largest CCC camps in the Black Hills, Camp Fechner taught skills in a variety of trades that would enable these men to perform jobs well when they were again available. Meanwhile, a small salary was received and a portion of this was required to be sent home to help the family.

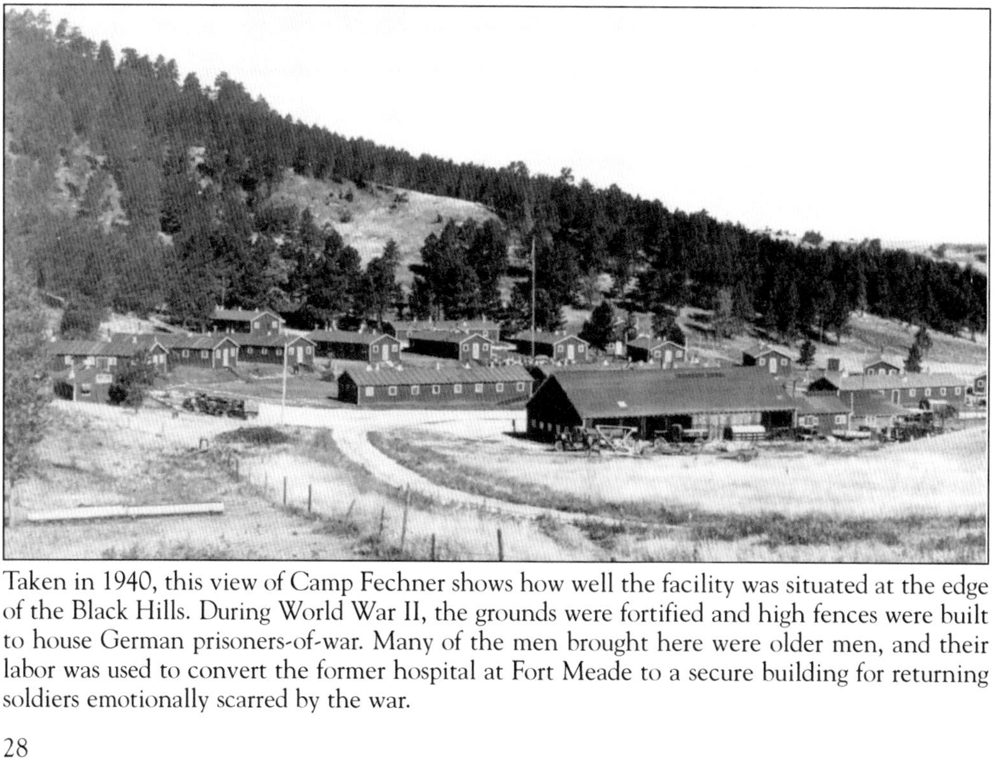

Taken in 1940, this view of Camp Fechner shows how well the facility was situated at the edge of the Black Hills. During World War II, the grounds were fortified and high fences were built to house German prisoners-of-war. Many of the men brought here were older men, and their labor was used to convert the former hospital at Fort Meade to a secure building for returning soldiers emotionally scarred by the war.

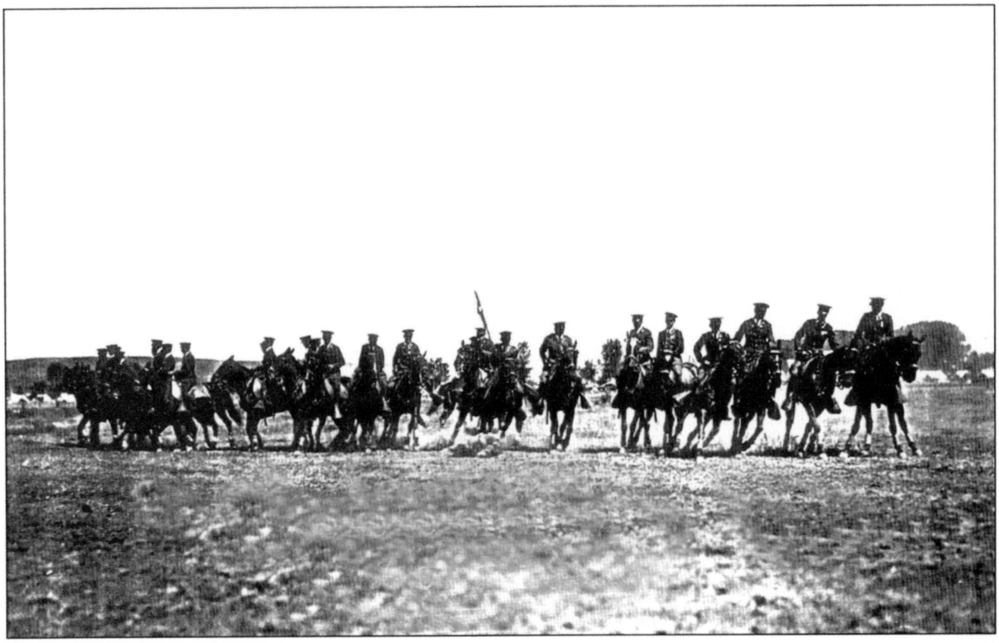

The Black Horse Troop, one of Fort Meade's most popular attractions, was a precision drill team of matched black horses with khaki and gold trappings, which performed to music at fairs and parades throughout the region in the 1920s. They were under the direction of Capt. J.A. Blankenship.

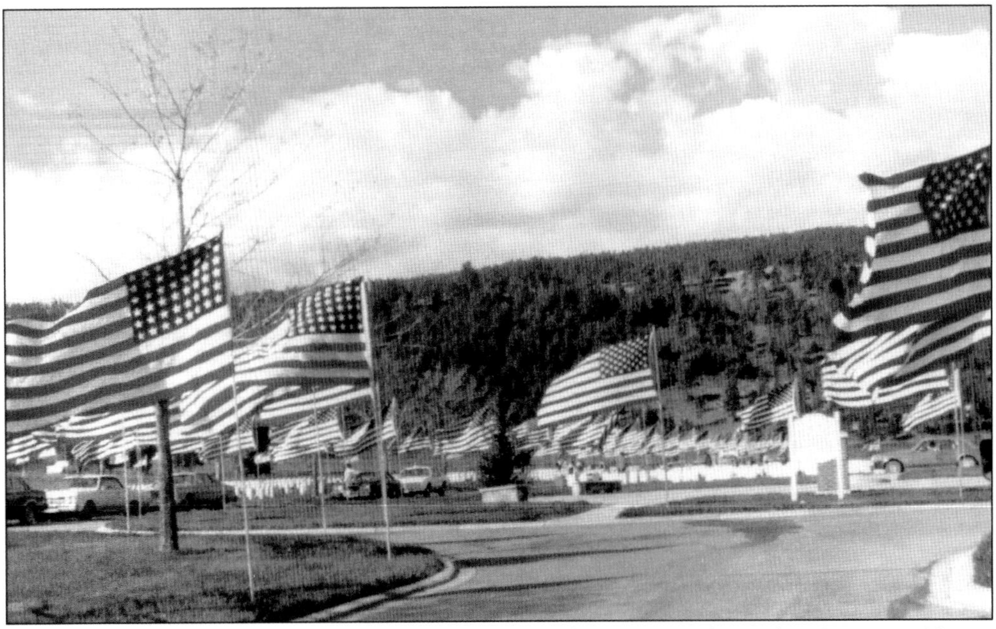

Called the "Arlington of the West," Black Hills National Cemetery is located on Interstate 90, just minutes south of Sturgis. The groomed acres were first used in 1948, replacing Fort Meade's old post cemetery. One of the early burials at the national cemetery was that of Sgt. Charles Windolph, survivor of the Little Big Horn fight and a Medal of Honor recipient who remained in the area.

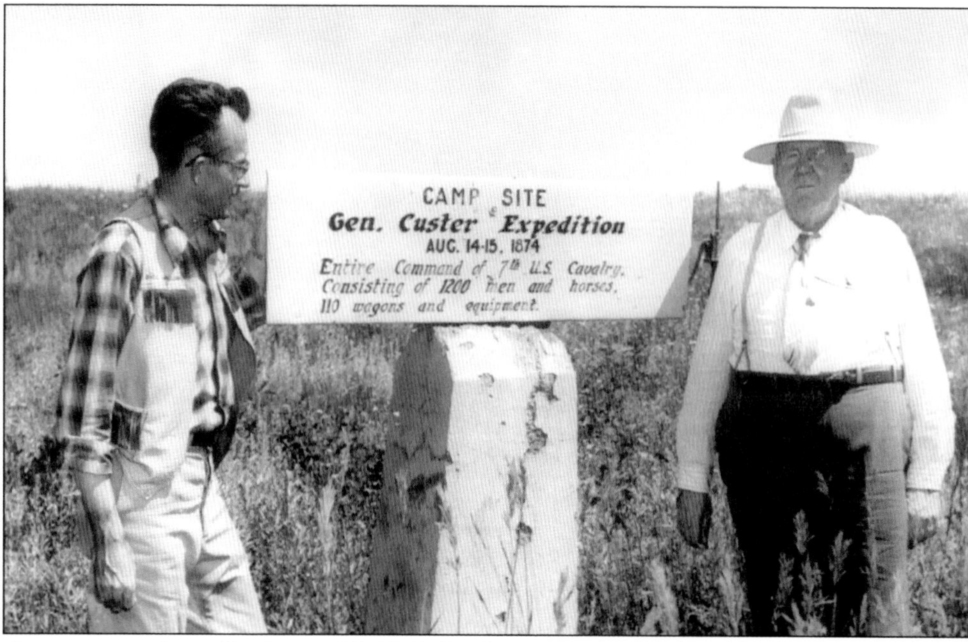

Custer camped here. On August 14–15, 1874, George Armstrong Custer and 1,200 men camped just south of Bear Butte on their returning route of exploring the Black Hills. Grasshopper Jim was already ensconced in the area and claimed to have watched the soldiers from his hideaway. Richard B. "Dick" Williams and Freeman Steele Sr. stand by a marker at the site.

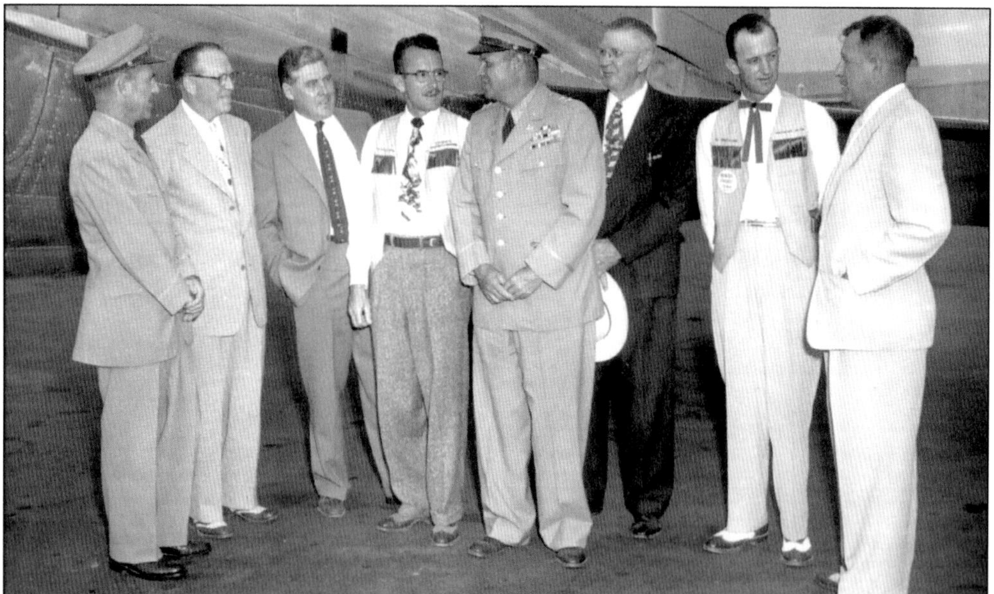

Gen. Samuel D. Sturgis III, grandson of Col. Samuel D. Sturgis and head of the US Corps of Engineers, arrives in town during the summer of 1949 to officially dedicate the Black Hills National Cemetery. Shown are, from left to right, an unidentified aide to General Sturgis, Mr. Loon (assistant VA Hospital director), Jarvis Davenport, Dick Williams, General Sturgis, Mayor Bruce Barnes, Al Matkins, and Fred Bradshaw II (VA Hospital director).

Three

Main Street and More

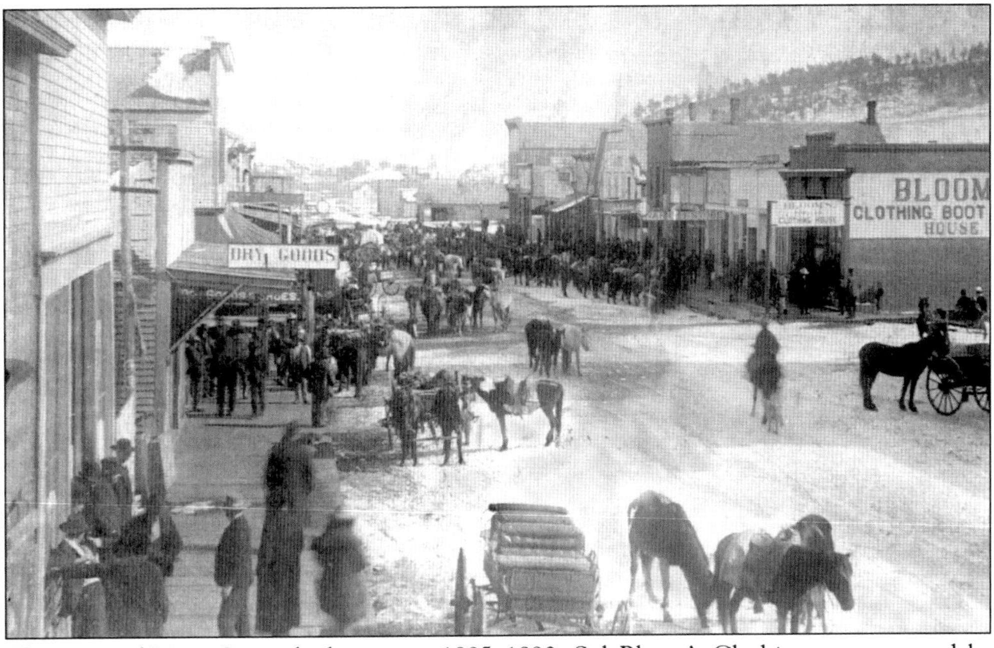

This view of Main Street looks east *c*. 1885–1890. Sol Bloom's Clothing was managed by Ed Galvin, Meade County's first state senator. Here we see a busy day in Sturgis—perhaps a Saturday. In 1890, the county population was 668. In 1888, the Sturgis City Council passed a law prohibiting selling, smoking, or using opium.

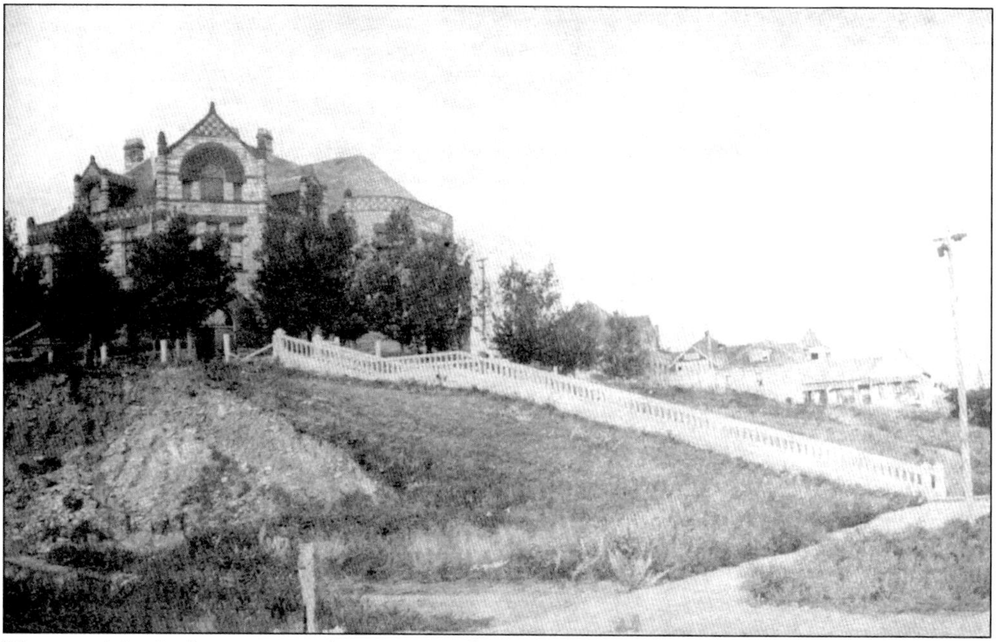

The new Meade County court house opened on West Main on September 26, 1896, and was constructed by William Grams' construction company with stone quarried within two miles of the city limits. The main entrance was at the northeast corner and it had a challenging wooden stairway. The modern structure had water closets on each floor, 20-foot ceilings, and was "absolutely fire proof and burglar proof."

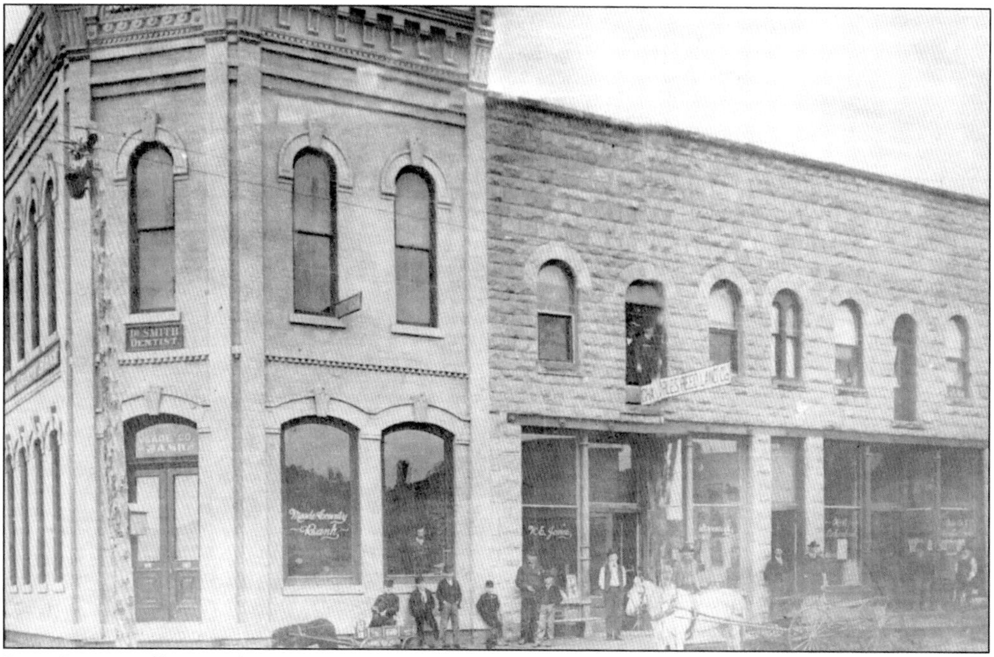

Bear Butte Valley Bank building was built in 1886 at 1100 Main. W.E. Jones had the grocery next door from 1885–1890 and provided fresh produce from his own gardens. In 1910, banks could no longer legally cash checks or notes for less than one dollar.

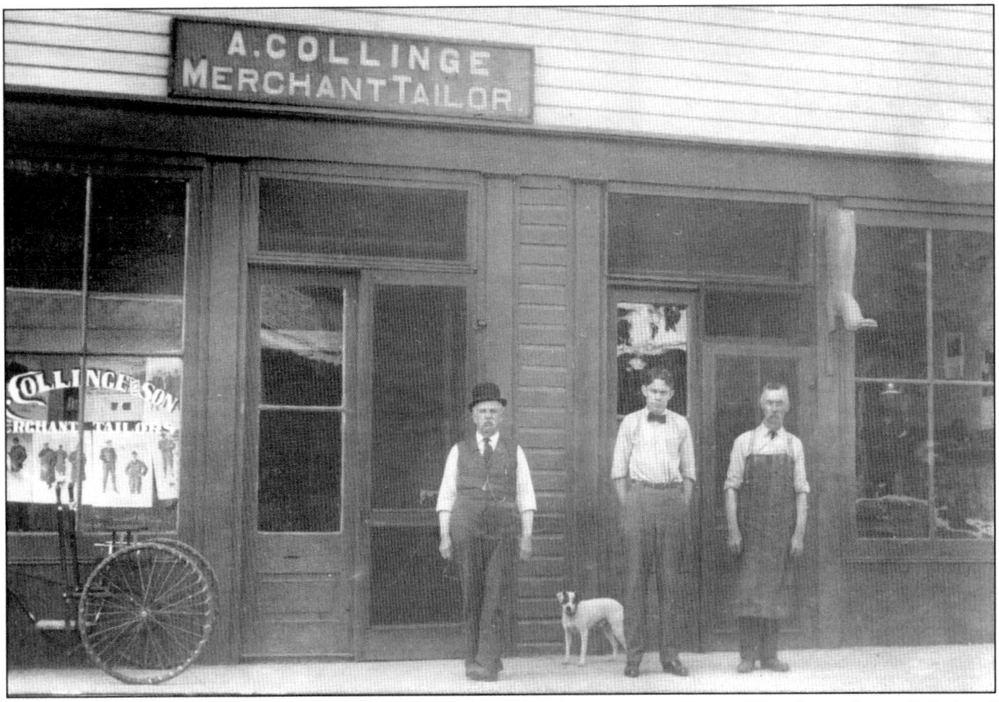

The store front of Collinge and Son, Merchant Tailors is seen here. The bicycle at left is of interest, as is the Jack Russell terrier.

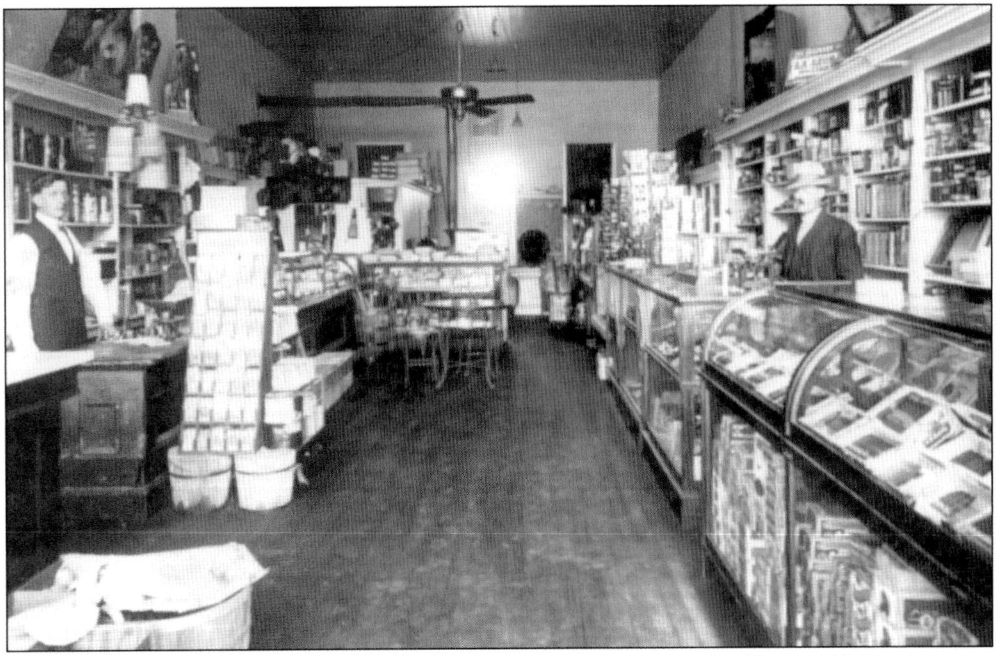

George Flavin and Herbert Hamblet had a confectionery store at the First and Main location where the Jones and Doran grocery stores were later located. Cigars seem to be a major item and took up a large amount of counter space. Both young men and ladies loved sweets, and often treated themselves to a weekly ice cream—hence the name "sundae."

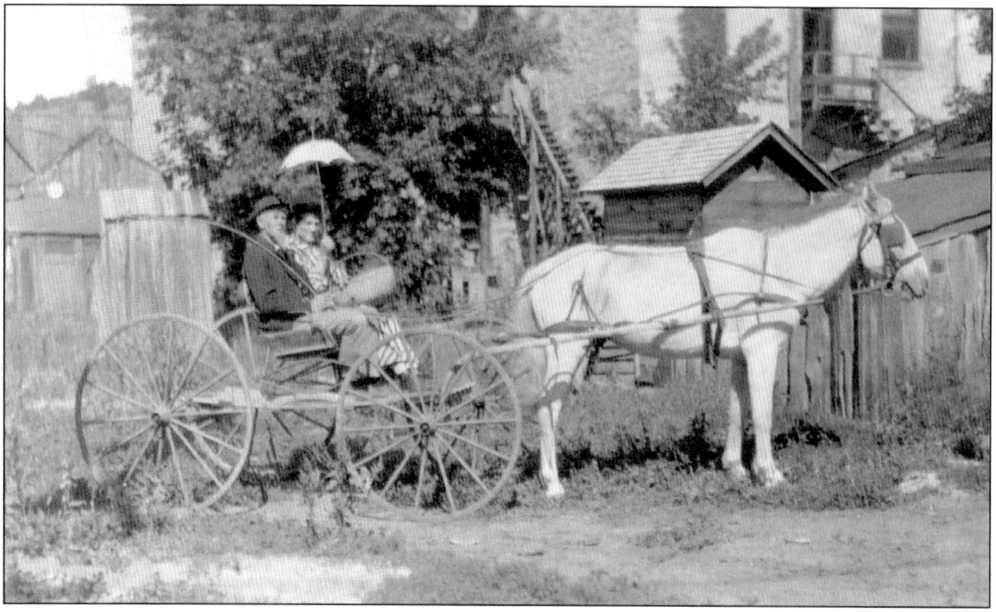

Uriah or U.S. Sparks and wife—parents of an early grocer, Roy Sparks, drive through the alley behind the store building next to the bank on Main Street. The horse looks like a gentle sort, and it is apparent that the elder Sparks needed the whip to coax it on. The parasol and big basket suggest that perhaps this trio is headed for a picnic.

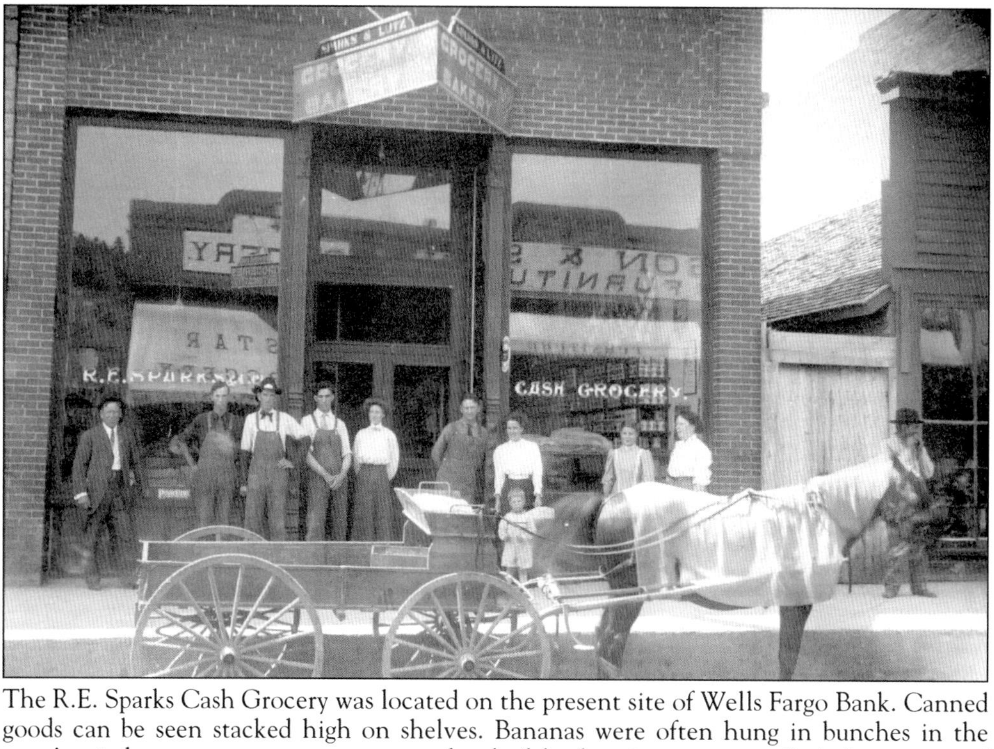

The R.E. Sparks Cash Grocery was located on the present site of Wells Fargo Bank. Canned goods can be seen stacked high on shelves. Bananas were often hung in bunches in the store's window to attract customers, and colorful advertisements extolled the virtues of wholesome products popular in their day.

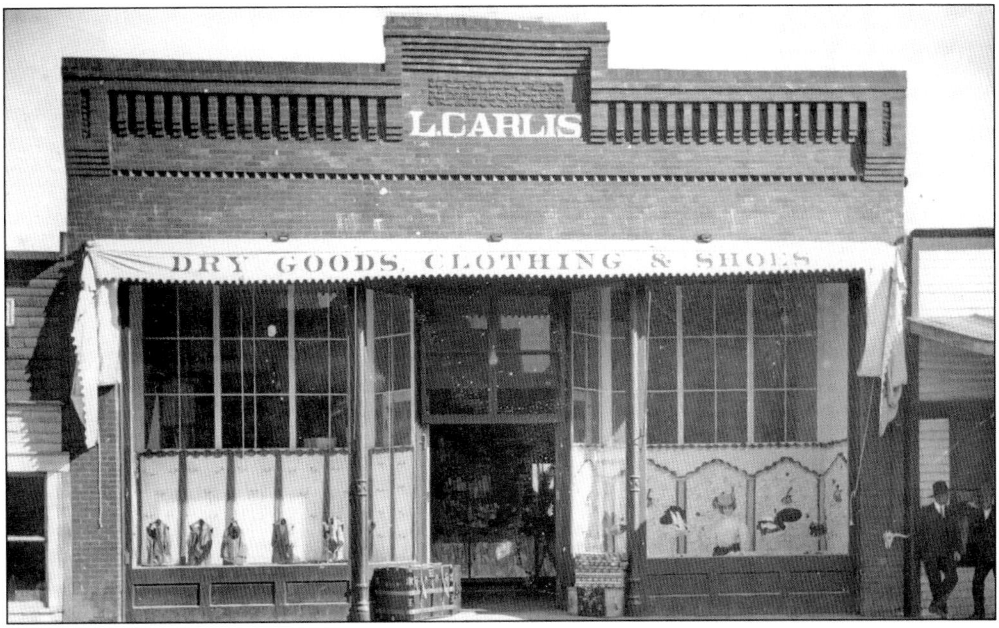

Dry goods and clothing were always needed. L. Carlis ran this establishment at 1063 Main in 1907. Elizabeth Bruch had a contract to make ladies' hats and sell them on the premises (see window display). The steamer trunk in the doorway was sturdy enough to withstand miles of rugged traveling over land and sea.

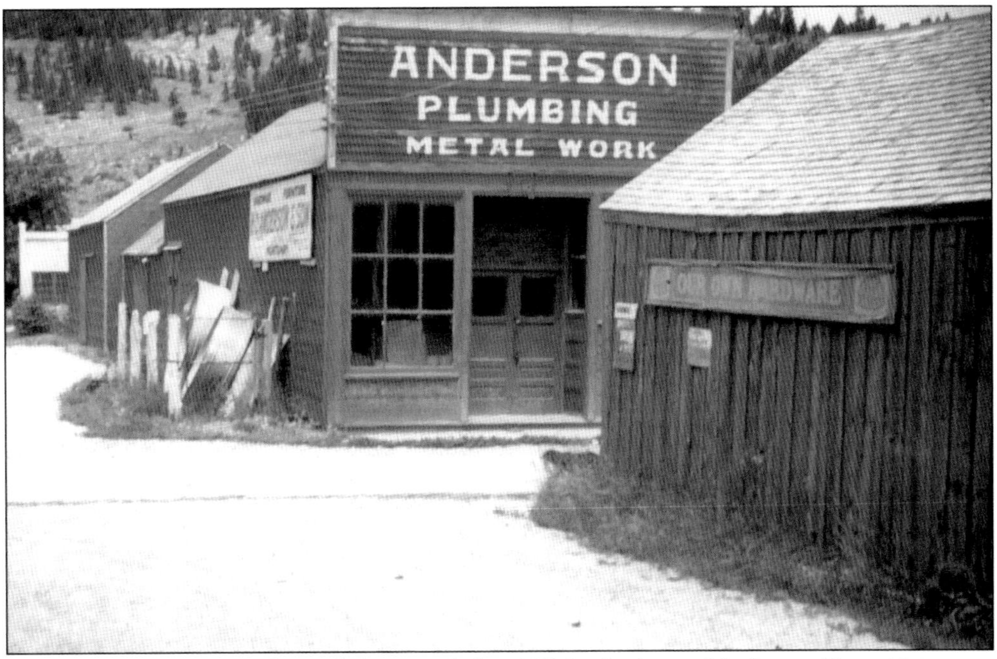

Anderson's plumbing and metal shop was behind H.O. Anderson Hardware. Tinsmithing was an important part of life in the days when throwing things away was unthinkable, and they were repaired rather than discarded.

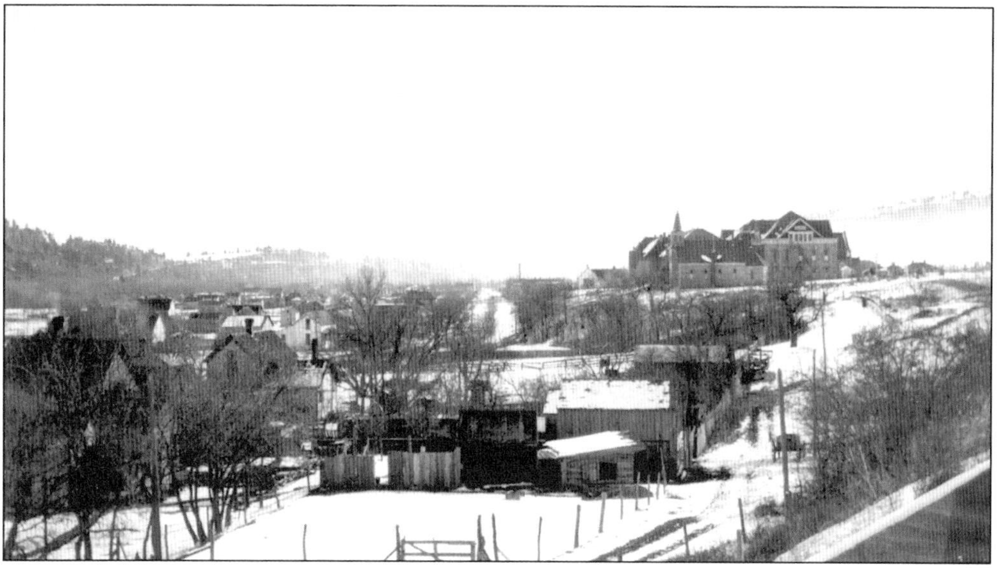

This view looks west on Main Street from the railroad trestle to St. Martin's Academy on the right. Founded by Father Peter Rosen in the spring of 1889, the first temporary classes were held in the Sage building on Lazelle Street. Judge Henry Clay Ash donated the land for the future school, chapel, and cemetery west of the court house. Mary Keffeler was one of the first students to receive communion.

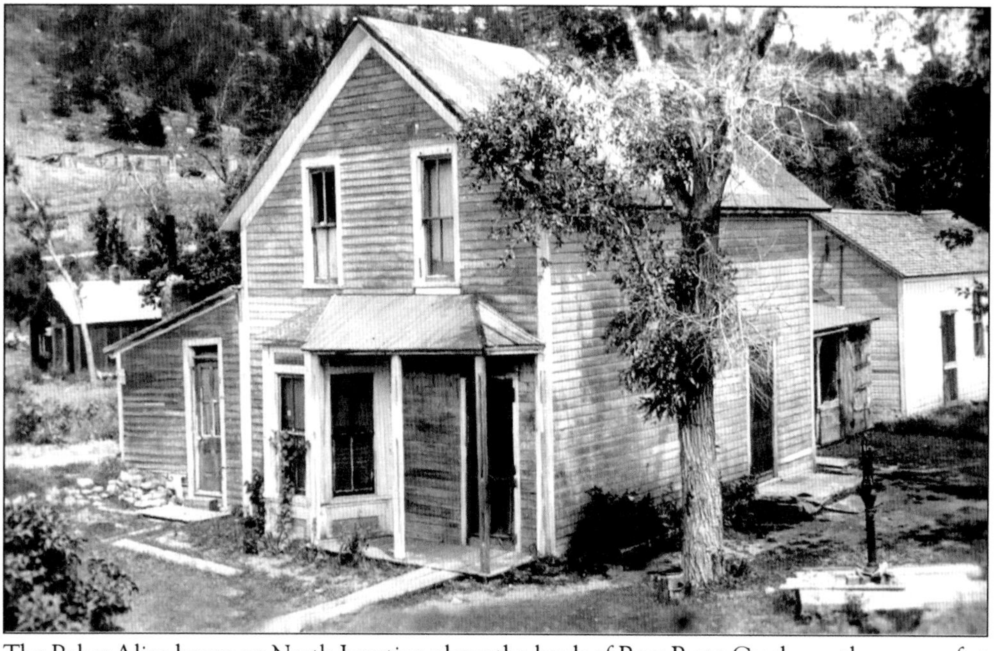

The Poker Alice house on North Junction along the bank of Bear Butte Creek was the scene of at least one shooting and was built on the "installment plan"—one room at a time being added to the others, until the thing now stretches out for quite a distance, said an early editor. It was moved to its present site on South Junction in 1990 and is preserved as a tourist attraction.

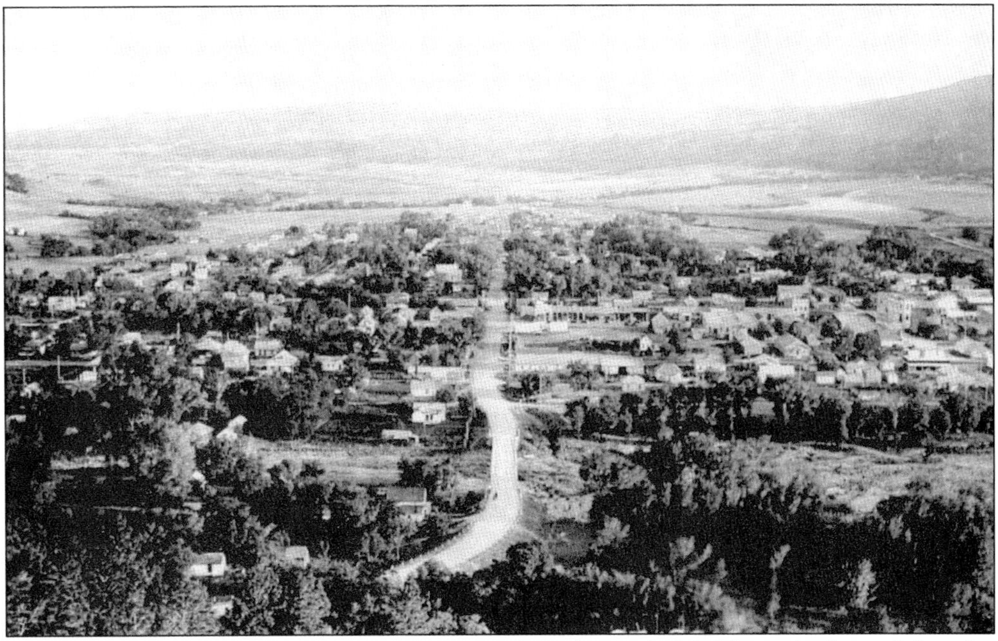

This bird's-eye view of Junction Avenue, *c.* 1920, looks south. Visible to the lower left is the Poker Alice house. Main and Lazelle Streets are center right in the distance.

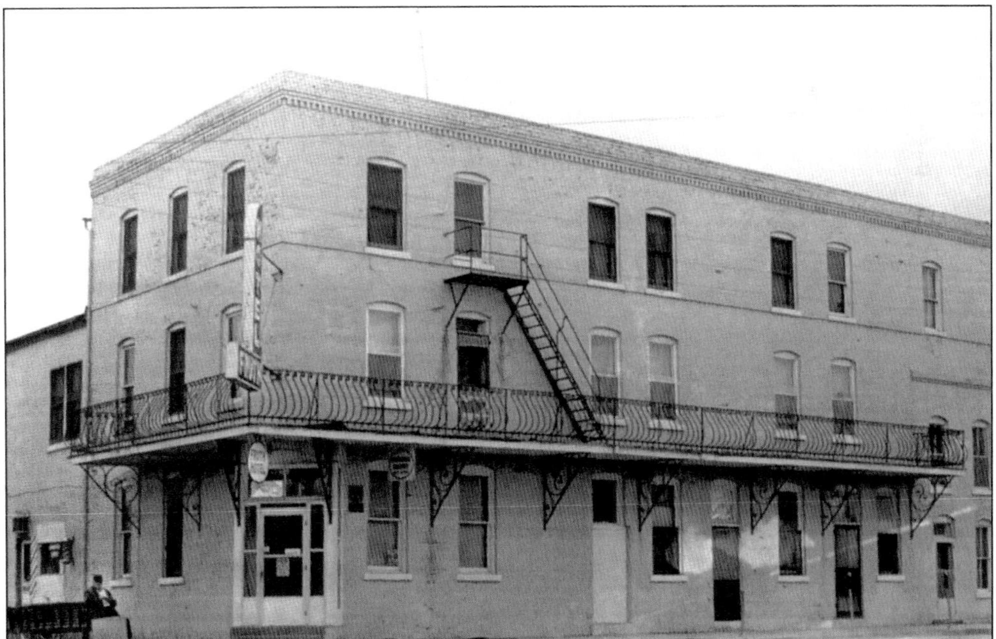

The Fruth Hotel at the corner of Main and Second Streets replaced the old Charles Hotel on that site. Henry Fruth, an employee, bought the building on January 22, 1908, and tore it down, replacing it with a brick structure that grew to 60 rooms by 1920.

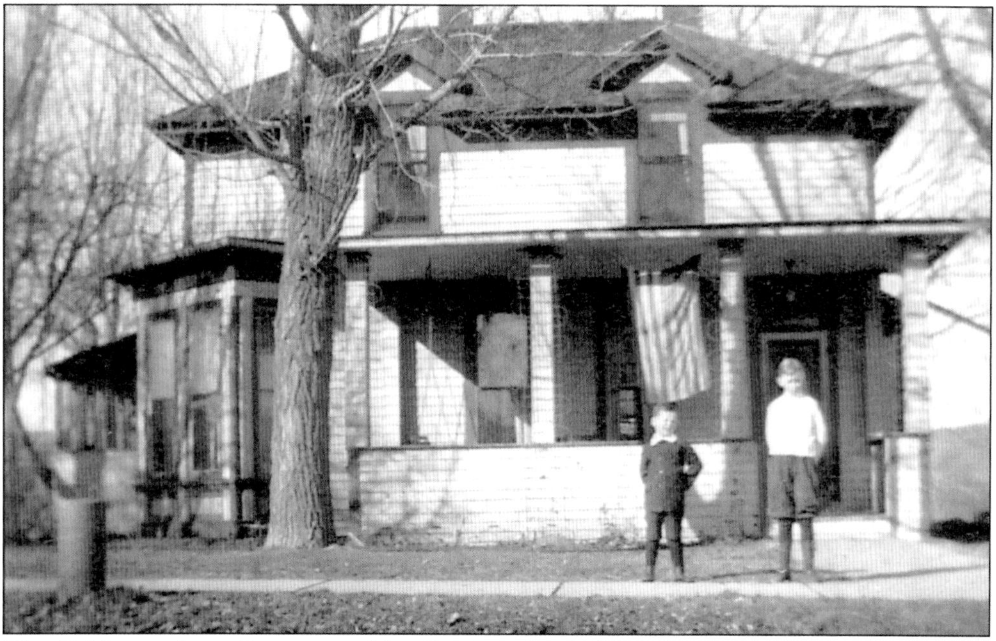

This 1916 view shows Freeman and Joe Steele in front of their home at 1439 Junction.

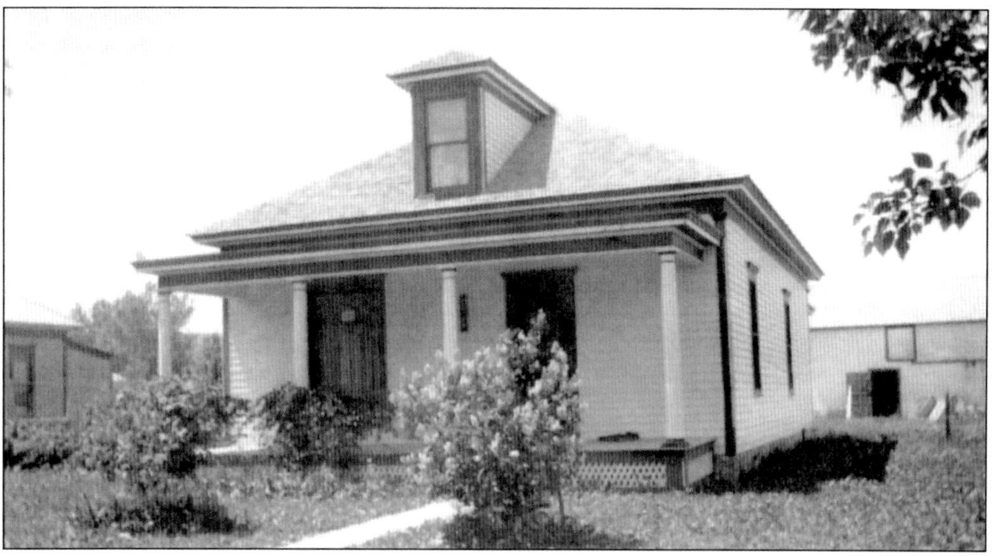

The residence of Jarvis J. Davenport was located at 1324 Junction. Jarvis was with his mother at an air show in Los Angeles in 1910, when a flight altitude of 4,600 feet was reached. The lad was so excited over the event, he shouted in his sleep "Oh, look Mama, look up," and fell out of bed.

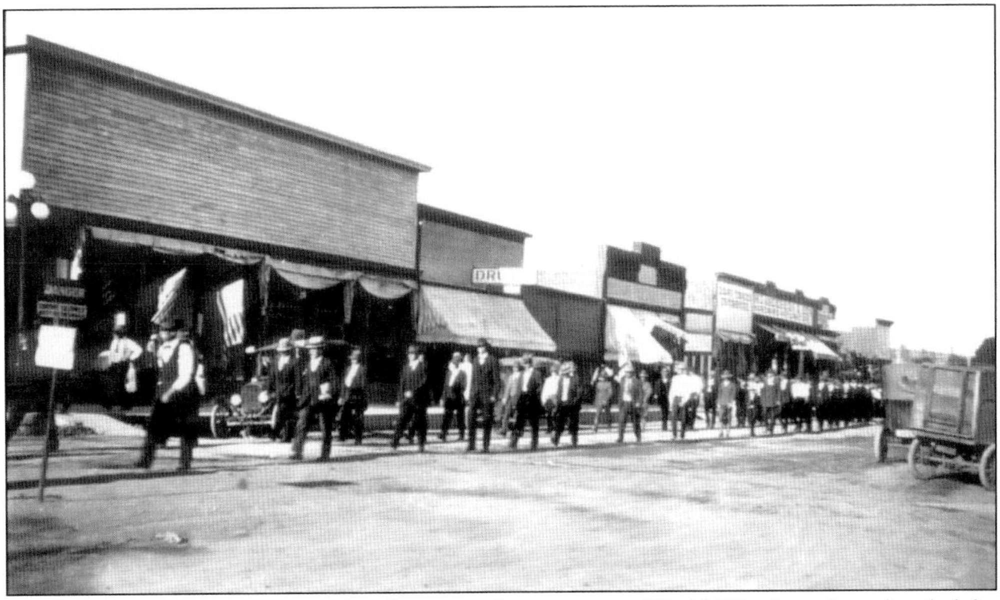

Striding down Main Street are local recruits for service in World War I, perhaps headed for the train depot. A sign on the left cautions persons to "drive slowly." The vehicle on the right resembles a "paddy wagon," but could be a delivery truck. Sturgis Drug Store and H.O. Anderson and Son buildings provide the background.

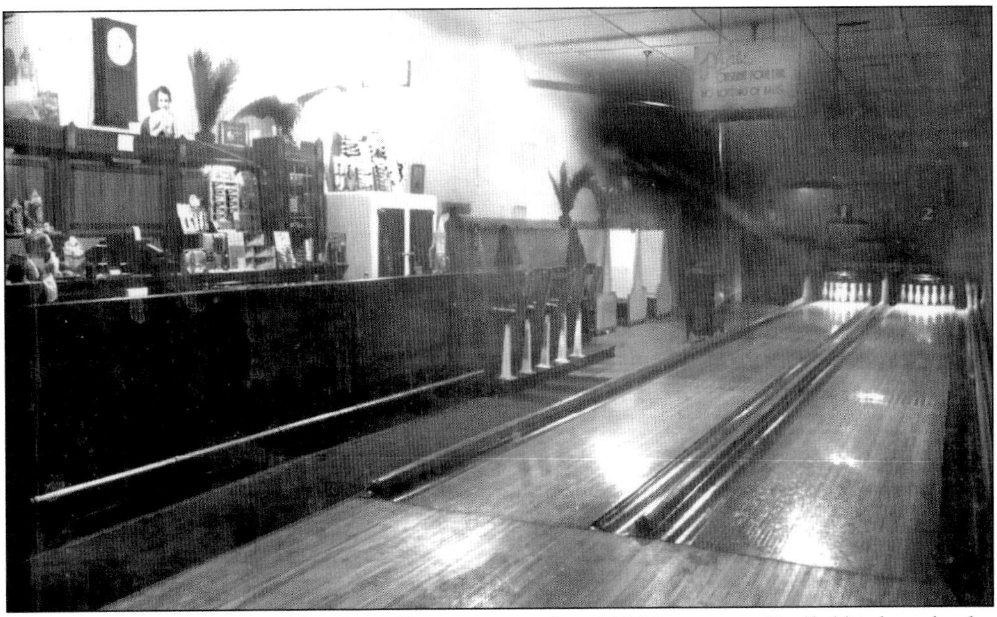

This photo of the Brass Rail bowling alley appears to be of 1920s vintage. Stuffed birds and palm fronds add to the rather curious decor. A backward misstep from a bar stool or an errant ball could wreak havoc here. The pipe smoking business appears to have been good, too.

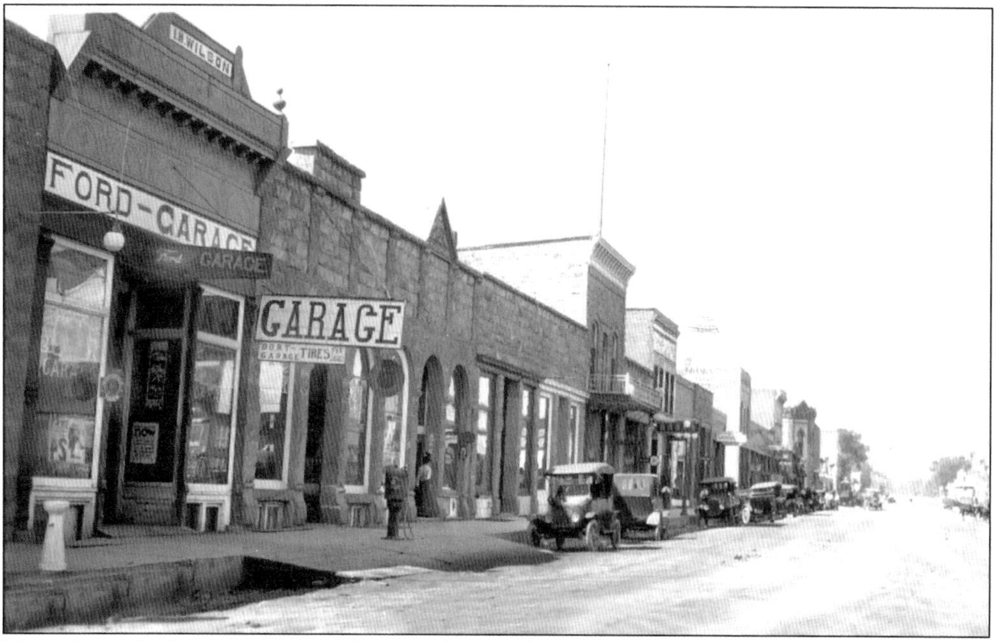

Main Street looking west c. 1915 is seen here. The row of stone buildings includes the Ford garage in the Wilson Building of the "commercial block," beginning at the south corner of Junction and Main. The cut stone buildings date from 1888 through the early 1900s.

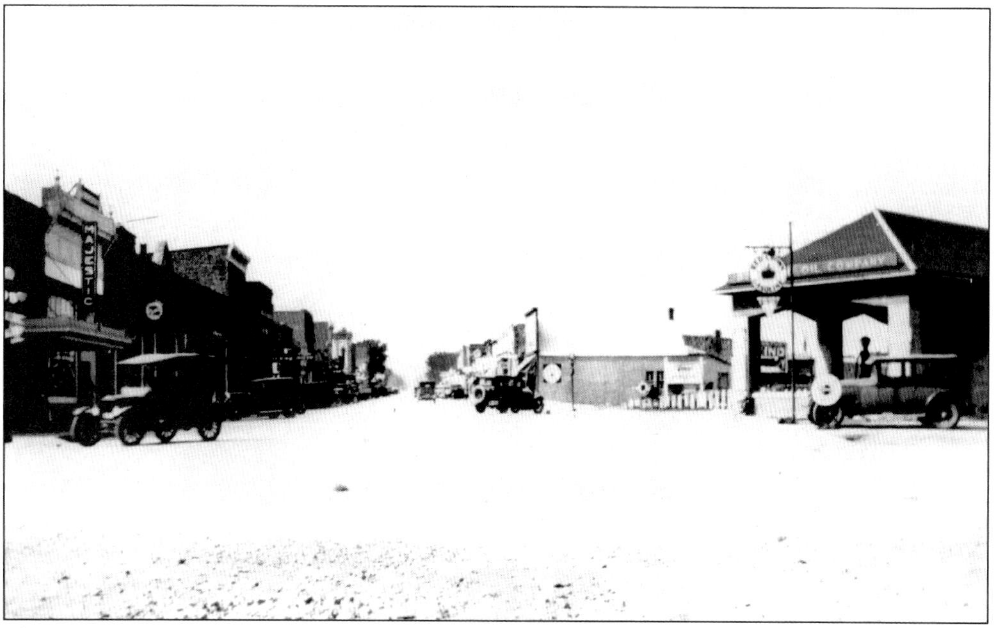

This is another view of lower Main looking west in the 1920s. The Majestic Theater is at the left, next to the Wilson Building. Across the street is the Standard Oil station, located on the future site of the city auditorium.

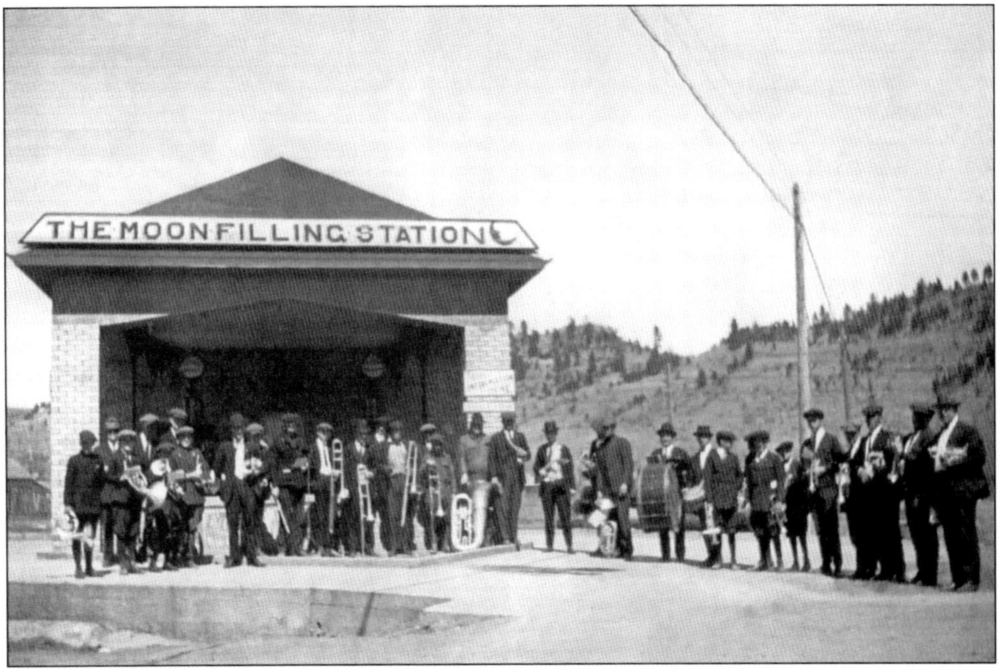

Now called the Moonfilling Station, posted signs offered tourist information to motorists. The brass band looks ready for the occasion, whatever it may have been. Clothing styles reflect the 1930s.

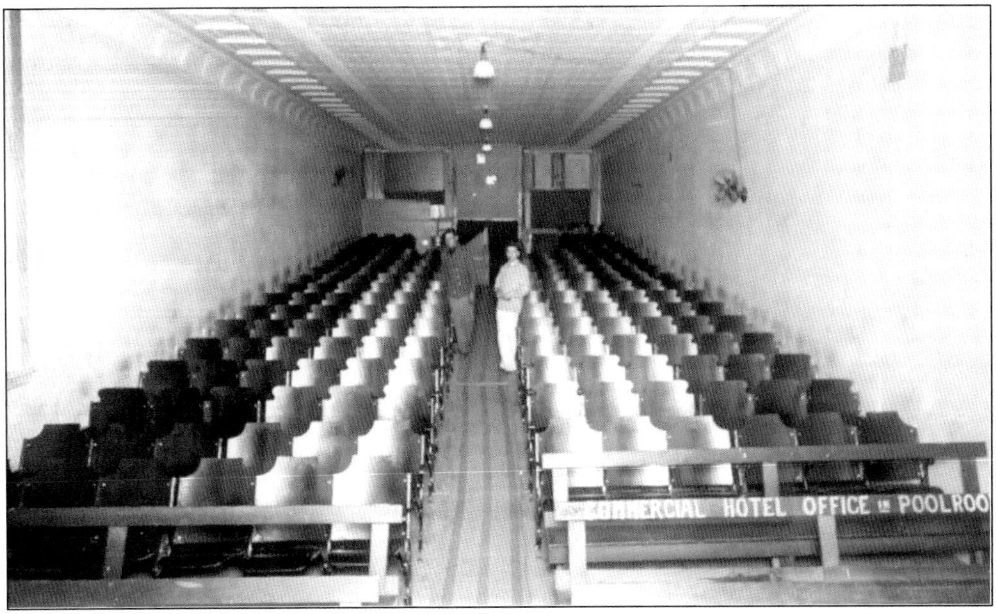

The interior of the Crook Theater doesn't look overly inviting with its rigid wooden seating and lack of exits. The bench at right says that the Commercial Hotel office is in the pool room. A date on the photo says 1913–1914, but this seems a little early for such a large movie house.

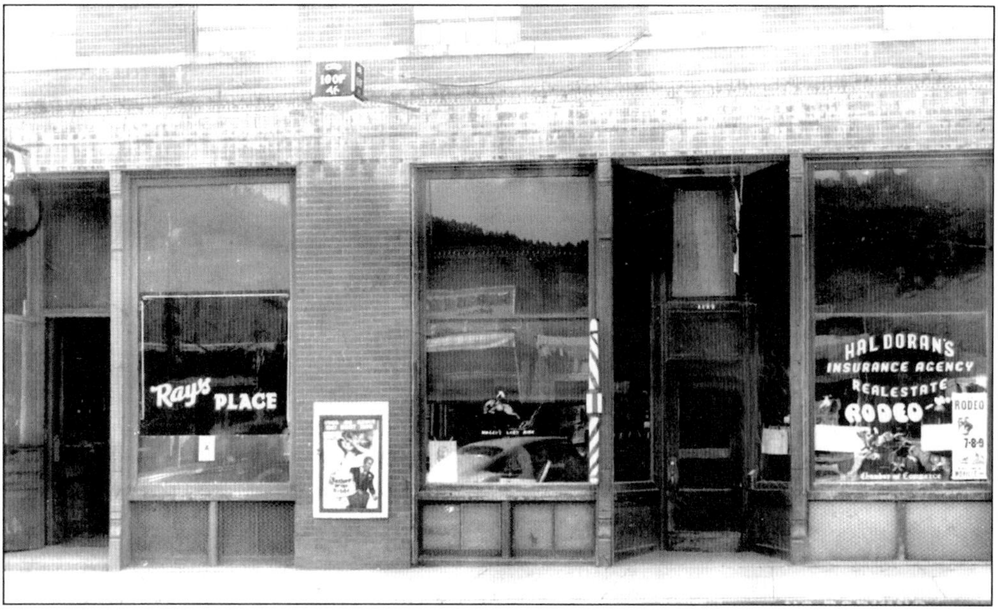

Doran's Insurance Agency and Ray's Place had a barber shop in-between. The brick building is shown before it became the J.C. Penney store in 1950. The Key City Rodeo is coming up and *Father of the Bride* with Spencer Tracy and Elizabeth Taylor is local movie fare. The Odd Fellows lodge and Masonic lodges were upstairs.

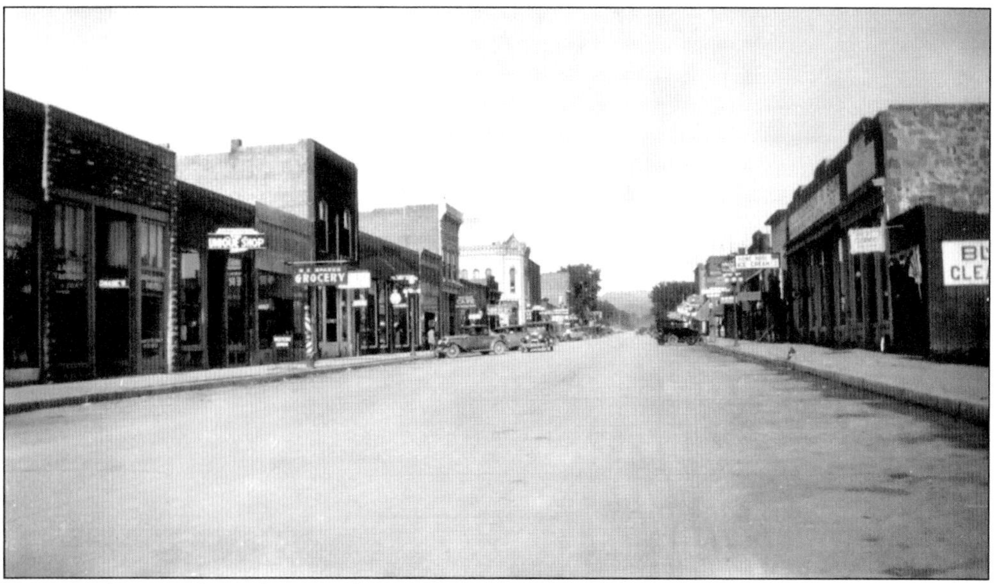

Pioneer photographer Ole A. Vik took this 1920s scene of Main Street, looking west. Ole and Della Vik recorded much early history of the northern Black Hills and knew many of the legendary characters who plied their trades here.

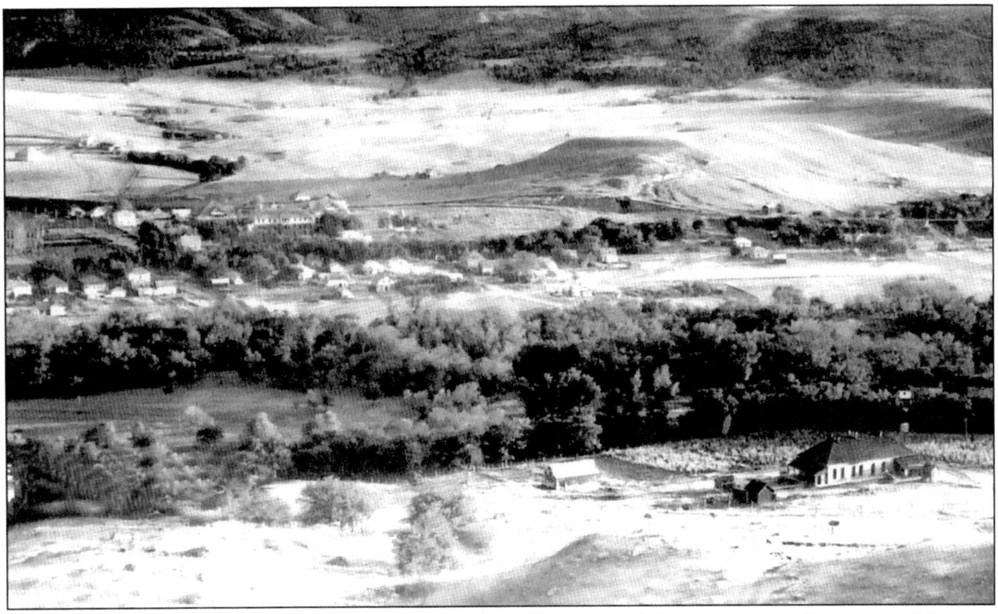

Harris Franklin bought 80 acres of land at a sheriff's sale and donated it to the town of Sturgis for the Meade County poor farm and pest house. Built in 1898, a large stone structure was constructed by Nick Schummer and was completed in six months at a cost of $2,639.08. The job superintendent, Walter Scott, was paid $50 for his labor. The poor farm closed around 1939, and based on a study from the previous year, it was disclosed that 28 poor farms remained in existence in South Dakota at that time.

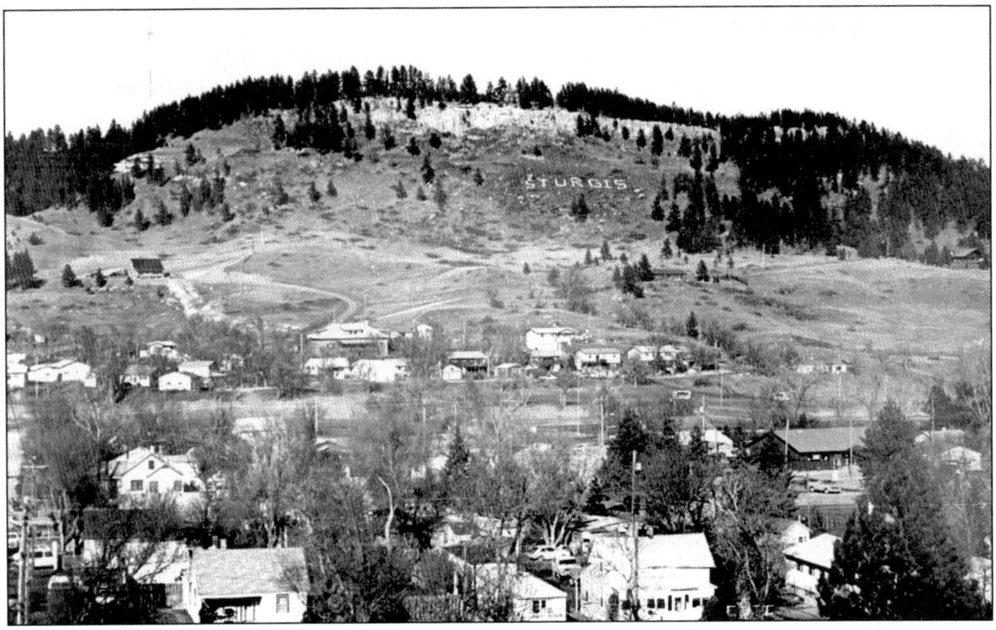

Looking north from Main Street, Sly Hill and "Sturgis" are plainly visible. In 1925, members of the Ku Klux Klan set off a dynamite charge to announce a cross-burning on Sly Hill. Fort Meade soldiers set up a machine gun on the opposite hill and with 1,500 rounds of ammunition, blasted away—bringing much discouragement to the hooded night riders.

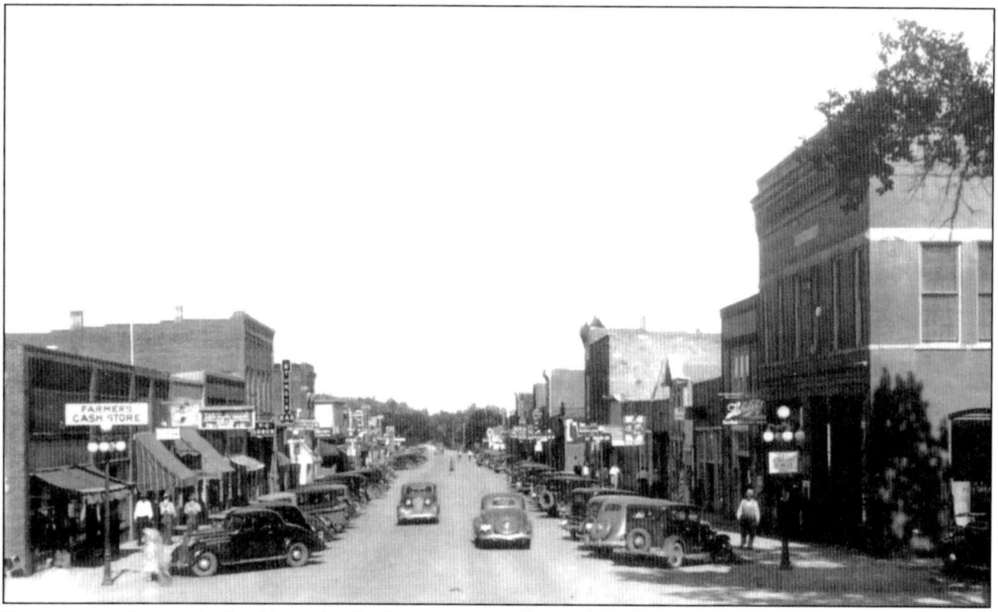

Downtown Sturgis looked like this before motorcycles replaced cars on Main Street in the heat of summer. Men in overalls are seen coming and going from the Farmer's Cash Store at left. Perhaps they will shop at Sturgis Drug; have a bite to eat at T.C. Lund's or down a cold brew at the Hi Hat or Sturgis Bar before heading home. The posted speed limit here is 15 miles per hour.

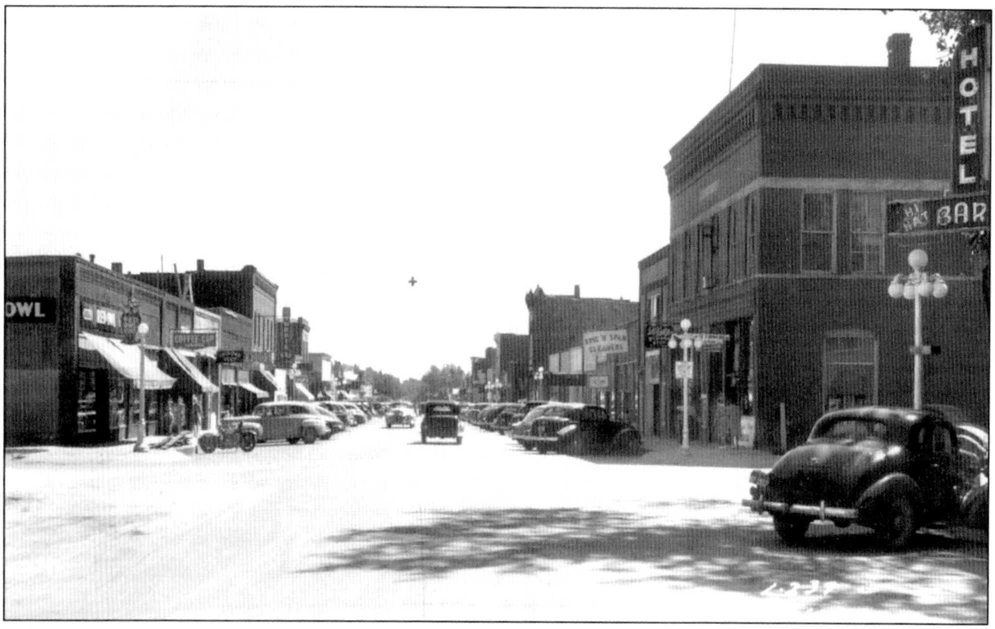

Taken at nearly the same spot in 1939, a Red Owl grocery has replaced the Farmer's store. Also new are the Coffee Cup café and Spic-N-Span Cleaners. And a motorcycle now sits at the curb.

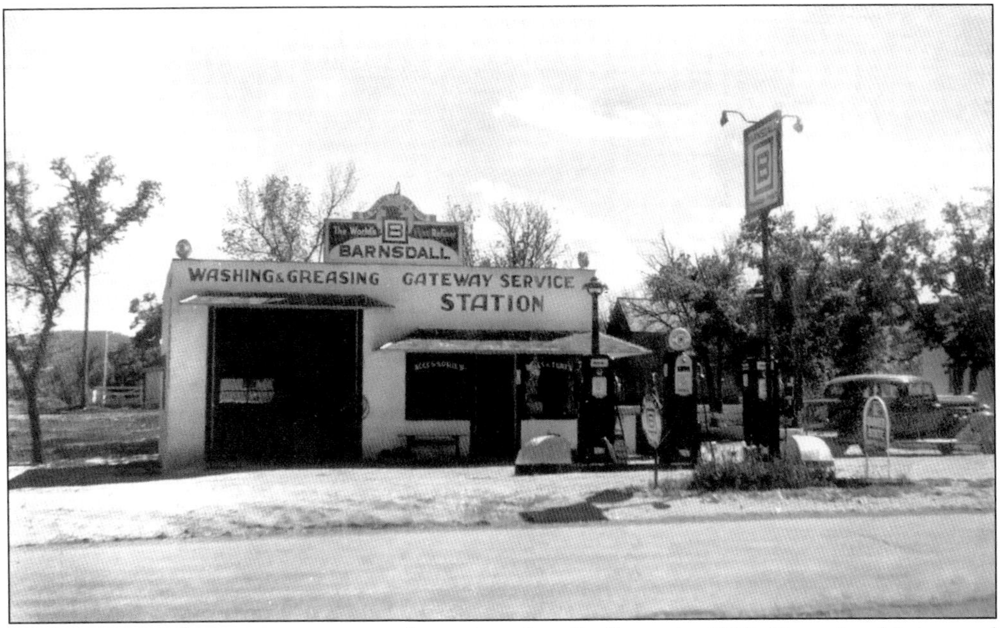

Regan's Barnsdall service station was located on Lazelle Street in 1937. Regan's sold tires and tubes, auto accessories, and Quaker State motor oil, according to their signs, besides washing and lubricating customer vehicles.

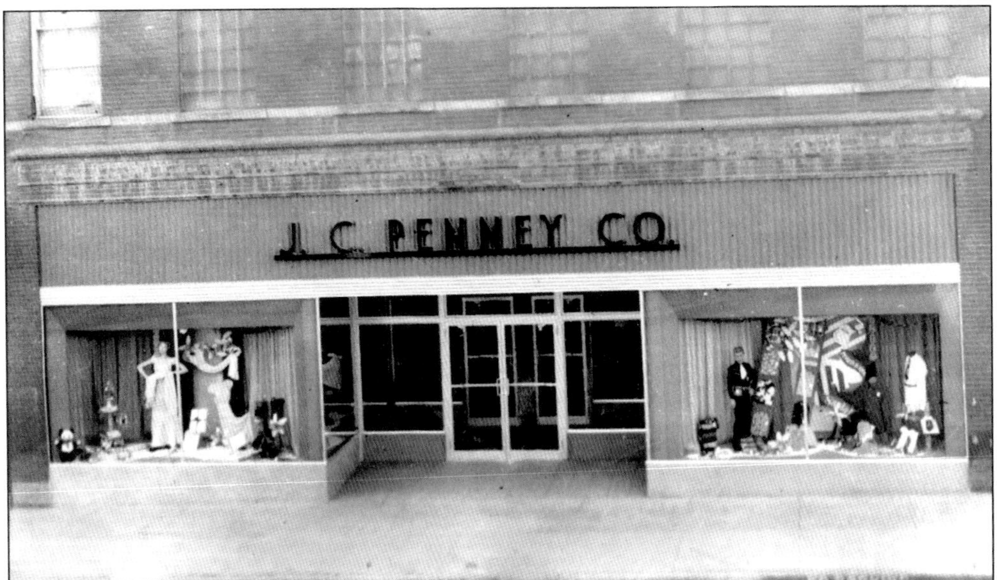

J.C. Penney's new store front on Main Street in 1950. The latest fashions for men and women are shown in an "ultramodern" setting with loads of shopping ideas, but the notice painted along the sidewalk says "No Parking."

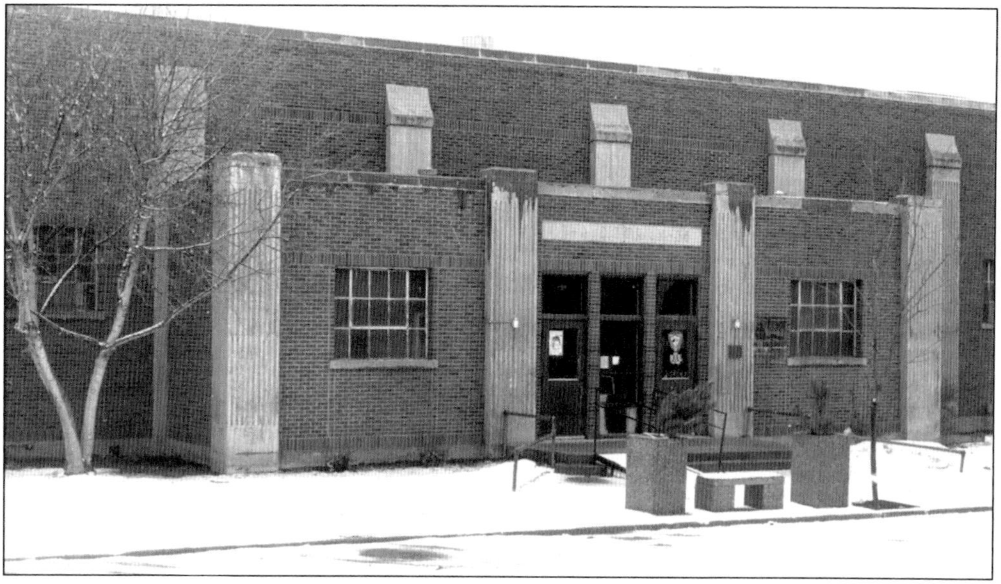

Located on the former site of the Commercial Hotel (also known as the Pierson Hotel), the new city building had an auditorium, gymnasium, library, and offices for the American Legion, who pledged $4,000 toward its construction. Between 1930 and 1940, Sturgis grew from 1,747 to 3,008 in population. Its biggest spurt of growth was in 1933, when the Meade County commissioners boasted of $50,792.70 in their general fund.

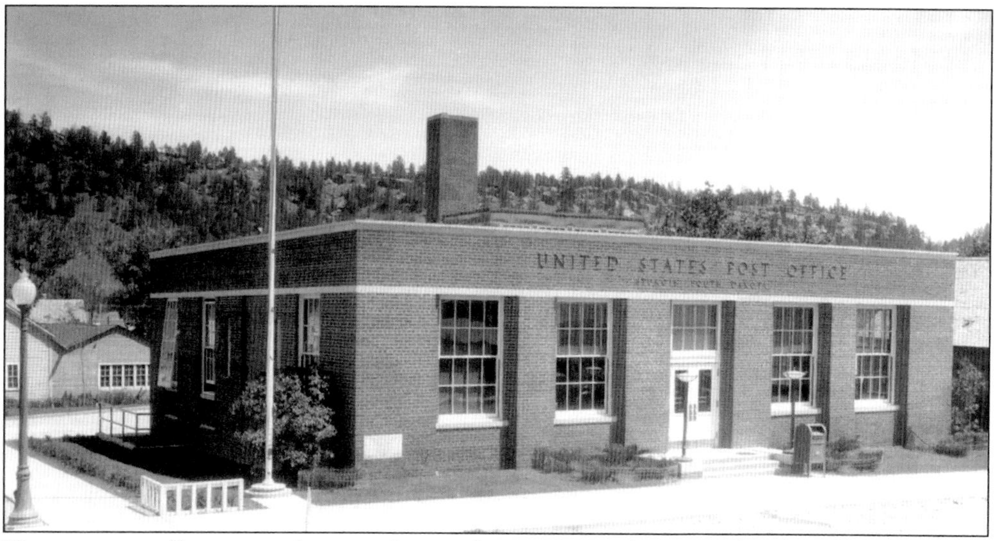

The new post office is seen here on the northeast corner of Main and Junction. Sturgis's first post office was operated in the winter of 1878–1879 by Sioux City newspaperman Charles Collins. Collins also wrote the first book published in the Black Hills. In February 1888, several bachelor mailmen sponsored a dance on Alkali Creek, serving up "half a critter and 40 yellow-legged spring chickens."

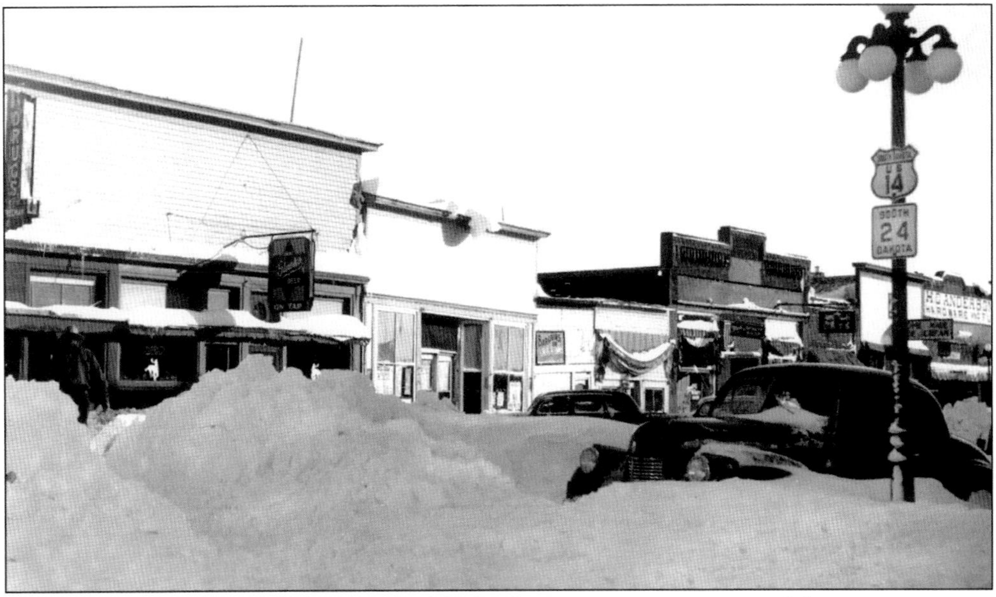

Dated November 14, 1944, this post card by Taylor was an ominous sign of things yet to come. Roads were blocked for six weeks due to the storm, a war was going on that America was deeply involved in, and an outbreak of scarlet fever just before Christmas closed schools and interrupted holiday shopping.

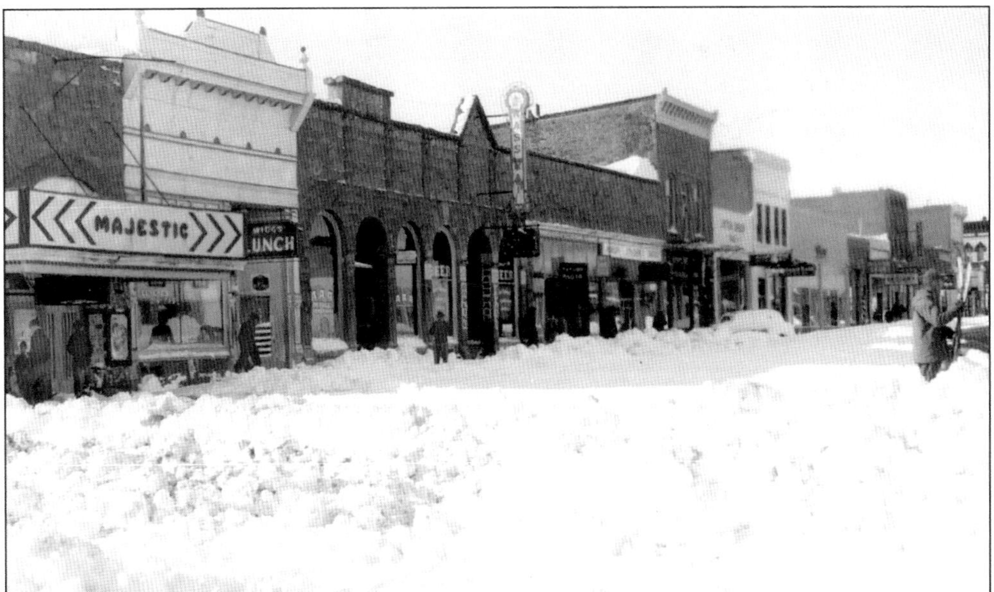

Here is the opposite side of Main Street taken on the same day. The Majestic Theater has some customers, but no children would be allowed to attend any public functions shortly thereafter, until the epidemic was over. Where are the snow plows?

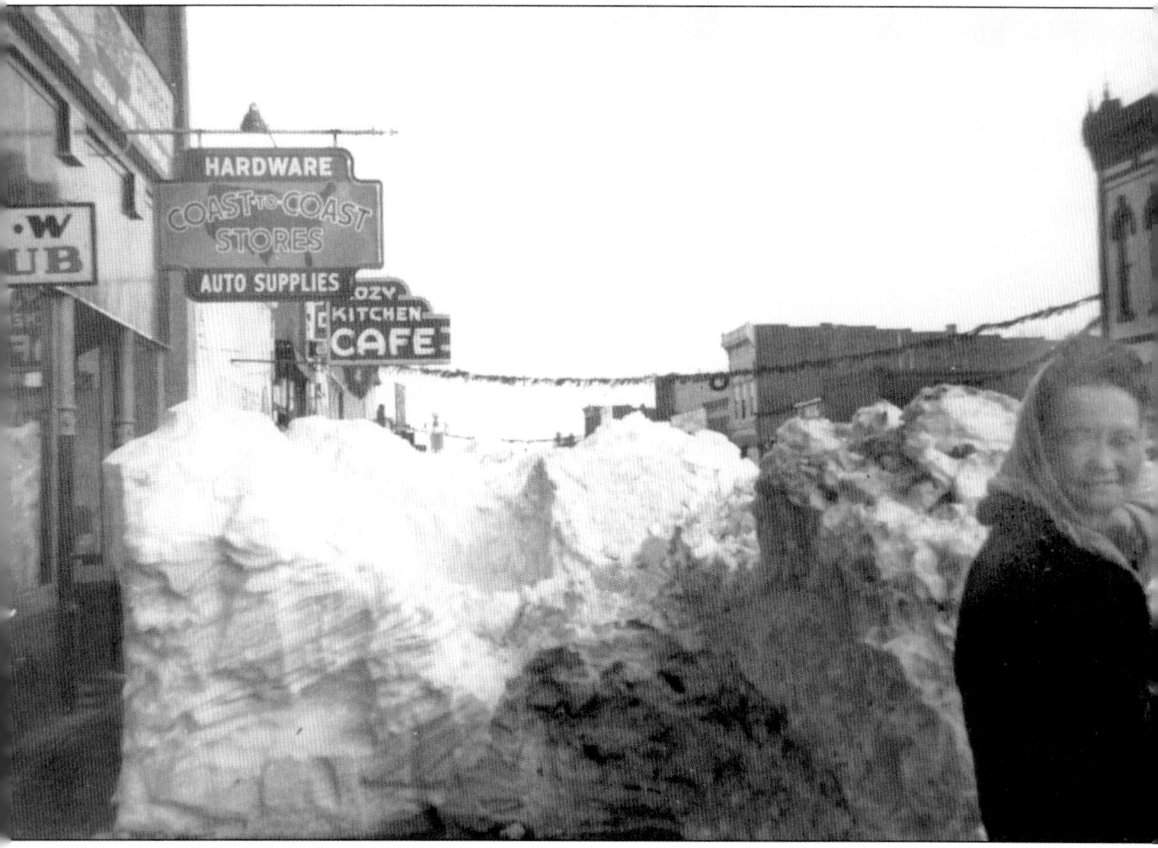

The "grand daddy" of all winter storms in memory was the "Blizzard of '49," burying much of the Midwest in hard-packed, wind-driven snow that piled up to rooftops and stalled trains on the prairies. On the 1100 block of Main, shown here, shop owners have apparently admitted defeat in the attempt to remove drifts taller than they were. Only a few brave customers were interested in venturing out before sunshine and warmer temperatures came to the rescue.

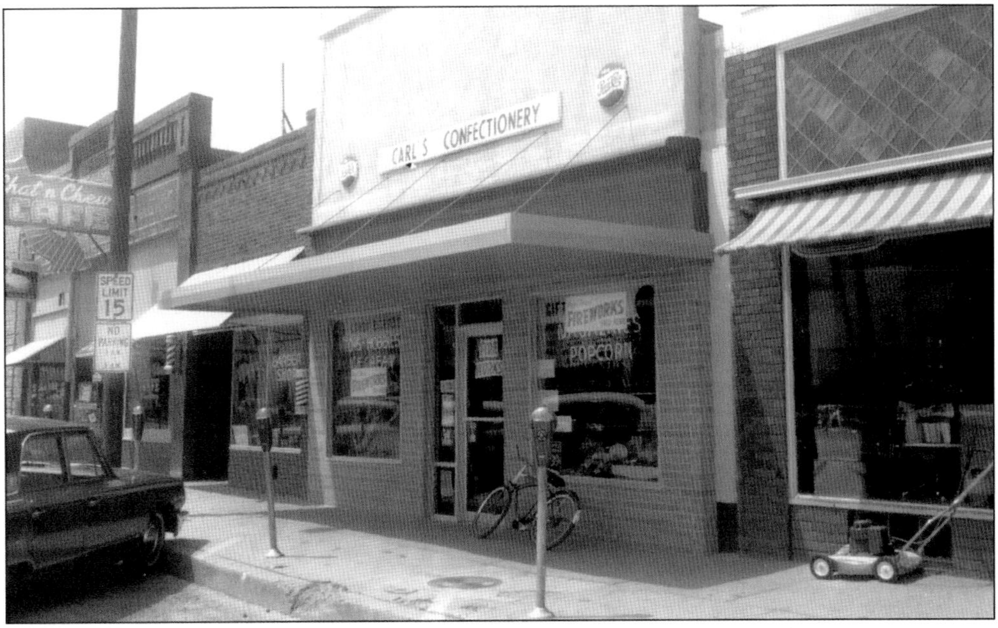

Carl's Confectionery at 1167 Main has a new front. It must be summer—a lawnmower awaits a new owner, a young customer's bike rests by the door, and signs in Carl's window are advertising fireworks for sale.

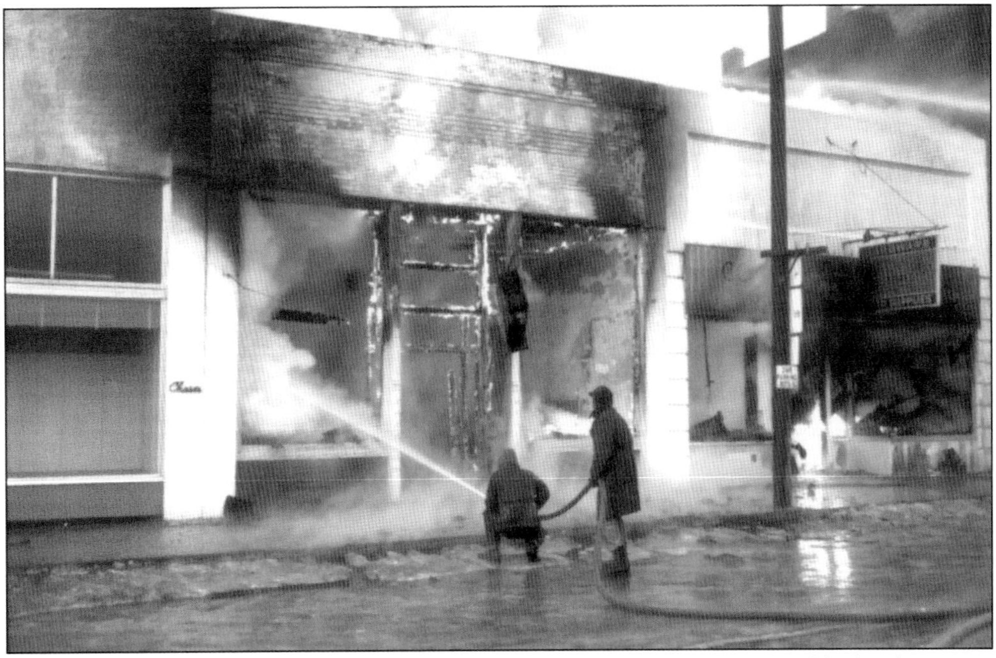

Firemen pour water on Knapp's and the Coast-to-Coast store in the 1100 block of Main in March 1960 as flames continue to erupt.

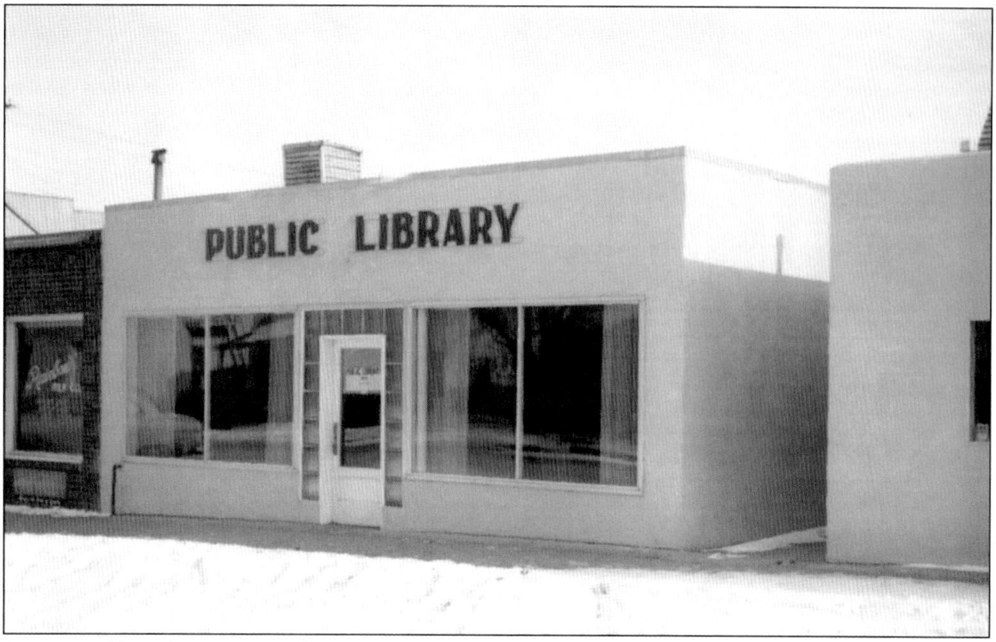

Sturgis Public Library is seen here in February 1956. Next door is the Rainbow Milk Company.

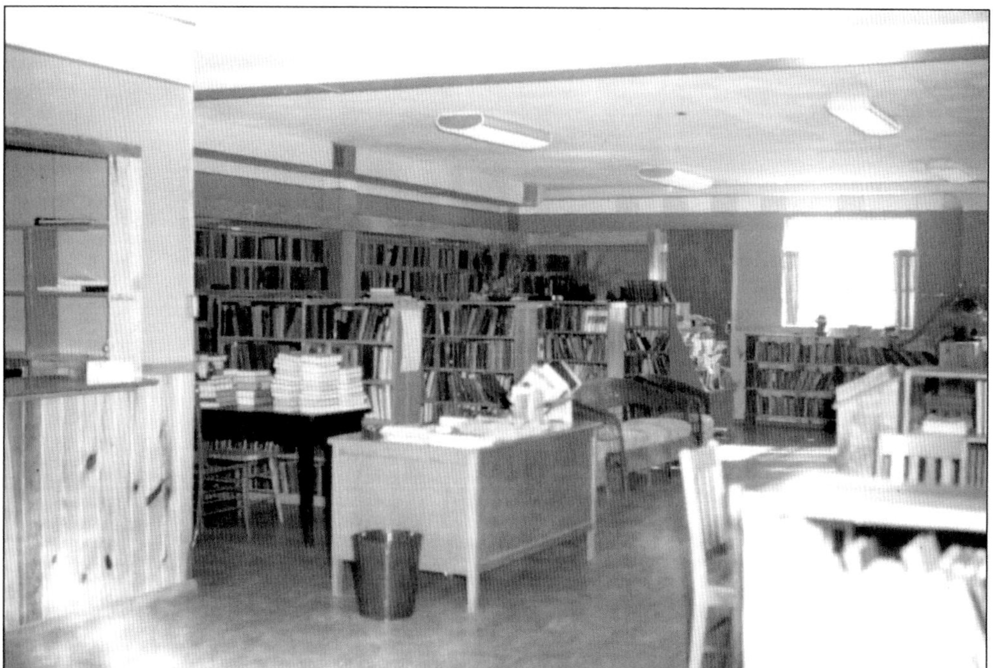

The interior of the library shows a reading area with wicker sofa and study areas. The library's collection of South Dakota books and related historical materials is a popular and busy section of the library today.

Four

Taking Care of Business

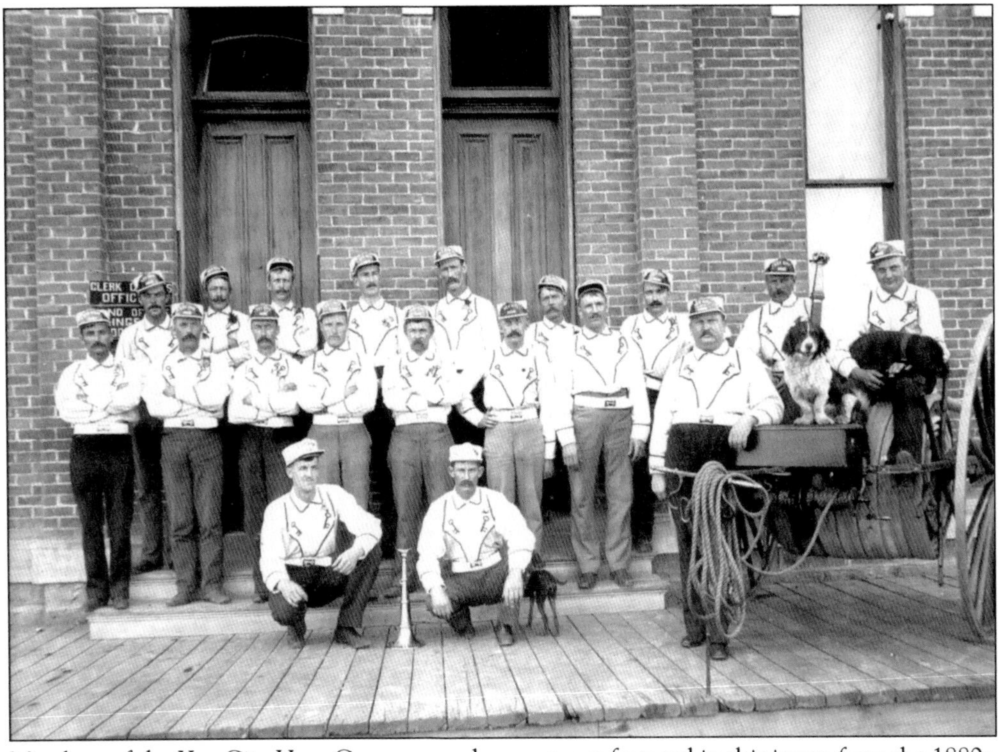

Members of the Key City Hose Company and mascots are featured in this image from the 1880s. On February 10, 1888, cooperative efforts of Sturgis firemen and those from Fort Meade performed "a narrow escape from the obliteration of the business portion of the town." Fanned by a strong northwest breeze, a fire in McLean's eatery quickly spread. Across the street, Elsenor's (later Charles) Hotel caught fire several times due to the heat. In 1906, two disastrous fires occurred within a month—the Francis Block on February 11, and Benevolent Hall on March 11.

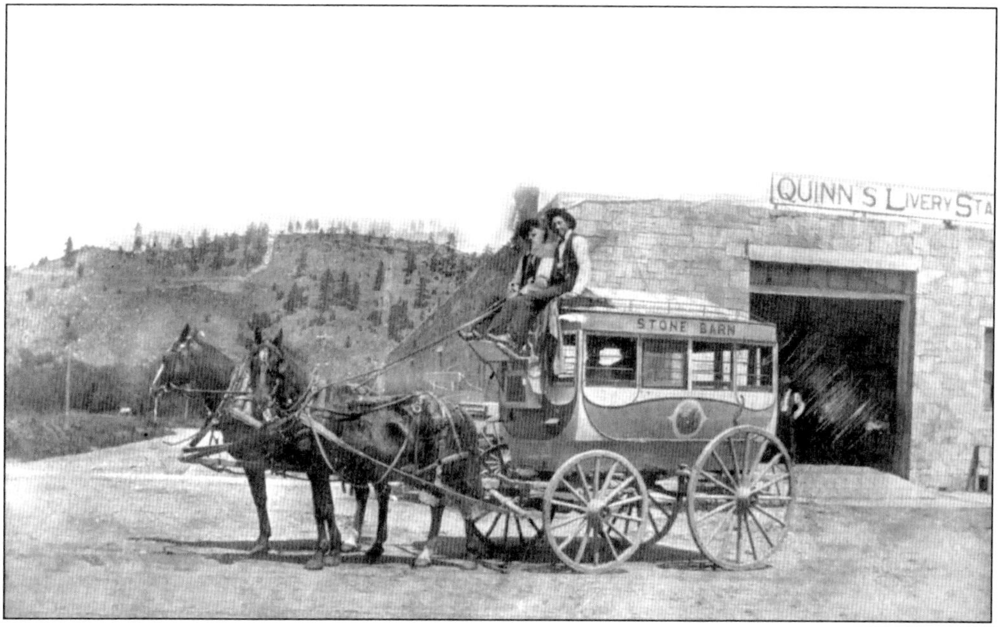

Fred Quinn ran this stagecoach, or hack, from his Quinn Livery Stable in 1907 at the northeast corner of Main and Junction, where the post office was located for many years.

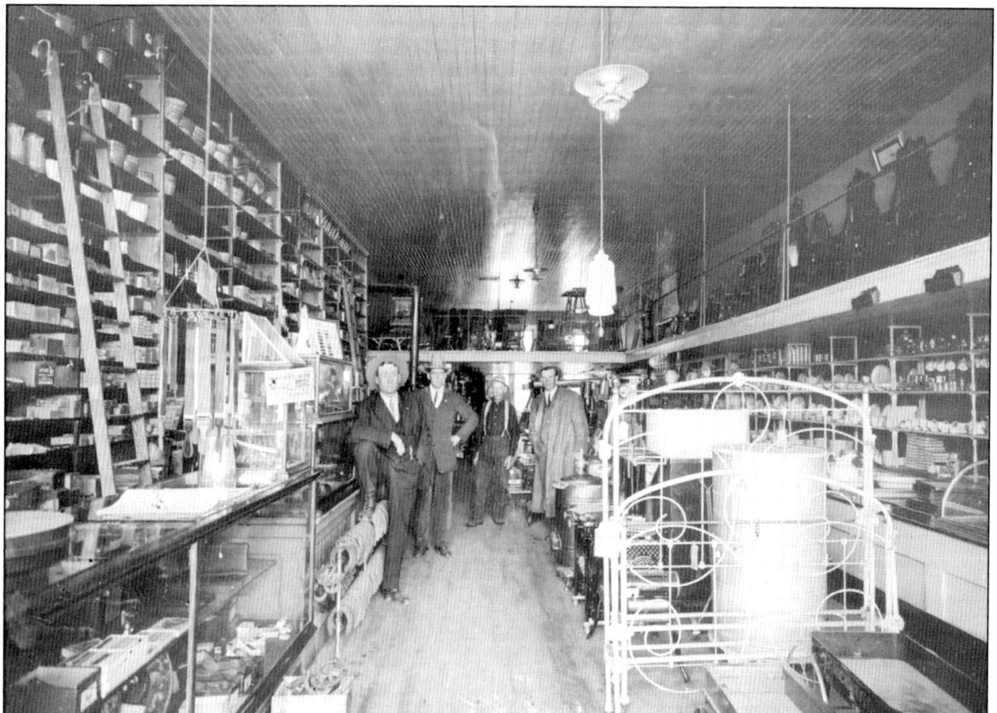

Star and Bullock Mercantile was the first business emporium in Sturgis. Built in 1877, it was reported to have seen "more money flow over its counters than any other building anywhere." The original log shack was hastily expanded several times and eventually became an eyesore. Torn down on March 17, 1905, it was replaced by James O'Neill's brick block.

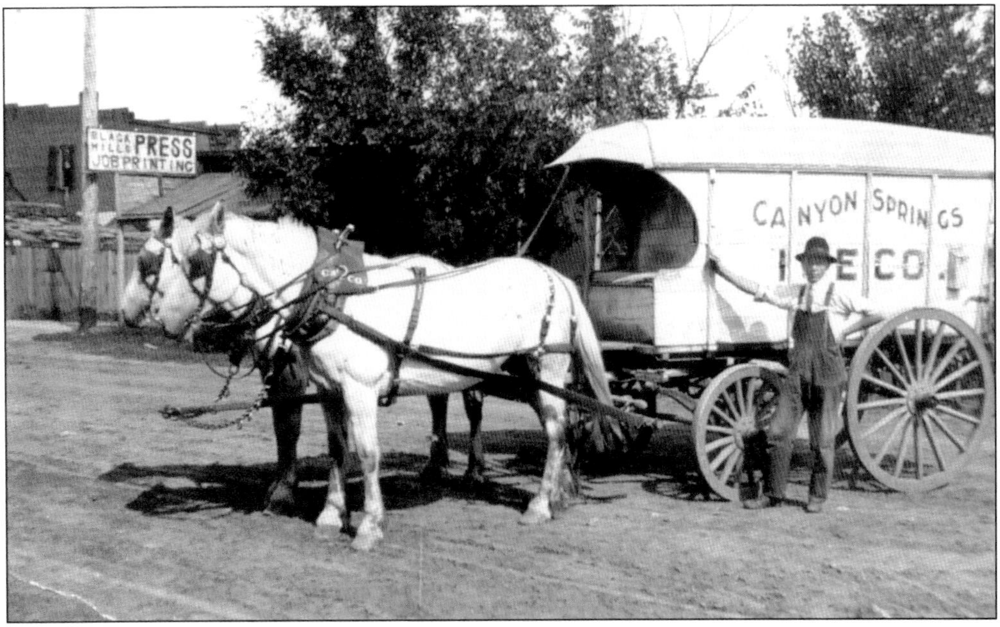

John Hoel began the Canyon Springs Ice Company, providing a valuable service before refrigeration. The ice wagon pictured here with George Norman had a canvas top and was manufactured by Studebaker. Ice was cut in large blocks and packed in sawdust for later delivery. The cost was 50¢ per hundred pounds to a business, or 60¢ per hundred pounds for home use.

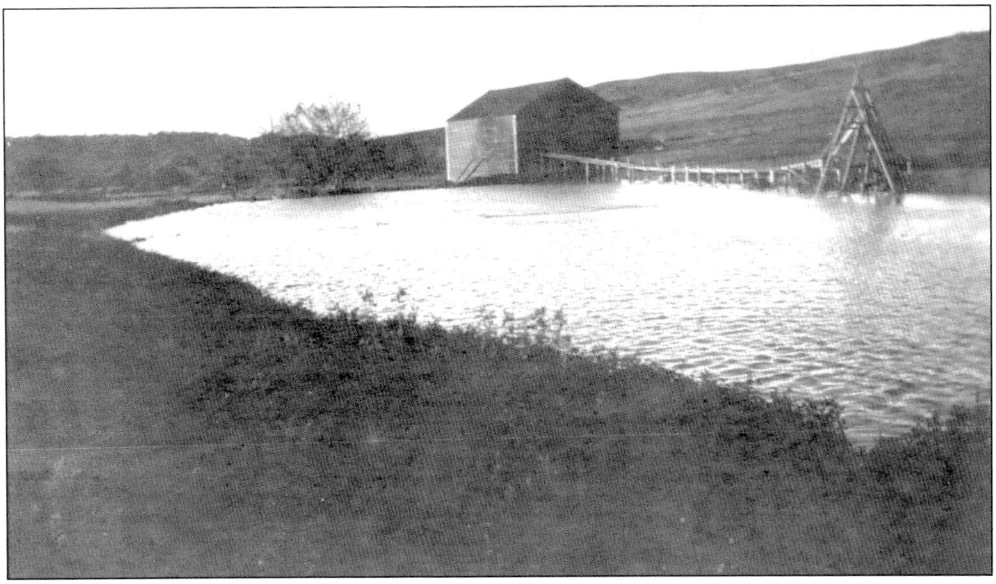
In 1903, John Hoel built a dam and ice house in Vanocker Canyon. In 1936, John's son, known to all as J.C. or "Pappy," took over the business, which remained in the family for 41 years. This dam was located on Baldwin Street in South Sturgis.

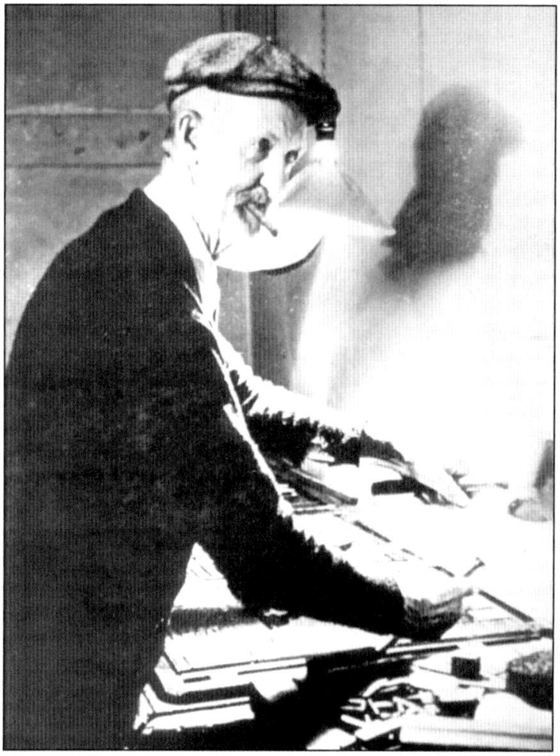

William F. Waldman worked for early newsman C.C. Moody and was president of the Key City Hose Company in 1904. The hand-cranked Taylor press was brought to the Black Hills by bull train. After working at all positions, Waldman became the owner of the *Sturgis Weekly Record* on January 1, 1925.

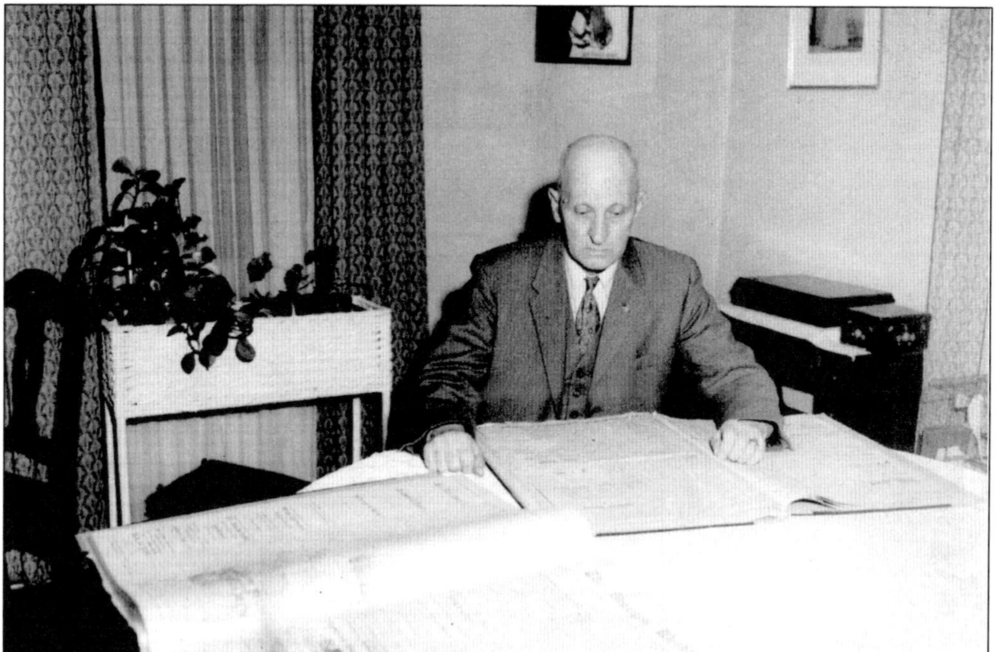

Charles Waldman looks over past issues from his father's newspaper enterprise. The *Sturgis Weekly Record* merged with the *Sturgis Tribune* on May 30, 1946, and was purchased by Morris Hallock in 1959. Hallock and Bob Lee formed Black Hills Publishing Company, purchasing the *Black Hills Press* in 1960 and starting *Tri-State Livestock News* in 1963.

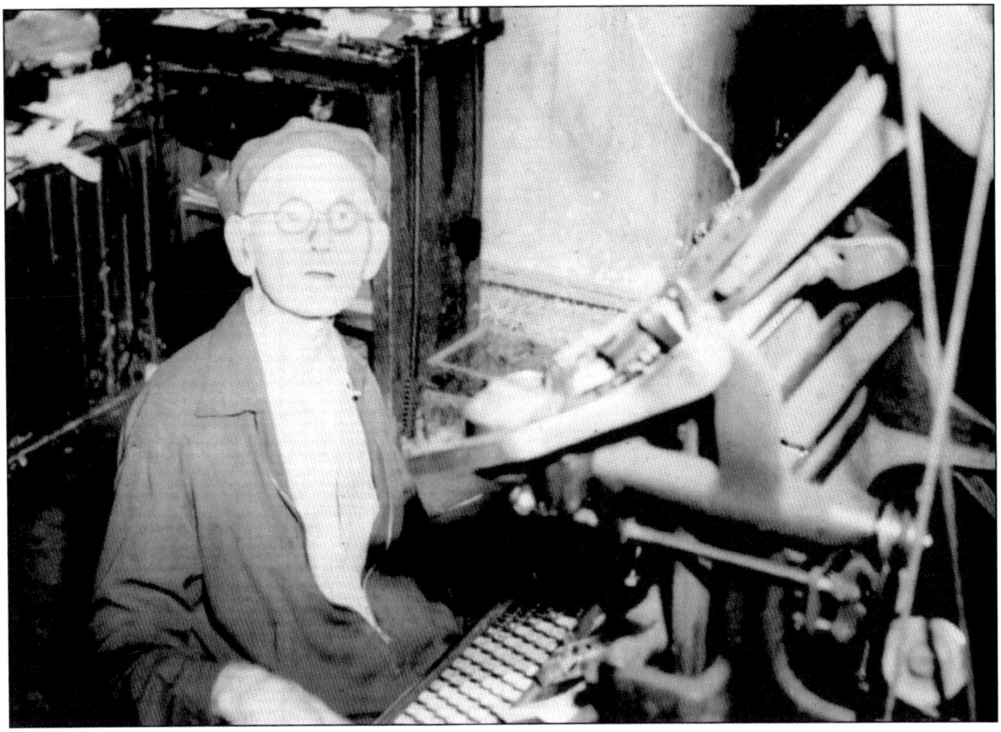

Scott Handlin, shown in the early 1900s, was one of the region's first newspapermen, and was editor of the *Black Hills Press*. On May 30, 1890, a fight between the town's competing publications broke out over the issue of women's suffrage. They told it like it was in the old days!

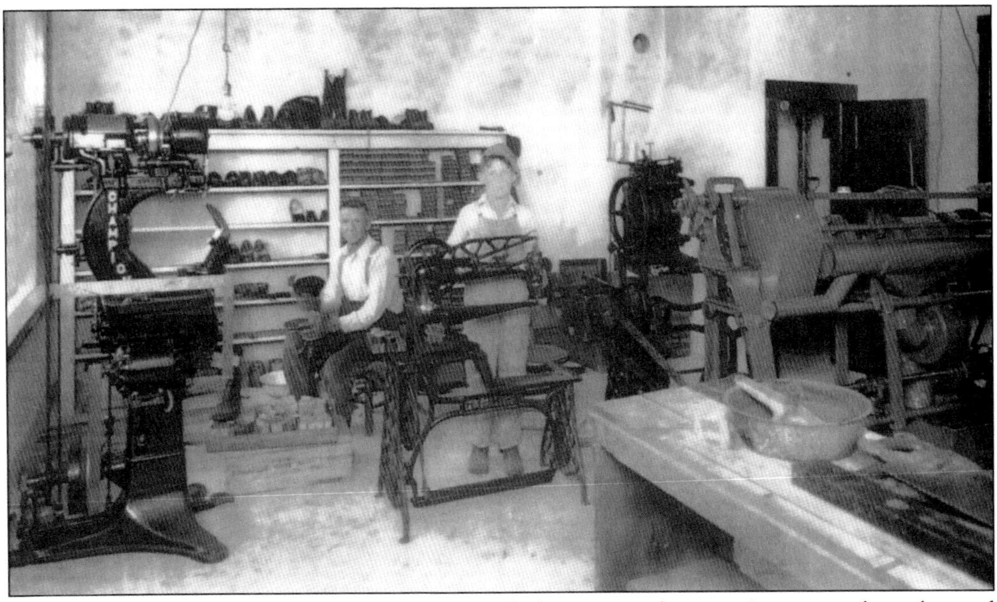

Lessard's Shoe Shop was one of several boot and shoe repair shops in Sturgis, and was located at 1036 Second Street, at the later site of the Rainbow Milk Company and the library. It was unheard of to throw out footwear with worn soles if the tops were still serviceable. The lad appears to be an apprentice and may be a family member.

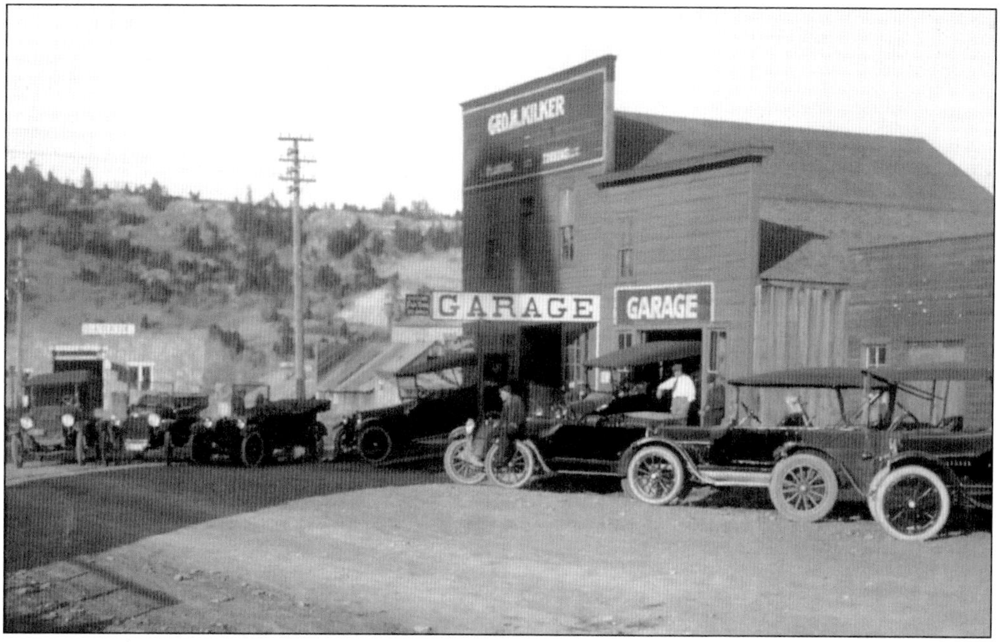

George and Art Kilker ran this garage on the east side of Junction, between Main and Sherman Streets probably prior to World War I. Art was the mechanic and George performed salesman duties.

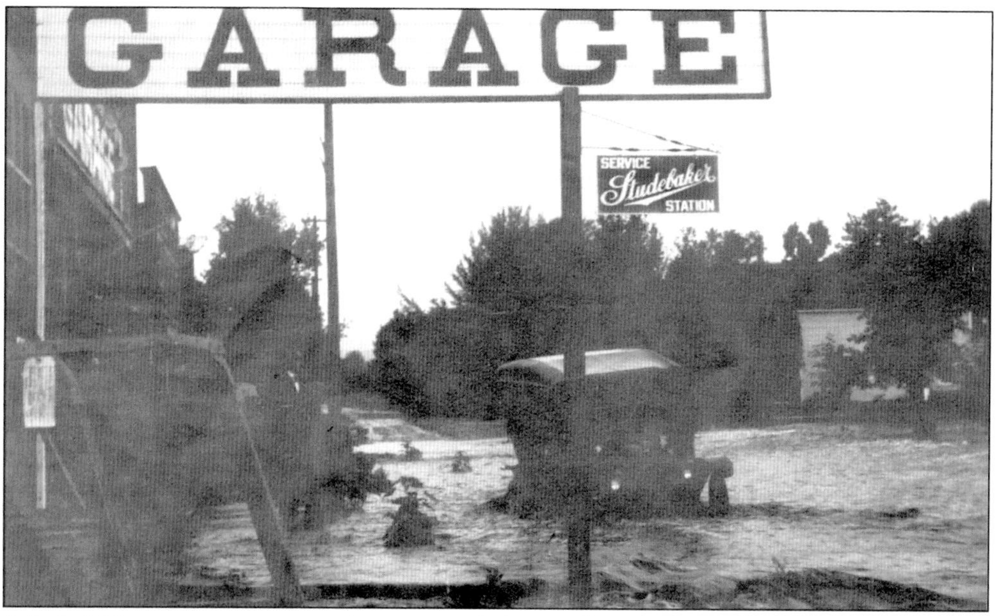

A little high water was commonplace now and then in Sturgis. Bigger floods occurred in 1883, 1907, 1908, 1916, 1922, 1946, 1962, and 1972. But in 1933, rushing water completely washed out "Lover's Lane," the road between Sturgis and Fort Meade.

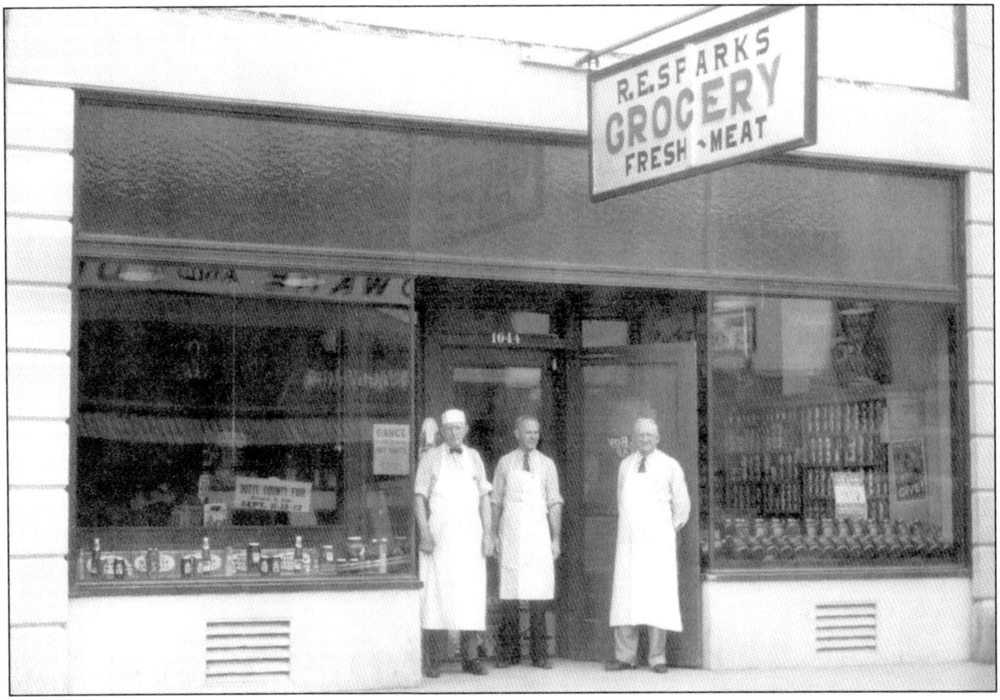

Many early businesses were still around decades later. Customers who were treated fairly were as loyal to local merchants as the merchants were to the generations of folks they served. Spark's Grocery is shown at a different location sometime after World War II.

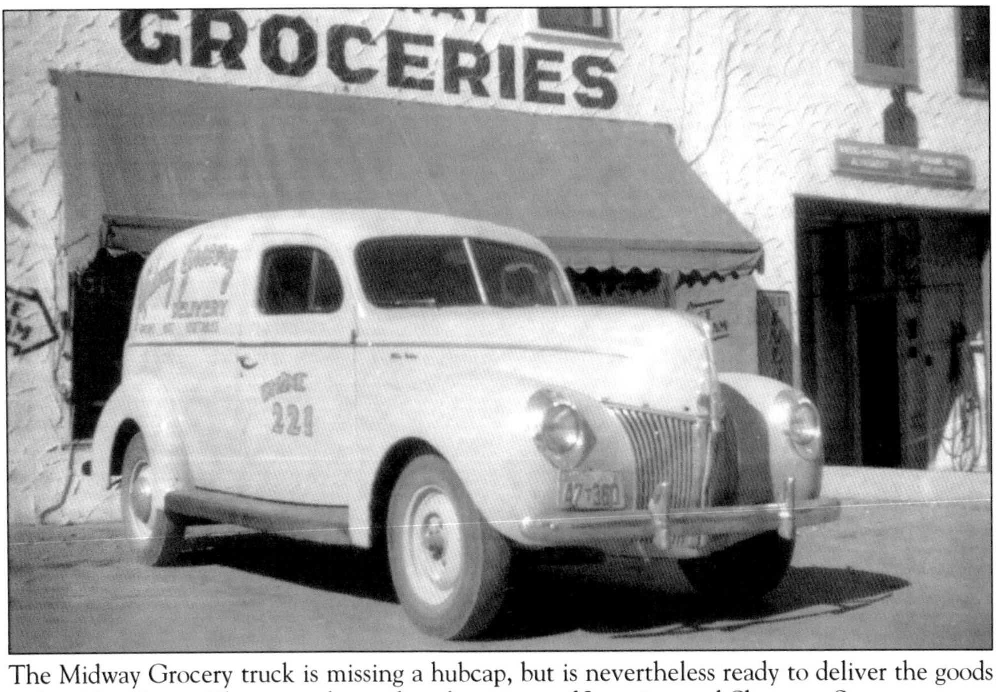

The Midway Grocery truck is missing a hubcap, but is nevertheless ready to deliver the goods ordered by phone. They were located at the corner of Junction and Sherman Streets, next to Ted's Auto Repair. The building was recently razed.

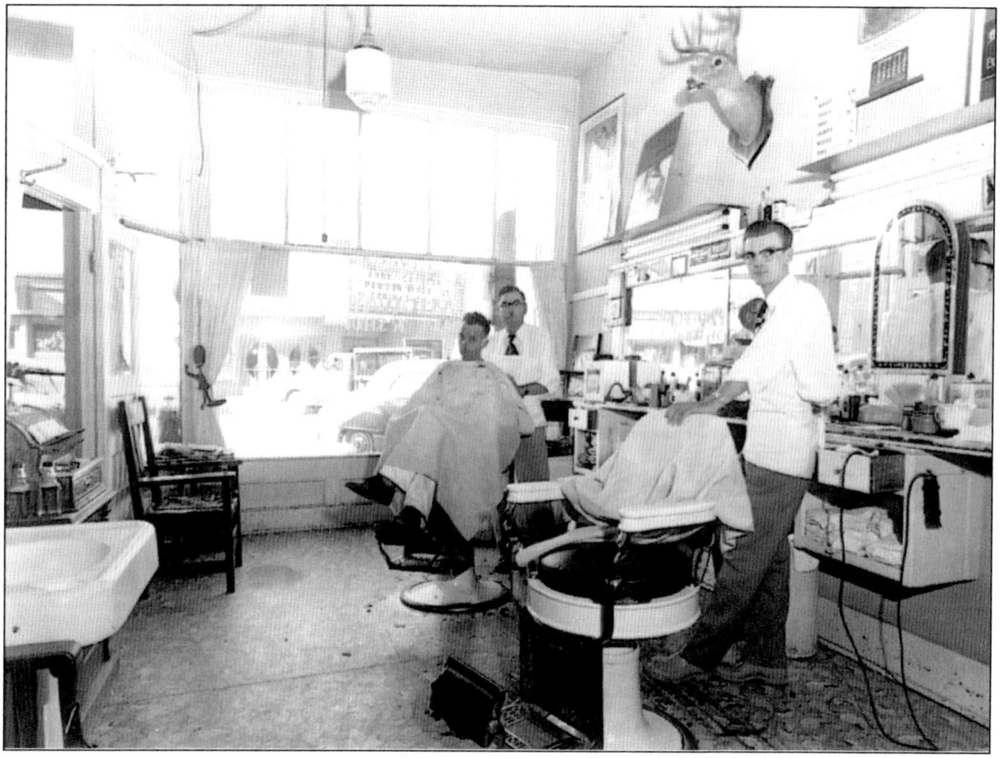

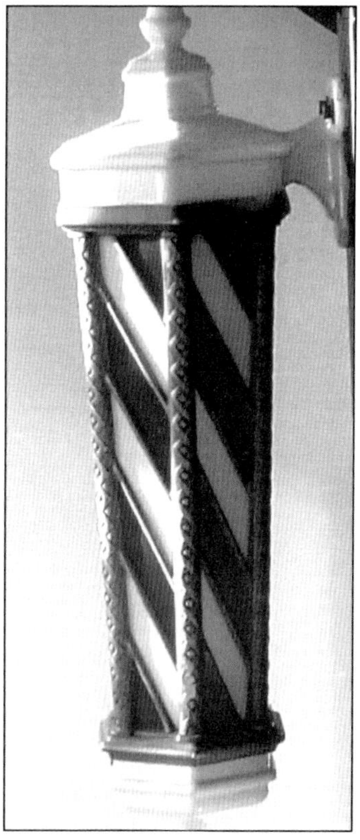

Shave and a hair cut at the Midway Barber Shop probably cost more than the proverbial "two bits" in January 1952. Pictured are customer "Shorty" Weimer, barber Joe DesJarlais, and Chuck Keuscher. It was at 1058 Main and Bea's Beauty Shop was located in the rear. The Majestic across the street was showing the Western feature, *Powder River*.

The unusual barber pole outside Joe DesJarlais' shop dates to 1884.

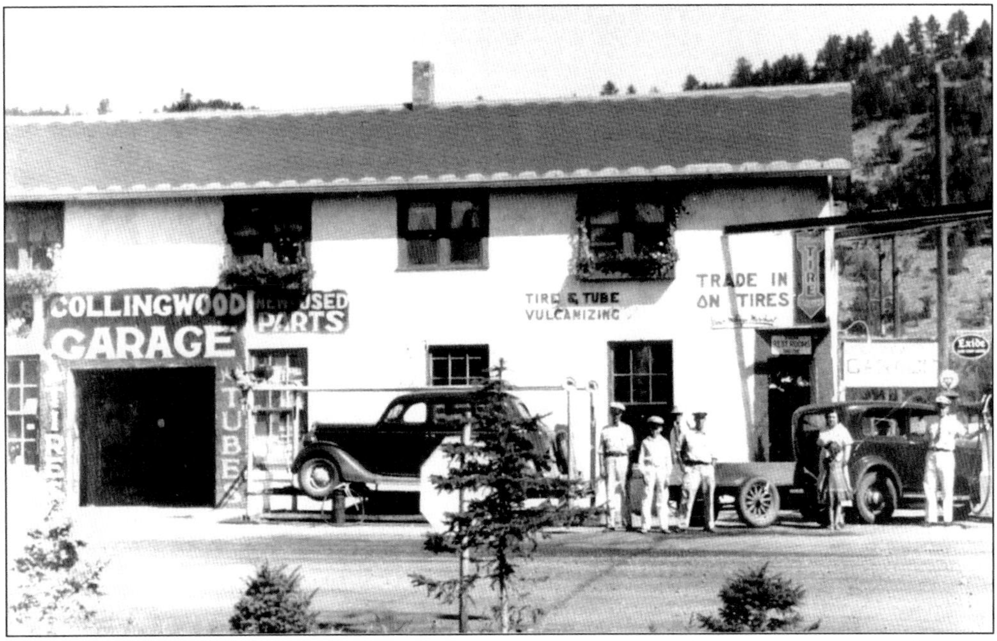

Collingwood Garage was another Sturgis enterprise catering to the new motoring and tourist industry. Later a Conoco station, the upscale operation at the northwestern side of Lazelle and Junction appears capable of handling any roadside emergency.

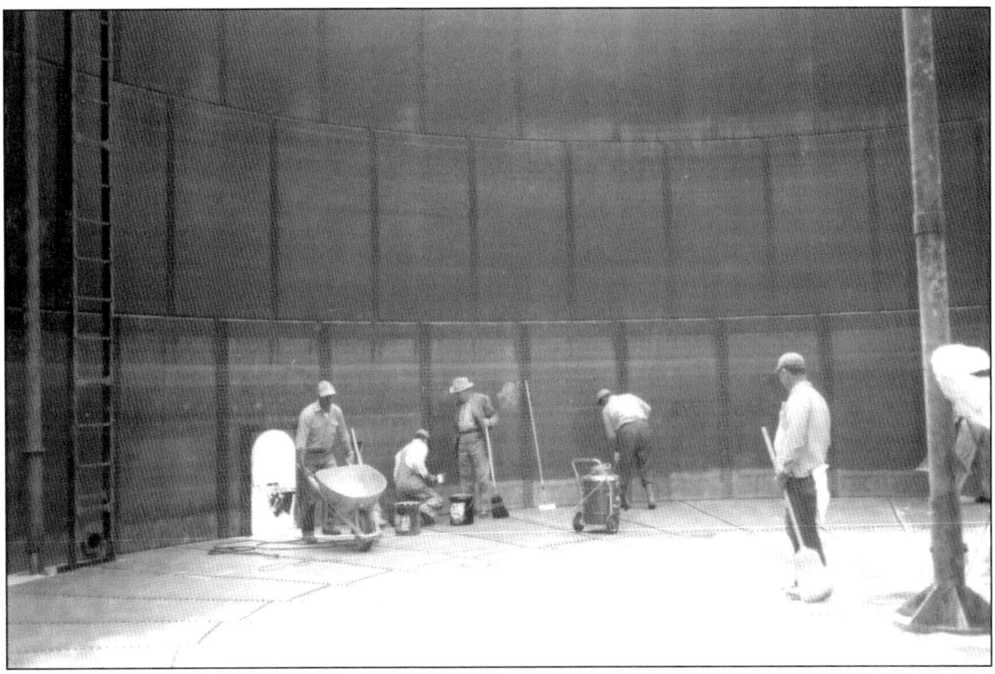
Building the Sturgis Water Works dam in 1959 was exacting and hard work, though broom pushing seems a little less demanding. The city bought the privately-owned operation from the Jarvis estate in 1977 for $2,037,689.

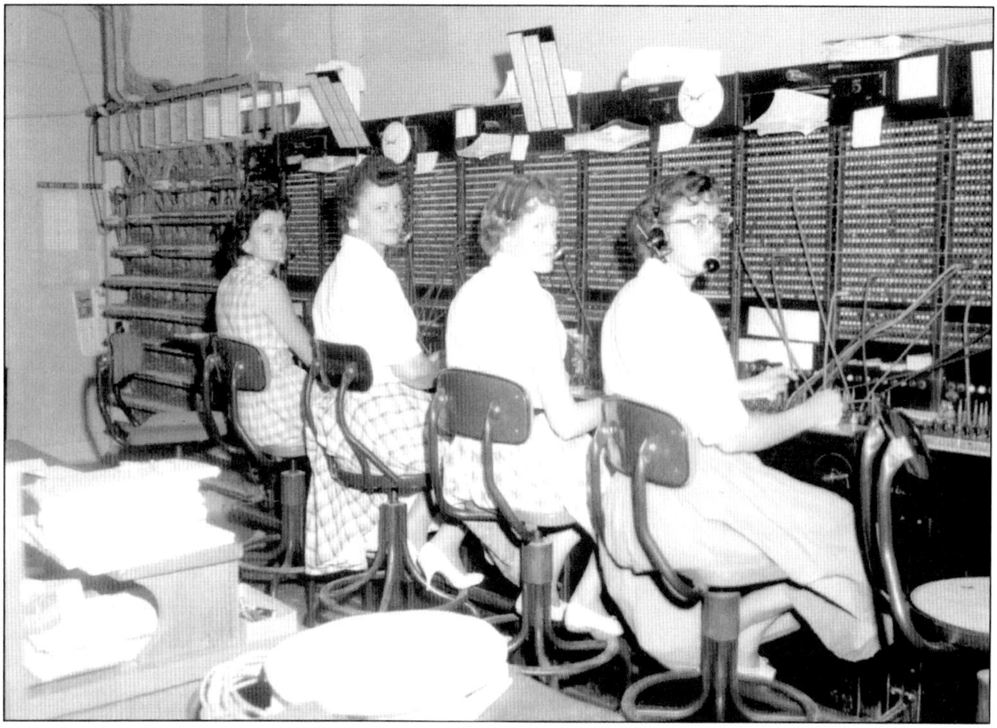

Telephone service was available in Sturgis as early as 1883. Dr. Lynch, who ran the post office and drug store, was the first customer. On July 21, 1936, systems were changed from magneto to battery and there were 409 customers. These young ladies are at the switchboard in 1950, but they were replaced by dial service in 1961. Long-distance direct dialing began in 1962.

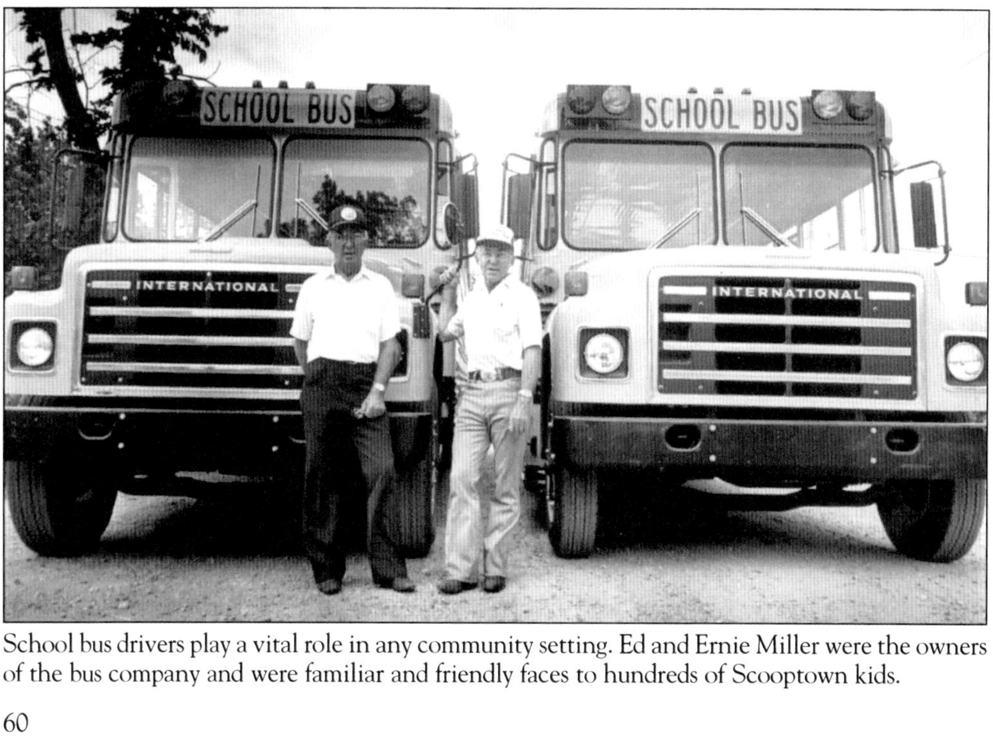

School bus drivers play a vital role in any community setting. Ed and Ernie Miller were the owners of the bus company and were familiar and friendly faces to hundreds of Scooptown kids.

Five

Around the Town

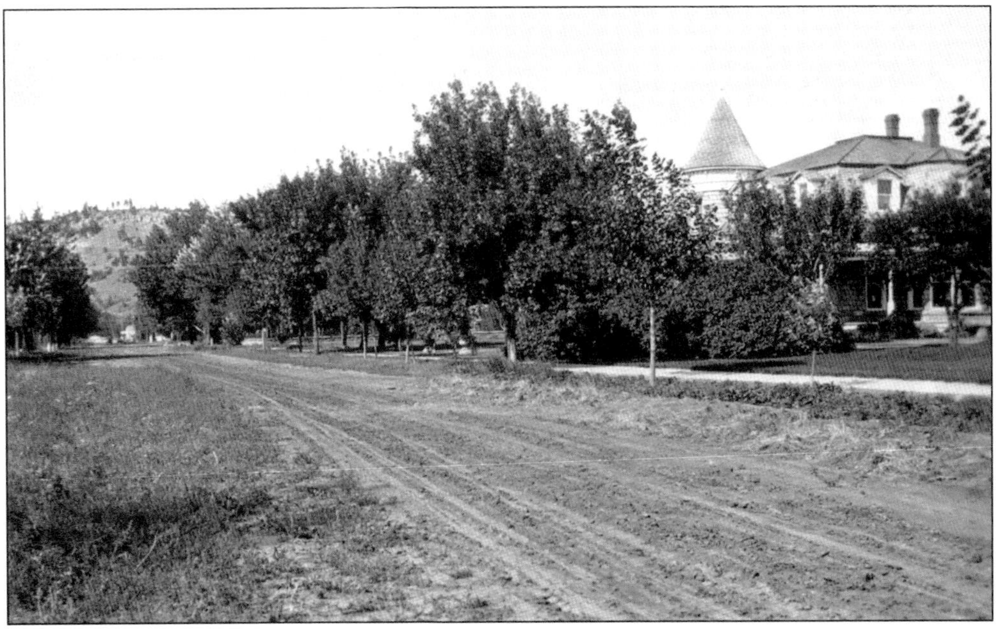

South Junction Avenue before paving was a challenge in both wet and dry weather, no matter how elegant the homes along the tree-lined boulevard may have been.

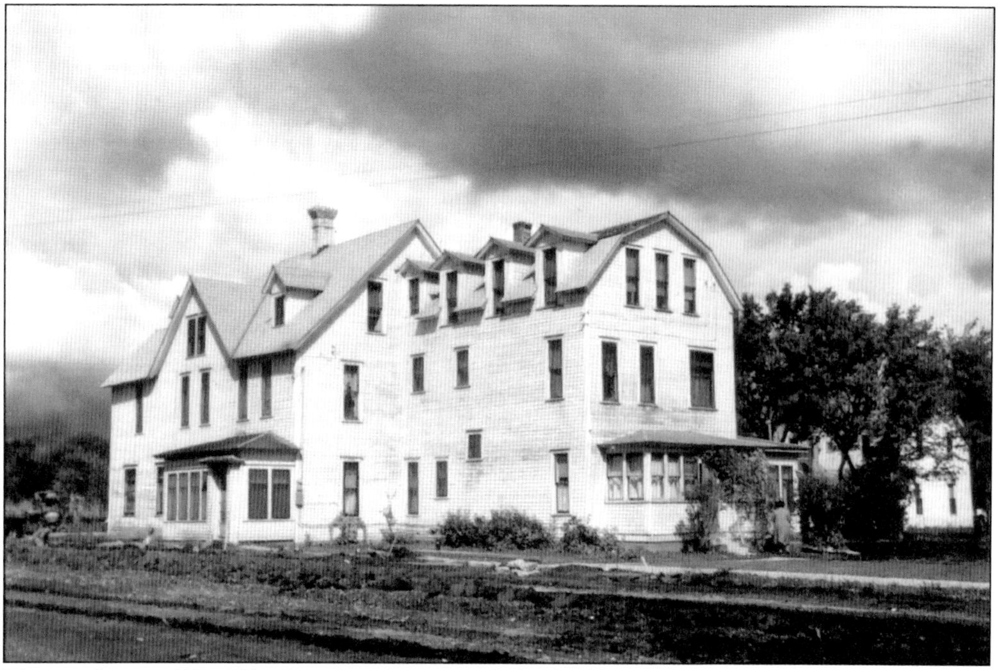

The residence of Dr. F.A. Brandt, who married the builder's widow, was at Howard and First Streets—where the present Catholic school is located. It had 40 rooms and though referred to as a hospital, the fact is disputed. In 1913, Miss Emma Israelson opened a millinery and dressmaking parlor there, and Msgr. Feuerbach was a boarder, prior to the opening of the rectory in 1954.

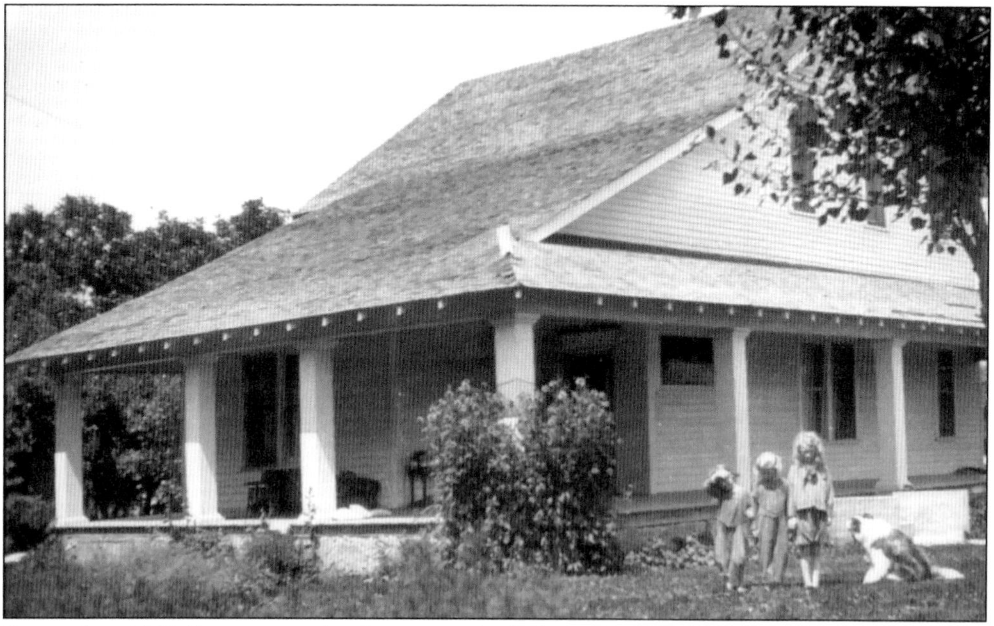

Situated at 1541 Davenport, this house was built by a Mr. Potter and was the birthplace of Jarvis Davenport. Barbara Cruickshank Lutz is one of the girls pictured. Can you guess who is who? The others are Barbara's sisters, Lois and Bonnie Jean. (Clue: Bonnie Jean is on the left, Barbara is in the center, and Lois is on the right.)

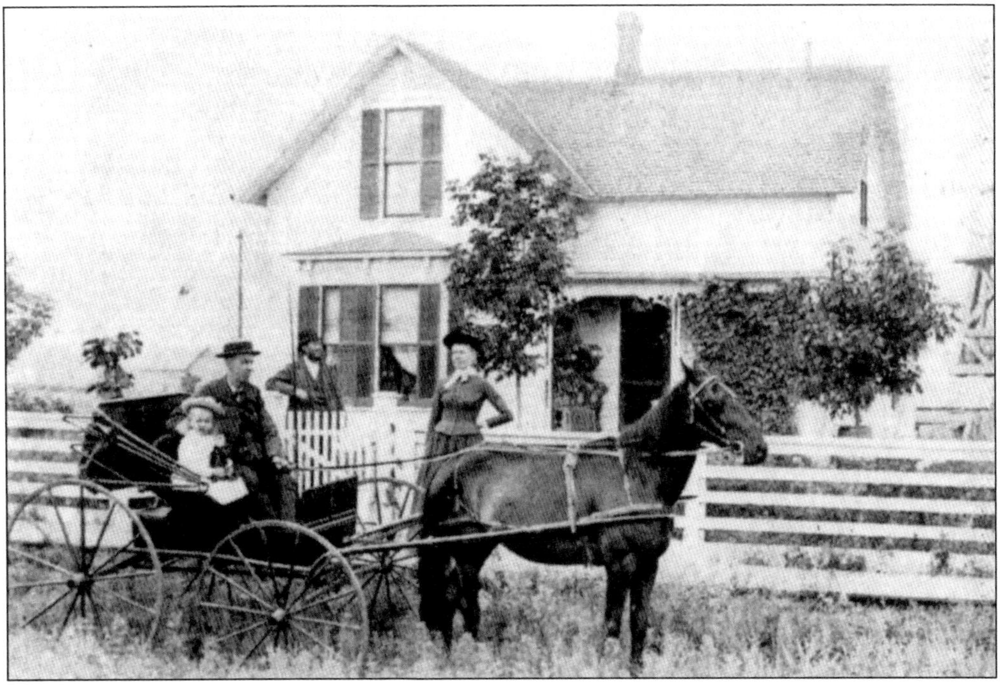

H.O. (Henry) Anderson, wife, son Albert, and daughter Edna are in a buggy in front of their home at Junction and Douglas in 1889—the year of South Dakota's statehood. The house was moved to Spearfish when the parking lot for Kinkade Funeral Chapel was expanded.

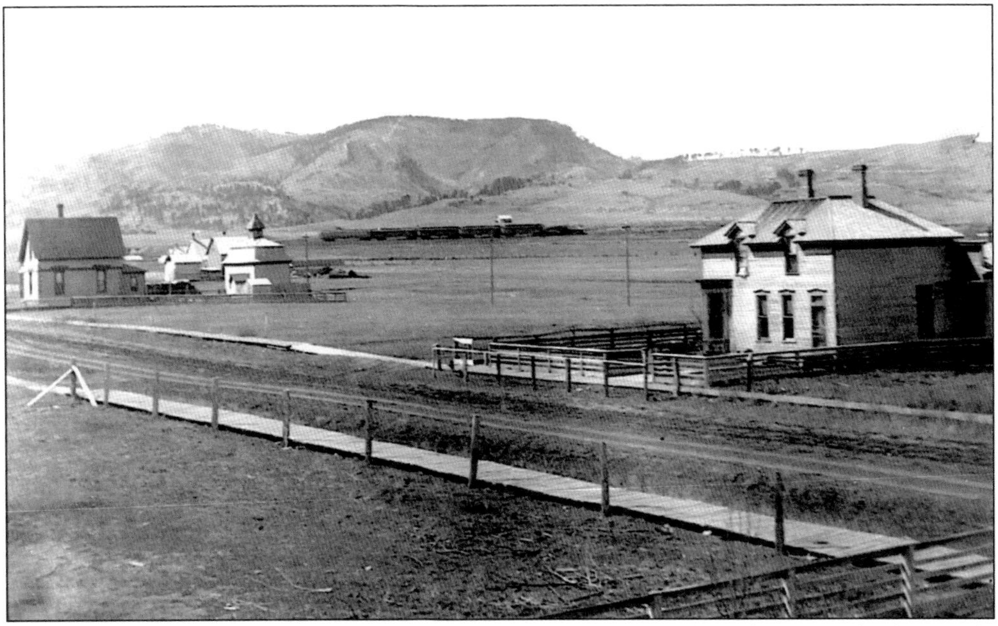

An early undated photo shows Junction Avenue looking south and west with the Steele residence in the right foreground. Note the boardwalk, which appears to be out in the country—and the train passing through town.

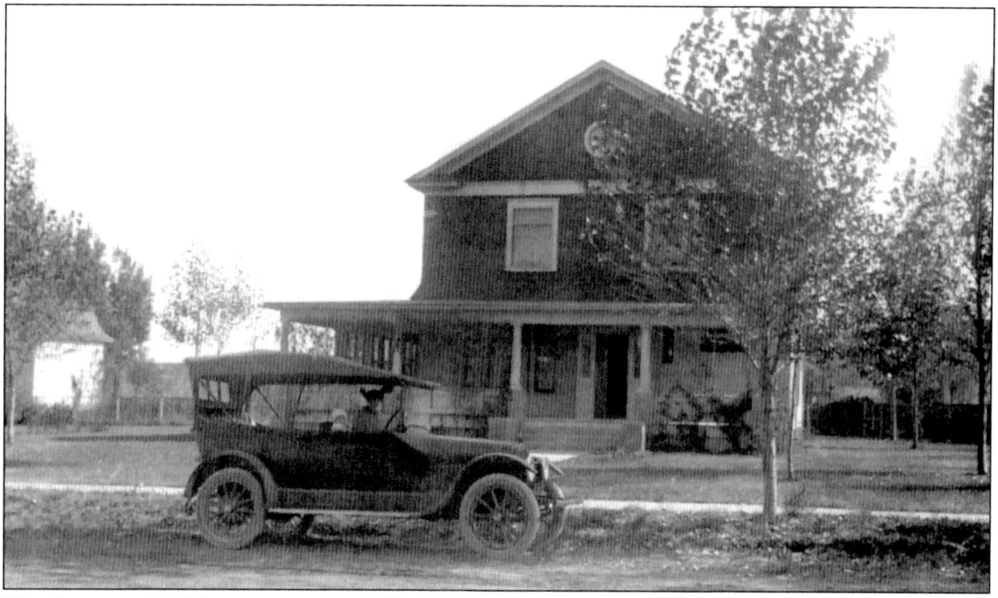

This home at 1440 Junction around World War I later became Jolley Funeral Home. The driver of the touring car is unidentified.

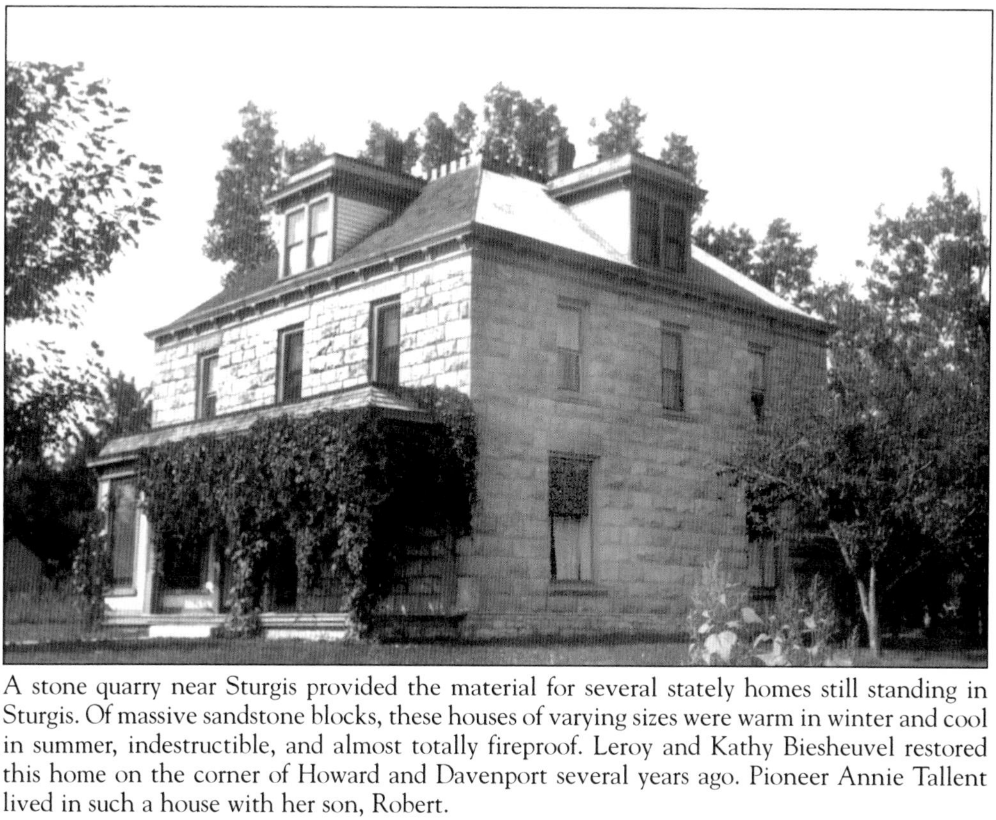

A stone quarry near Sturgis provided the material for several stately homes still standing in Sturgis. Of massive sandstone blocks, these houses of varying sizes were warm in winter and cool in summer, indestructible, and almost totally fireproof. Leroy and Kathy Biesheuvel restored this home on the corner of Howard and Davenport several years ago. Pioneer Annie Tallent lived in such a house with her son, Robert.

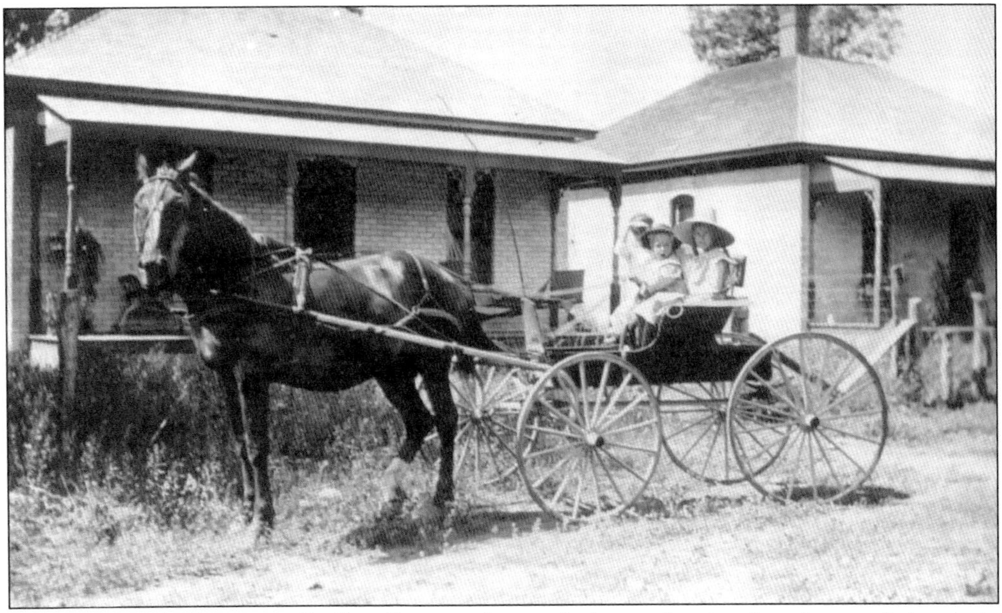

The Roy Sparks home on Dudley Street is featured above. A trio of sunbonnet babes is in the buggy.

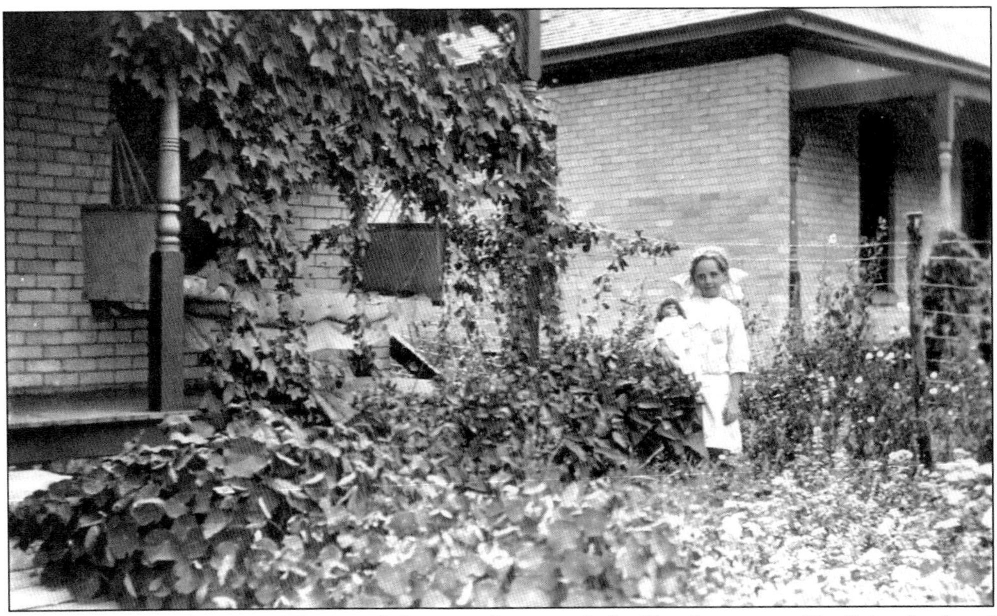

My, how things do grow! The porch hammock is nearly hidden by ivy, and hollyhocks dwarf the young lady with the doll (who has also gotten much bigger since the above photo was taken). She is Blanche Sparks.

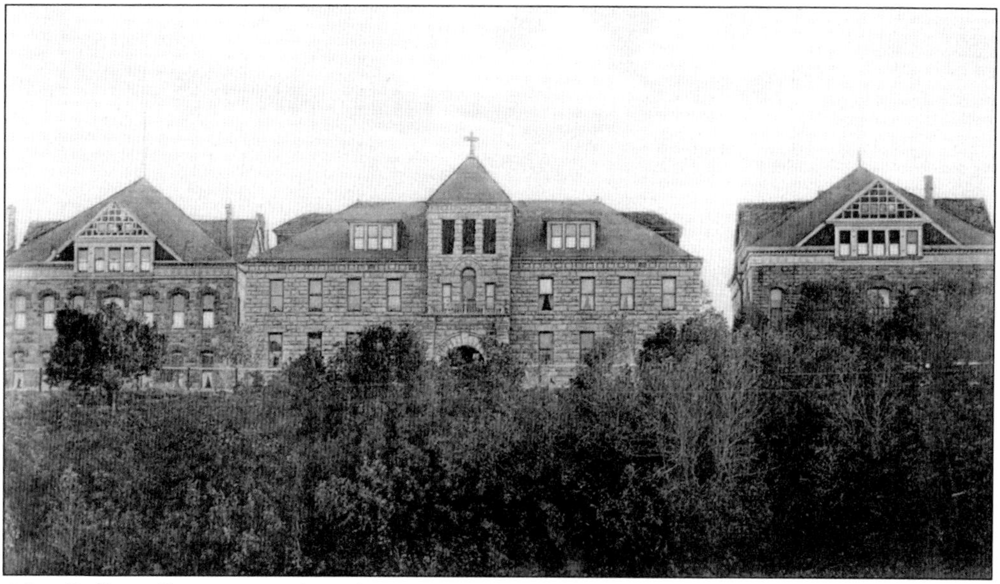

After Fr. Peter Rosen was ordained a priest at Notre Dame University, he arrived in Deadwood in 1882 and later came to Sturgis. An amateur geologist, he located the stone quarry on the property of Judge Ash, and the latter offered to donate the raw material to build the Catholic learning center, which Father Rosen named for his good friend, Bishop Martin Marty.

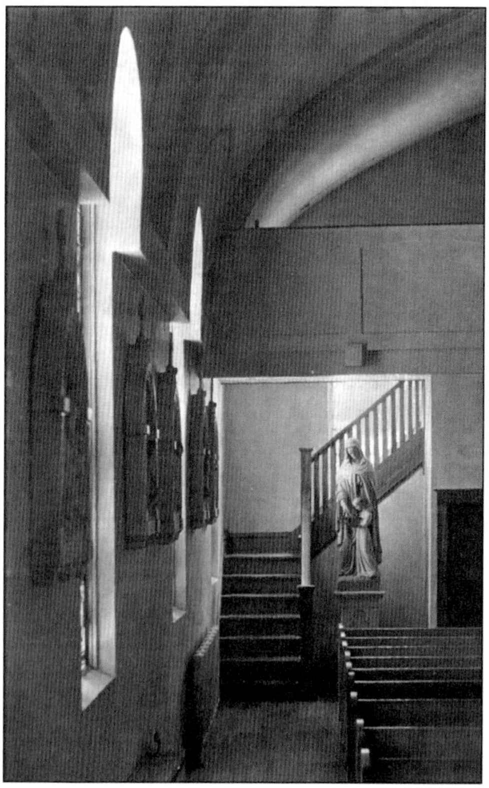

St. Martin's chapel interior is pictured here showing the Stations of the Cross at left and a stairway leading to the upper rooms at the back of the building.

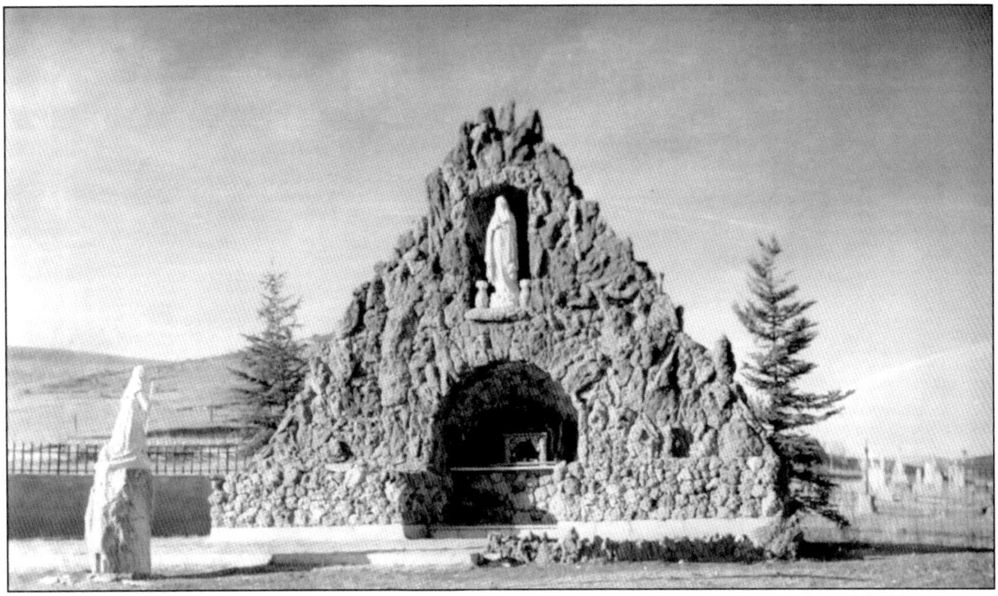

This is the grotto at St. Martin's. Father Rosen beautified the grounds, and he loved bells. He was responsible for the construction of bell towers in Sturgis, Deadwood, and Galena. Father Rosen performed his first wedding May 17, 1883, but almost drowned that day trying to cross flooded Bear Butte Creek. Saved by Fort Meade soldiers, his team and buggy were retrieved downstream.

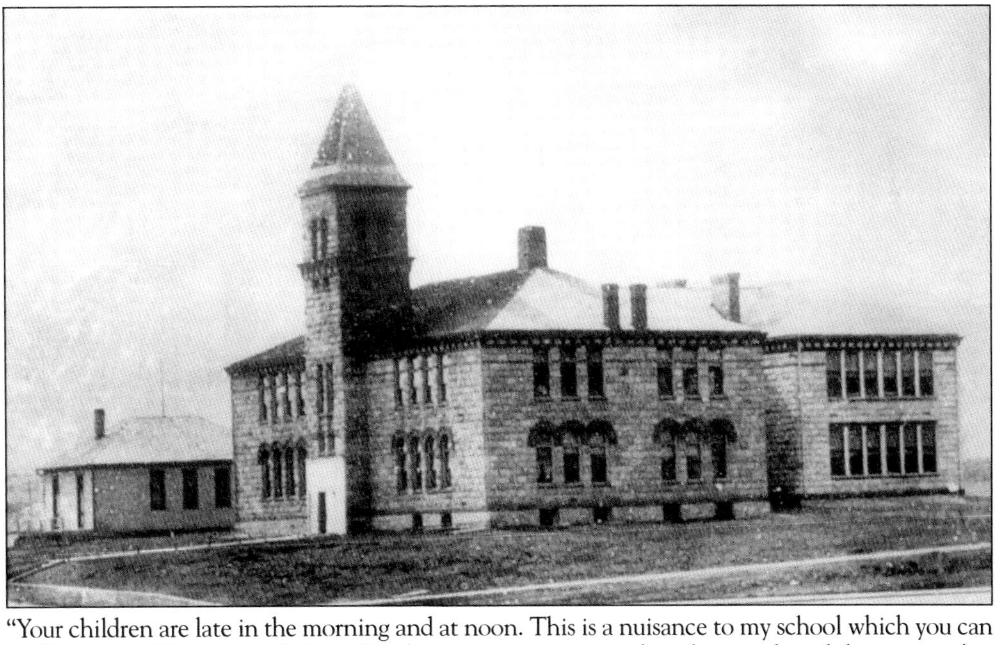

"Your children are late in the morning and at noon. This is a nuisance to my school which you can easily remove. Please rise a little earlier, be more prompt in sending them and send them every day. . . . " H.B. Lorrimer placed this notice in local papers March 19, 1888. Pictured is the new school, built in 1902. It replaced Lorrimer's, which burned in 1900. It is still in use today and called Erskine School, after the Rev. C.D. Erskine, who became very involved in community affairs.

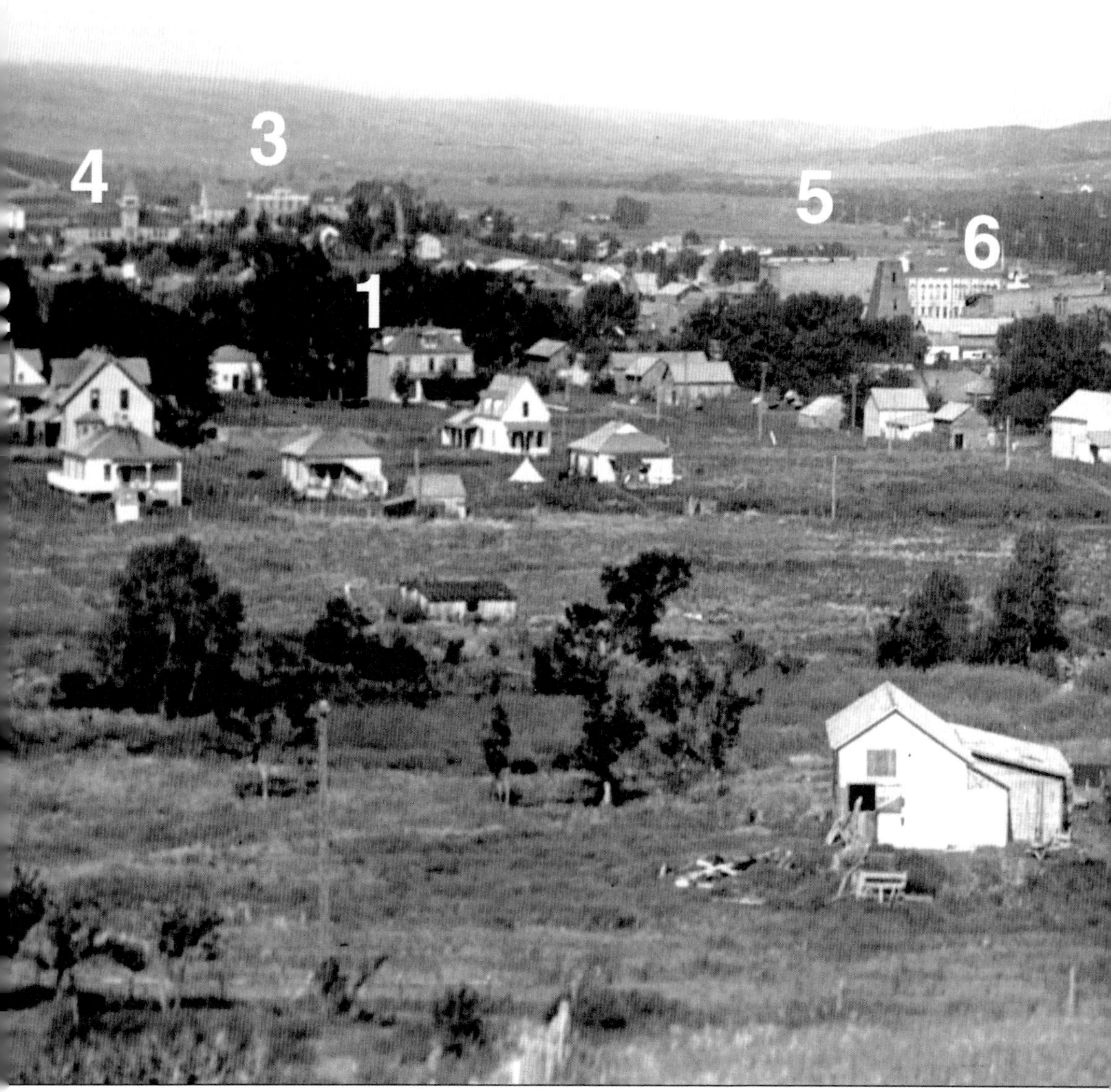

Sturgis points of interest looking west in the early 1900s include: 1) home of Jack Hale; 2) home of V.J. Skutt; 3) St. Martin's—courthouse row; 4) Erskine School; 5) Fruth Hotel; 6) Bear Butte

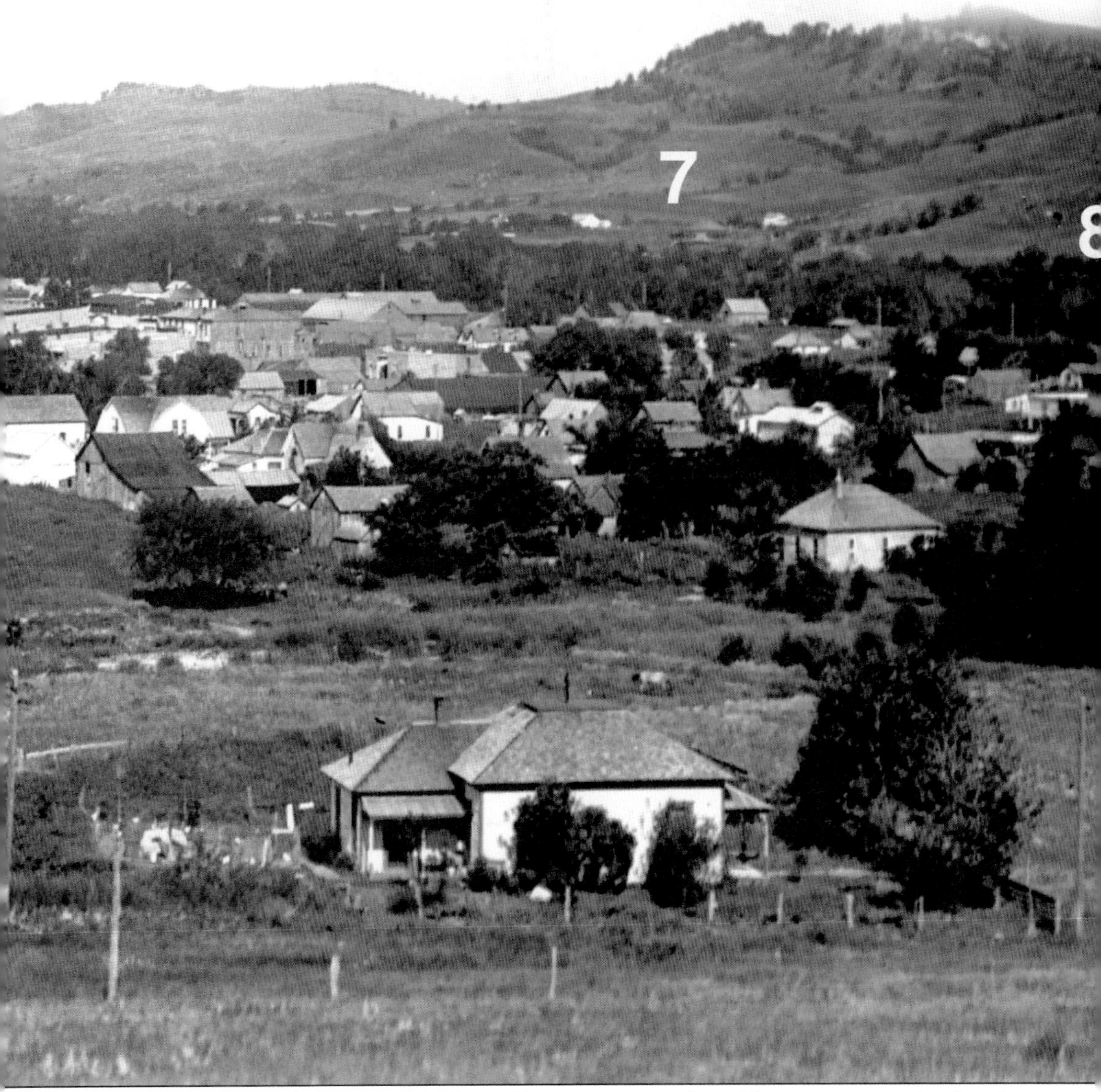

Valley Bank; 7) Meade County poor farm; 8) steam power plant. How many more landmarks can you find? V.J. Skutt was the founder of the Mutual of Omaha Insurance Company.

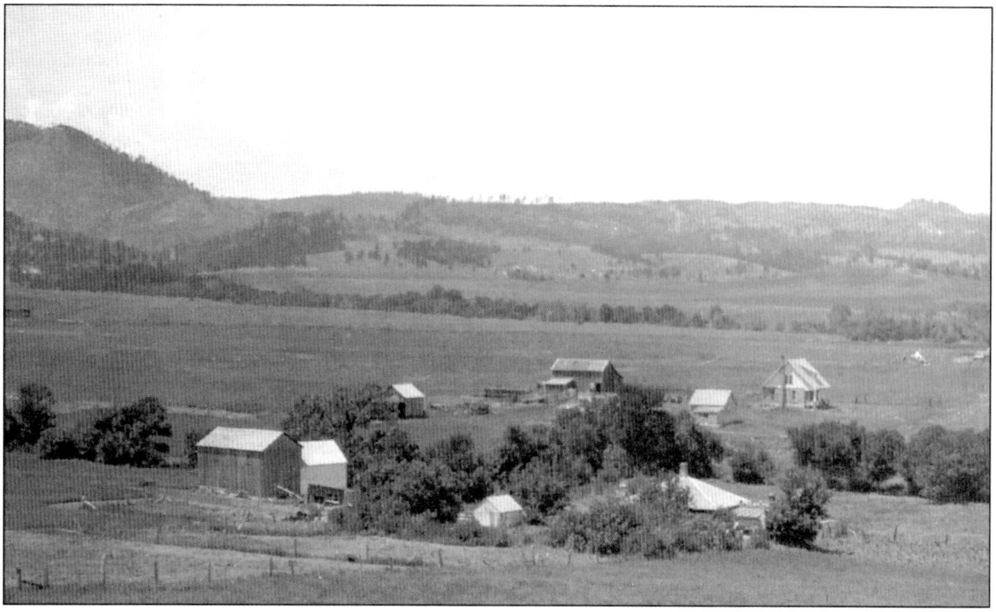

East looking west shows the John Hoel place in center of photo, and Caton home. Later streets that would run north to south are Baldwin, Fulton, Davenport, Junction, Harmon, and Marshall. Park ran east to west.

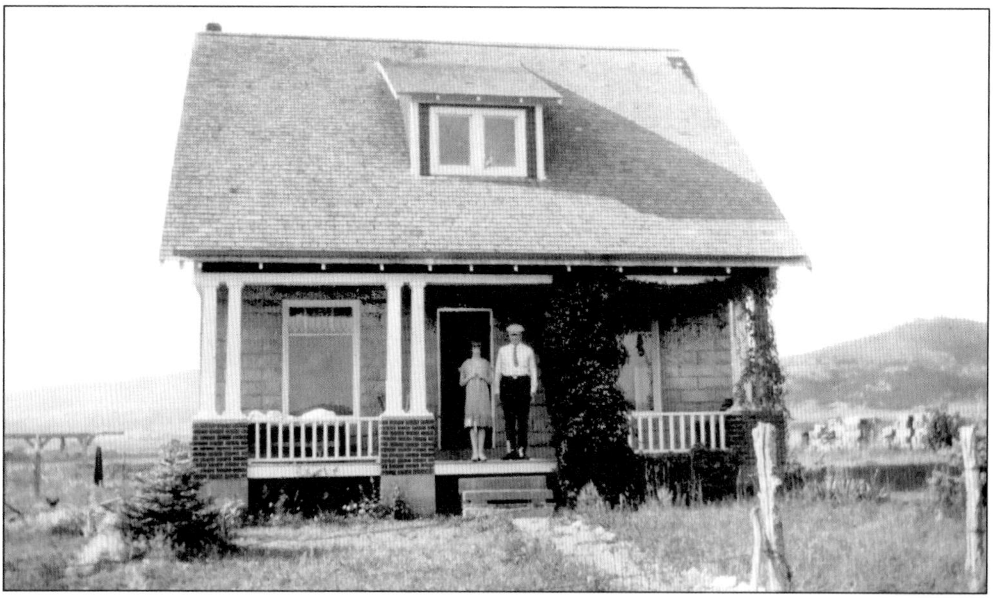

The home of John and Ivy Hoel is in the country now, but will later be placed in the 700 block of Harmon Street at Baldwin. This photo was taken in the early 1900s.

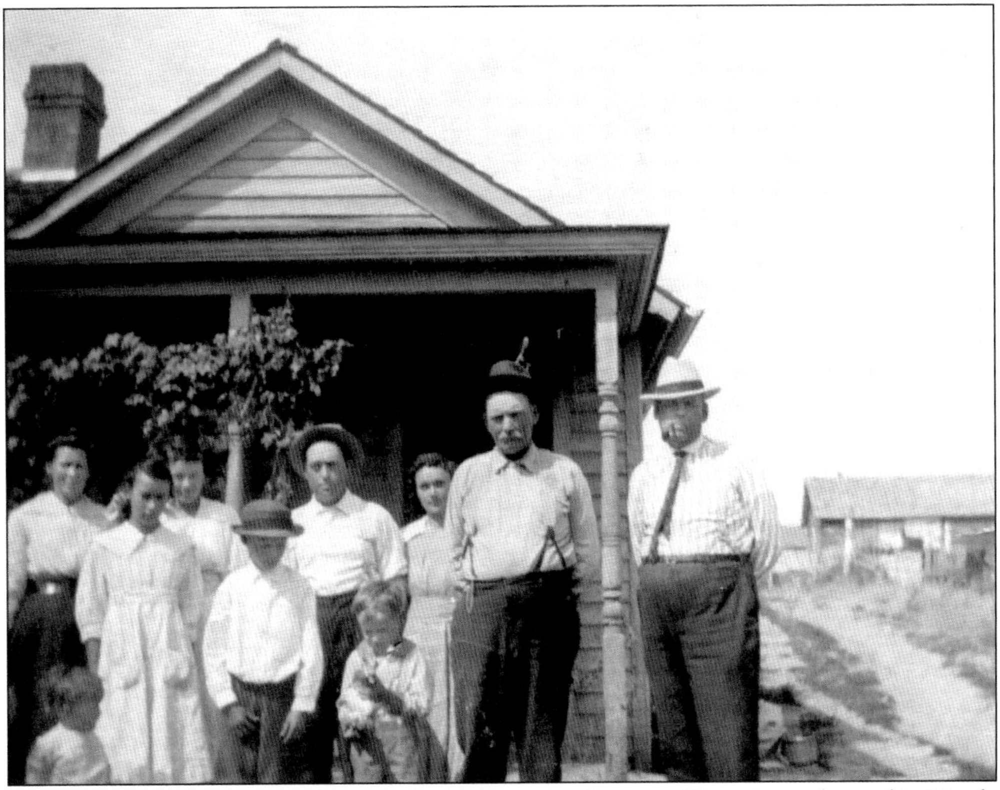

The Murray place was unique because the house, one mile west of Sturgis, was located in Meade County, and the barn, shown in the background, was in Lawrence County in 1918. Pictured here are, from let to right: (front row) Earl, Ruth, Glen, Bartley, Charles, and Ira Murray; (back row) Edith and Fern Murray, Arden and Bertha Hannat.

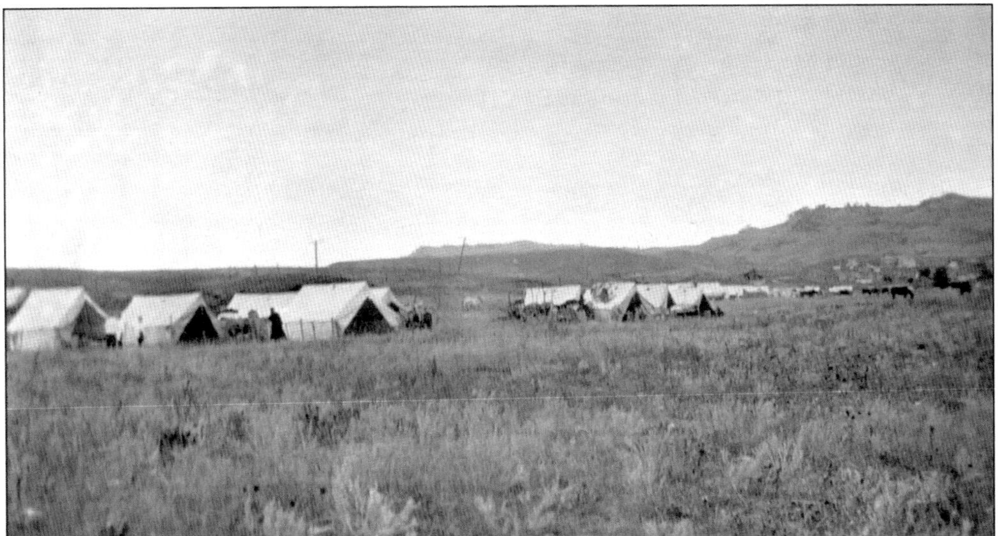

An Indian summer camp south of town is provided with army tents. The year is uncertain, but probably pre-1910. Note Meade County court house in distant right, completed in 1896.

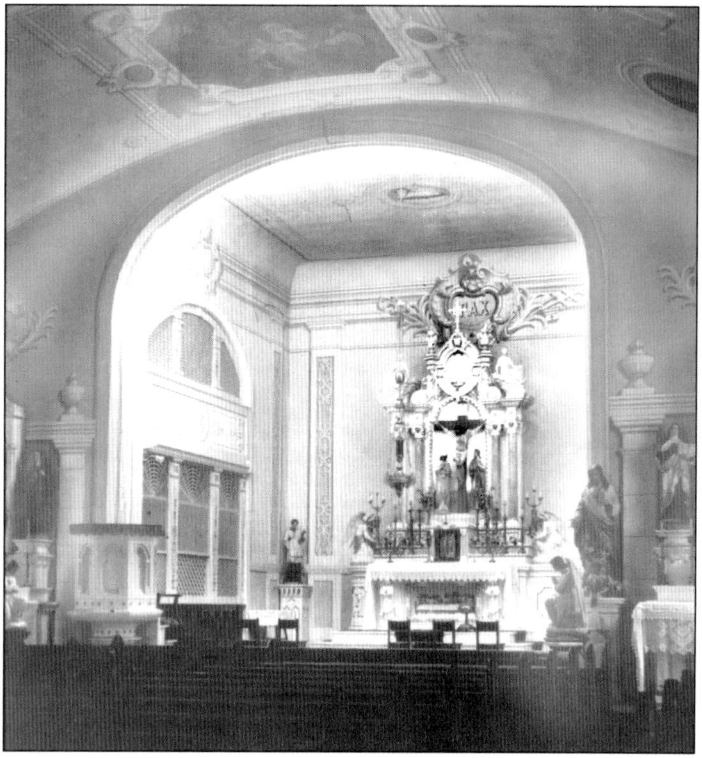

The lovely altar of St. Aloysius Catholic church was donated by Louis II and Mary Grubl. It was purchased in Europe by Fr. Columban Bregenzer, who served the Sturgis community from 1903 to 1946.

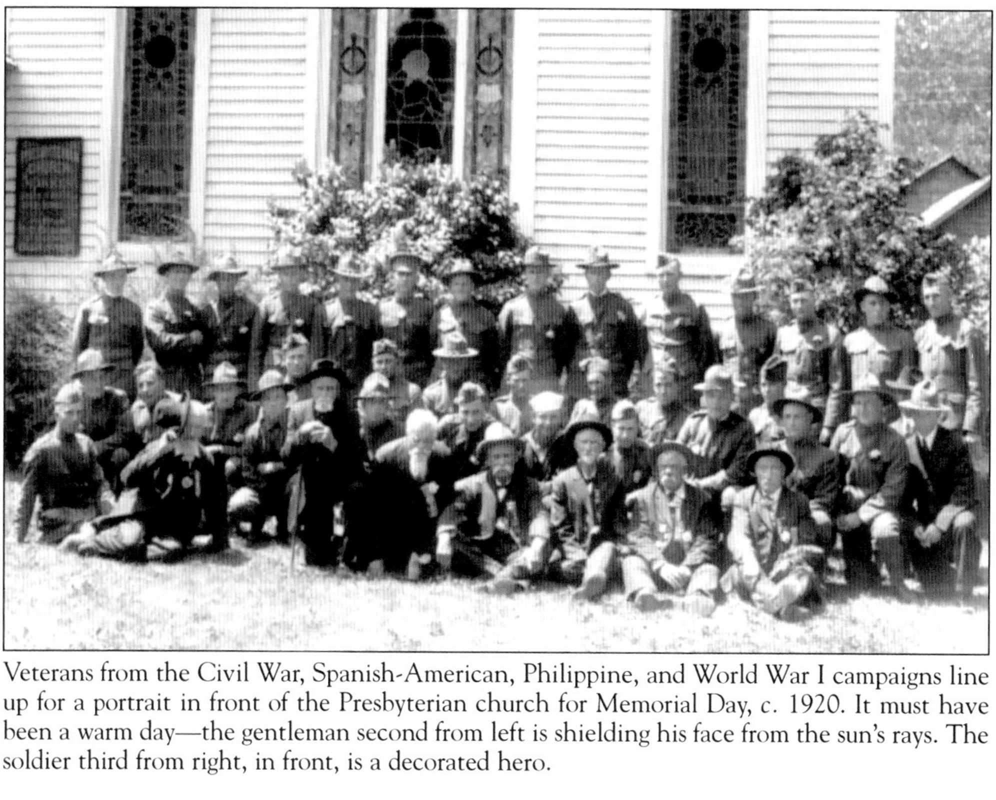

Veterans from the Civil War, Spanish-American, Philippine, and World War I campaigns line up for a portrait in front of the Presbyterian church for Memorial Day, c. 1920. It must have been a warm day—the gentleman second from left is shielding his face from the sun's rays. The soldier third from right, in front, is a decorated hero.

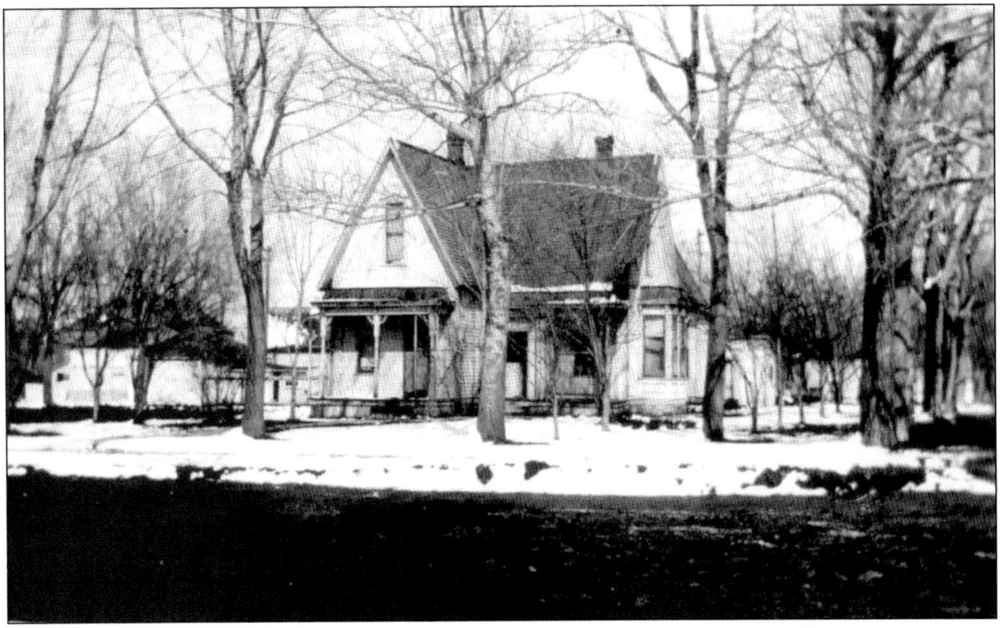

This spacious turn-of-the-century home at 1240 Junction and the northeast corner of Douglas has more recently been the location of Flowers by Rose. Many of the stately trees seen here have been removed.

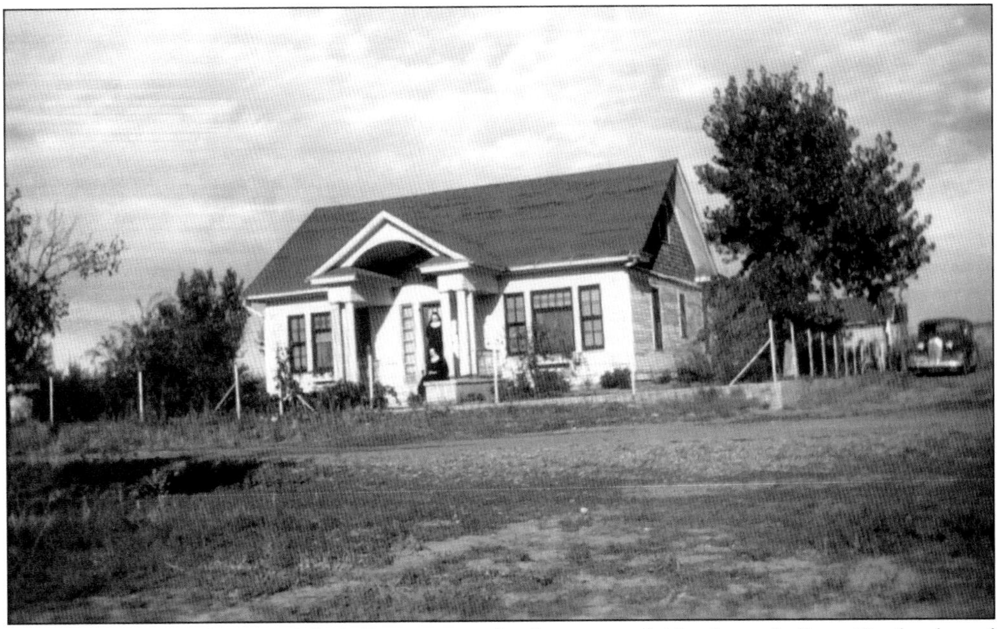

Edna Long's bungalow on Alkali Drive was a kit home available through Sears Roebuck and Company. Sears sold several styles of houses up to and including the 1920s and even into the 1930s at reasonable prices. It was up to the buyer to properly assemble the materials, however.

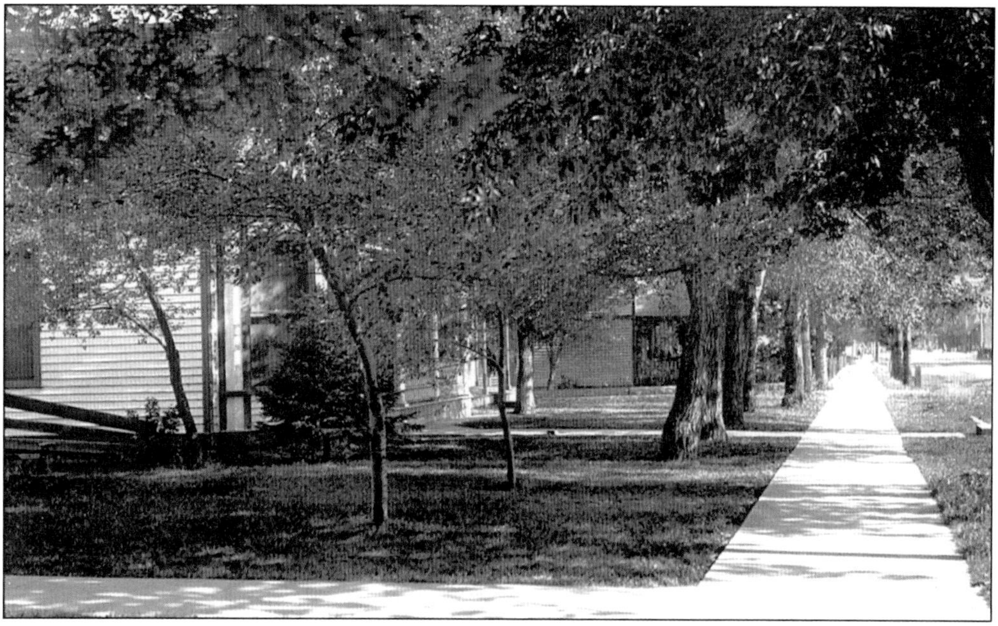

Residential areas of Junction Avenue appeared shady and inviting, but the street was either muddy or dusty—depending on the time of year. One of these early boulevard homes belonged to the Allison family on Howard Street.

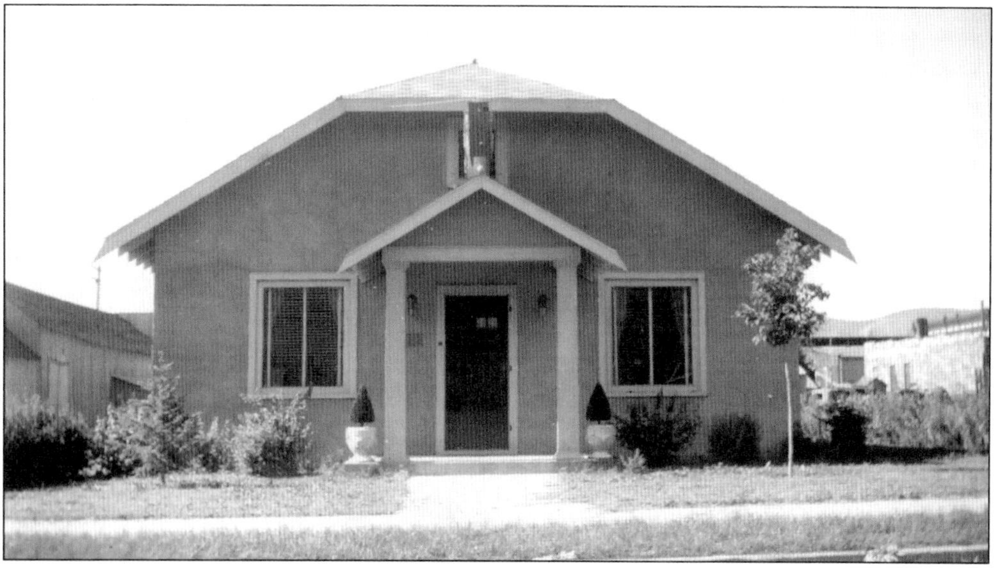

The Anderson Funeral Home at 1238 South Junction is seen here in the 1930s. In 1932, Meade County had 854 births, 354 deaths, 778 marriages, and 40 divorces. The leading cause of death was due to heart disease—followed by cancer and fewer cases of tuberculosis and pneumonia.

Grace Lutheran Church congregation is nearly as old as the town of Sturgis itself. Early services were held in the old city hall. This building was completed in 1927. Trinity Lutheran Church later purchased the old church and moved it to its present location on Baldwin Street.

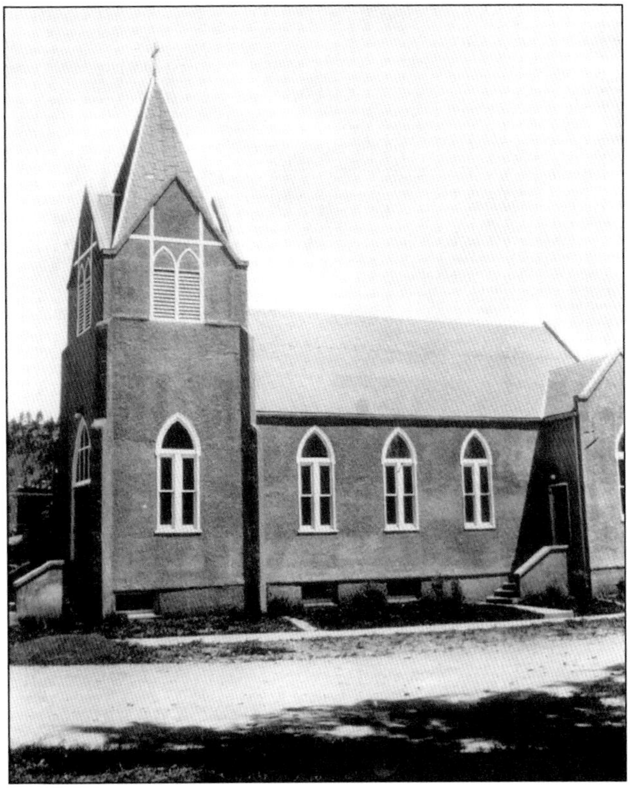

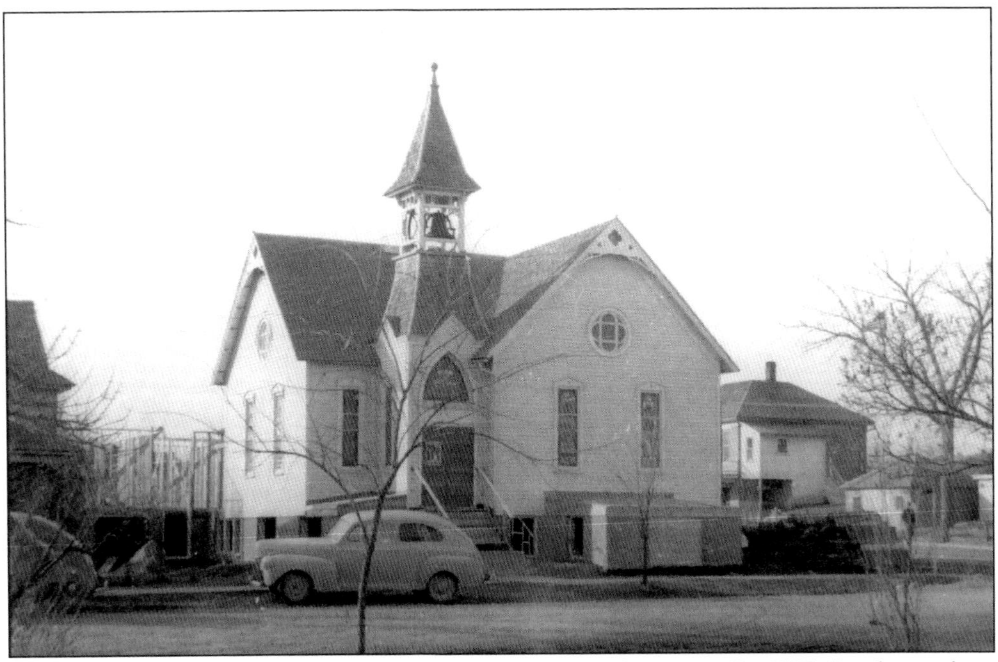

Sturgis's Methodist (M.E.) church was also established in the 1880s. Dr. W.E. Smith was the pastor when the church and parsonage flooded during the storm of June 14, 1907, which took three lives in the community.

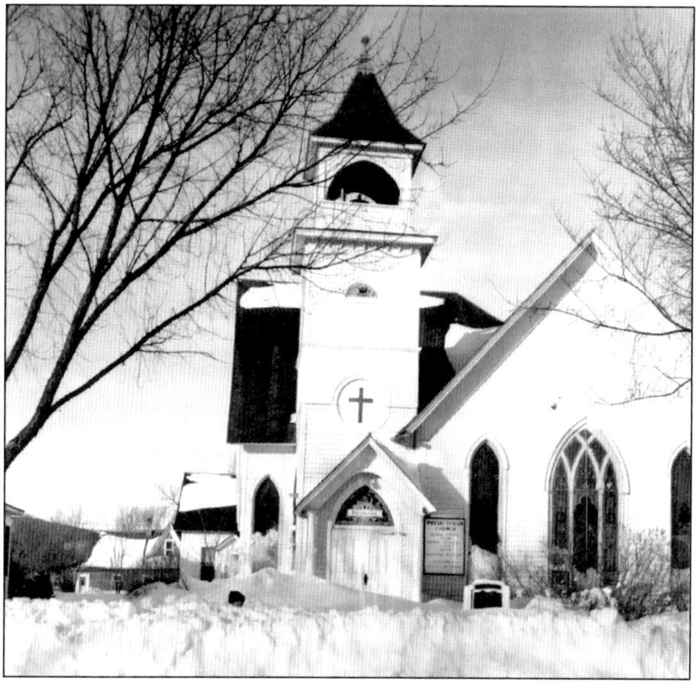

The Presbyterian church is pictured in 1949. Several denominations worshiped here together, and each parishioner contributed to the overall well-being of the town, regardless of whether or not they lived within the city limits.

The cornerstone of St. Francis of Assisi Catholic Church was laid on July 1, 1949. The parish priest was Fr. Leo O'Doherty, who arrived in 1948. In 1947, Fr. Innocent Amhof, Fr. Gilbert Stack, and Most Reverend Bishop Dvorshack conducted masses.

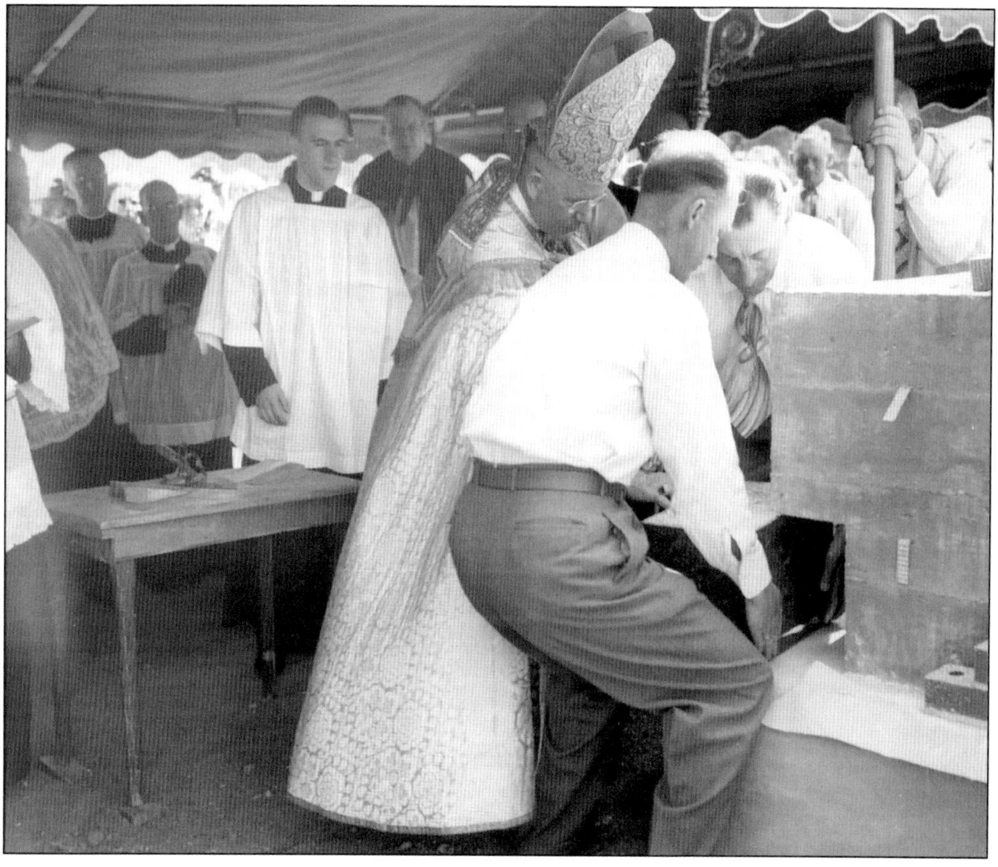

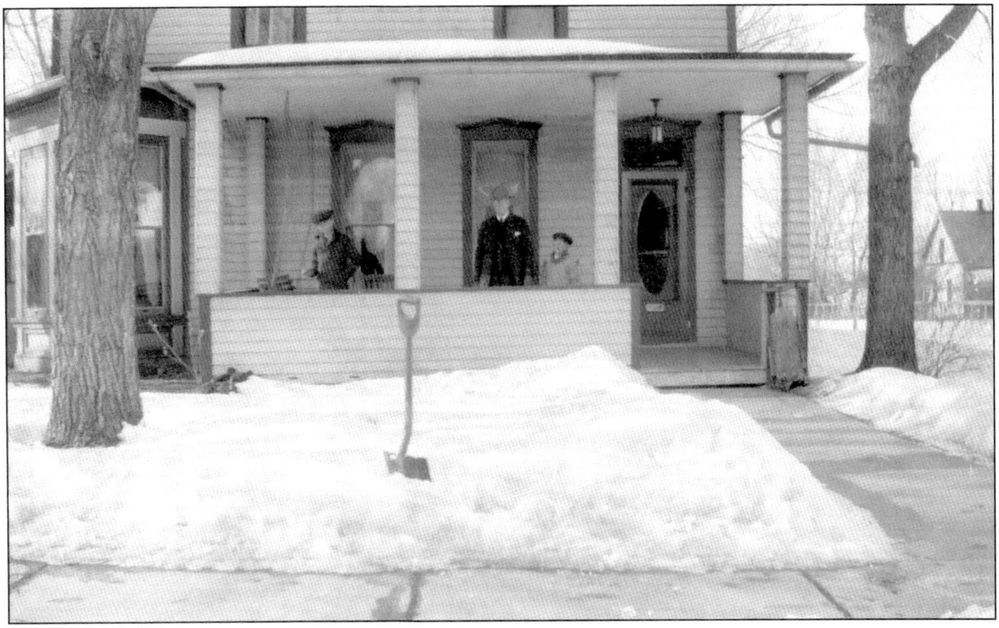

This elegant home is the Steele residence on South Junction Avenue, as shown on page 63. The porch was added later.

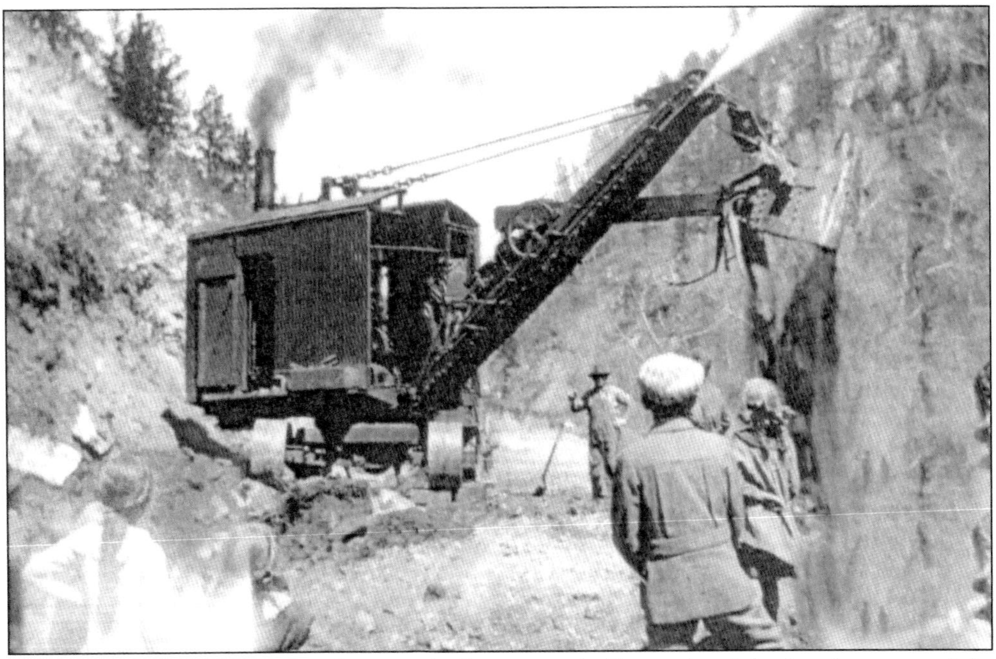

Building Boulder Canyon Road was a challenging task. Tons of rock had to be removed. In the very early days, a toll road existed at one end of the canyon for a much more primitive passageway. The date on this photo suggests it was taken around the World War I period.

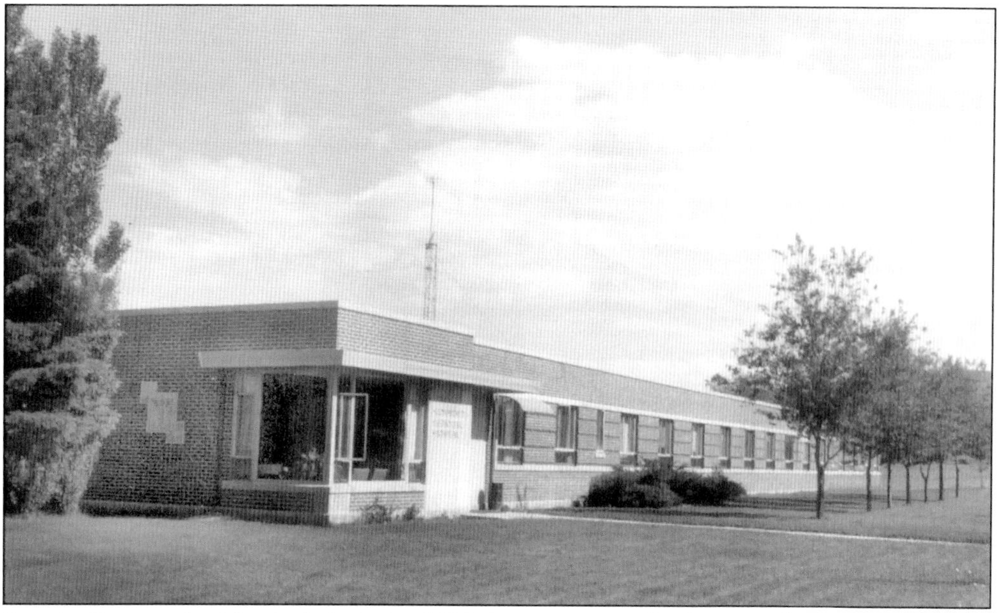

Sturgis Community Hospital, built in 1953, became part of a busy medical center for the region. A dispute broke out over some of the issues involved in the new enterprise that provoke animated conversations among townsfolk to this day.

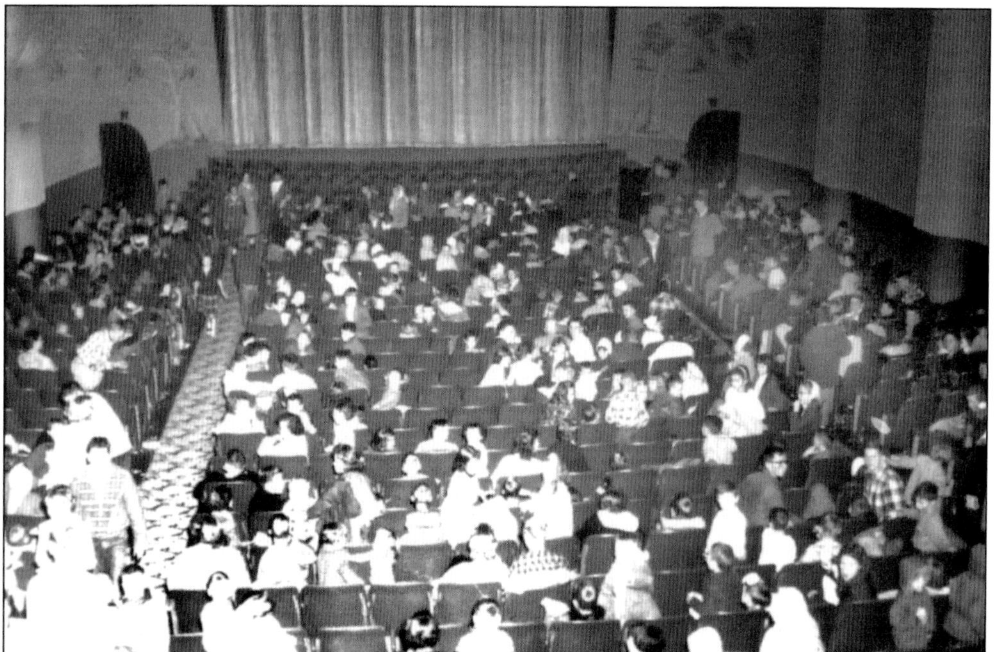

Interior of the Dakota Theater in December of 1959. The occasion is a special Christmas show for the kiddies.

Six

FAMILIAR FACES

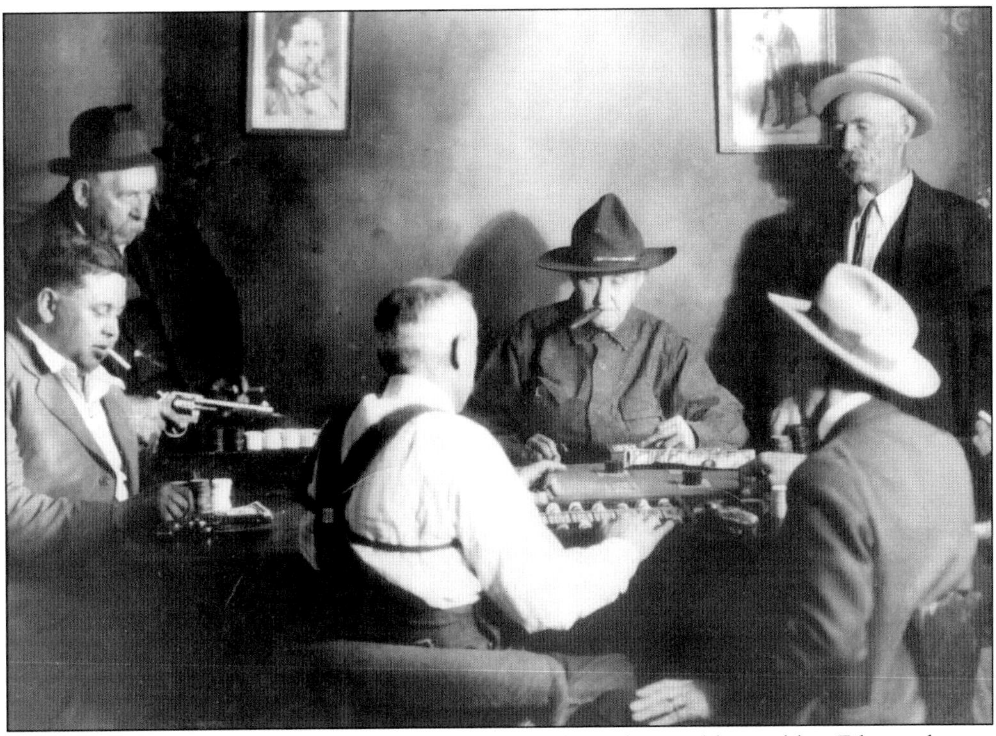

Poker Alice is seen here with a cigar, plying her trade at the gambling tables. Educated at an exclusive Southern girls' school, Alice Ivers—thrice married—lost her first husband in a mine accident and began dealing cards to support herself. In Deadwood, she received the name "Poker Alice." It was rumored she could "hit a bull's eye with a pistol at 100 yards." Alice (Duffield-Huckert-Tubbs) raised seven children, plus chickens, cats, and a garden and gave generously to those in need.

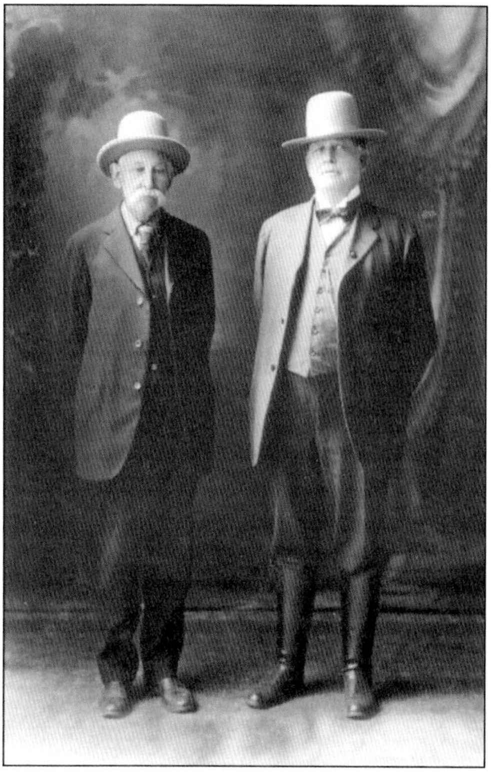

Jesse Brown and Scott Davis are pictured here. Brown came to Deadwood from Fort Laramie, riding "shotgun" on the Deadwood to Sidney (Nebraska) stage. Davis, a steely-nerved guard on the metal-clad treasure coach, was aboard during the legendary Canyon Springs Stage Coach holdup in 1876. Heavily loaded with gold bullion, robbers staged a shoot out with Davis. Brown later teamed up with Capt. A.M. Willard to write a colorful history of that era.

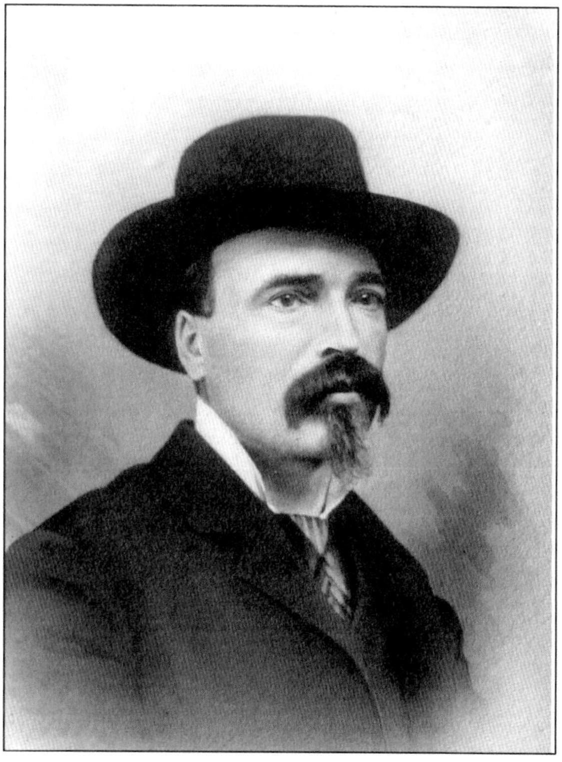

Freighter, railroad worker, and rancher, Miles M. Cooper helped to lay out the Boulder Canyon toll road from Sturgis to Deadwood. He was elected to the Grand Assembly at Yankton and was a representative from Meade County to the Territorial Legislature. In the 1880s, Miles Cooper was commissioned a colonel of a local militia by Governor Mellette prior to the Battle of Wounded Knee.

Shown in 1883 with one of his handmade violins, William Grams was one of Sturgis's most versatile citizens. He built a cabinet shop at the Sturgis Drug location, and started a sawmill and construction business. Grams and company built the Meade County court house, the Sturgis city hall, and several buildings at Fort Meade. In addition, he operated portable sawmills throughout the Black Hills, and in 1910 began a phone service to Belle Fourche.

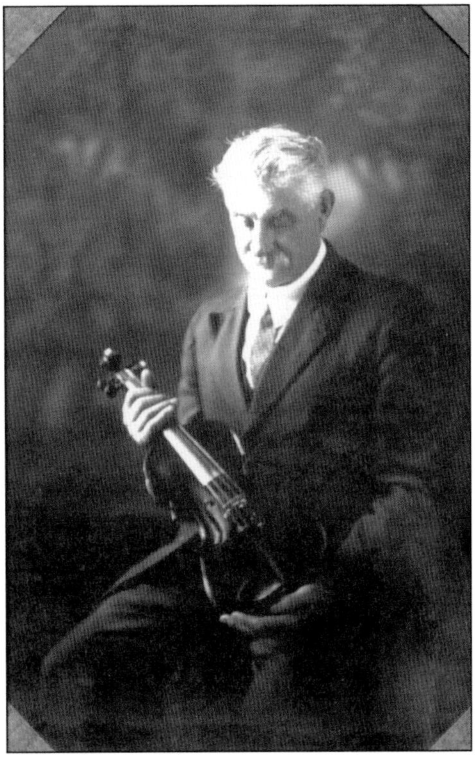

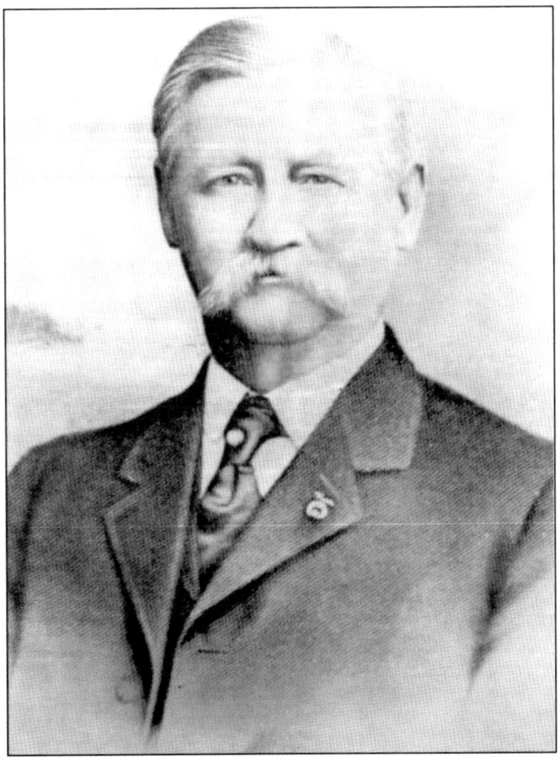

Joseph Davenport provided Sturgis with its most valuable commodity—water. Arriving in Sturgis in 1884, he started the First National Bank and soon after located the springs that would provide water to Sturgis and Fort Meade. Davenport planned and operated a water works system in 1893 that served the town for nearly a century. Additional wells and a reservoir were added in the 1940s–1950s. The city purchased the operation in 1977.

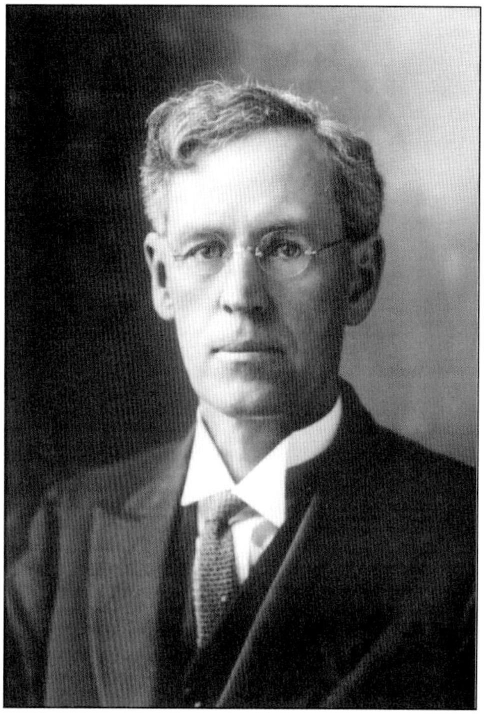

Lawyer John T. Milek was in the first graduating class from Sturgis high school. Besides publishing the *Black Hills Press* from 1915–1955, John Milek was twice state's attorney, operated a roller skating rink, and raised prize Holstein cattle. While mayor (1938–1940), he obtained a city sewer system and the new post office and armory. He was president of the South Dakota State Historical Society and amassed a huge collection of historical artifacts prior to 1935.

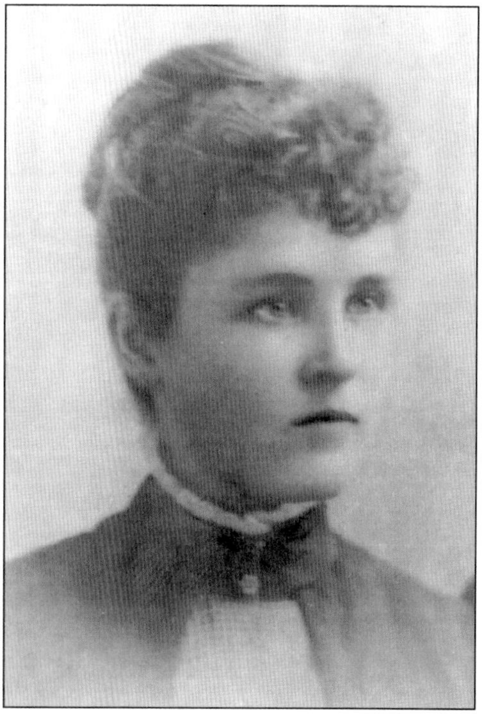

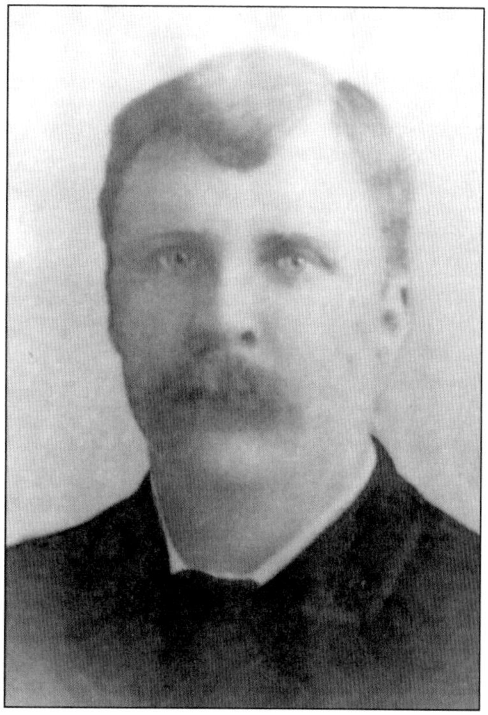

John and Nellie (Rodebank) Wenke owned the finest home in Sturgis, which took five years to build. A successful merchant, John Wenke owned several hardware stores in different towns and was active in civic and governmental affairs. Nellie was the first school teacher in Sturgis in 1879. They had five daughters: Freida, Flora, Margaret, Nellie, and Esther.

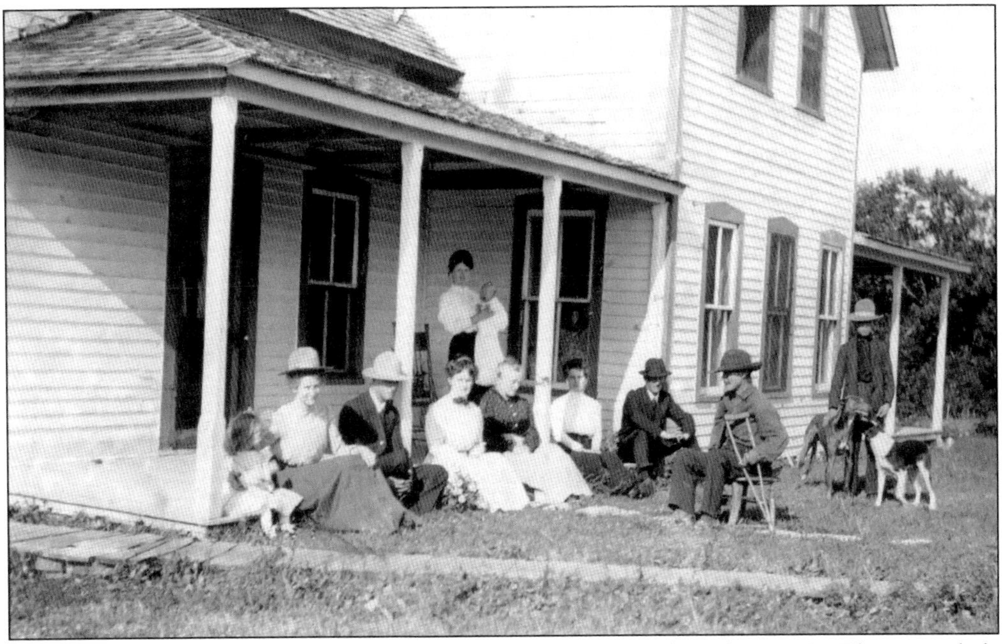

The home of Mr. and Mrs. George Harvey Blair is seen in this photo from 1909. The young lady second from left is dressed in riding fashion. Early cowgirls were first called "cowboy girls" for lack of a better term. Hounds were often used for running down game or four-legged predators.

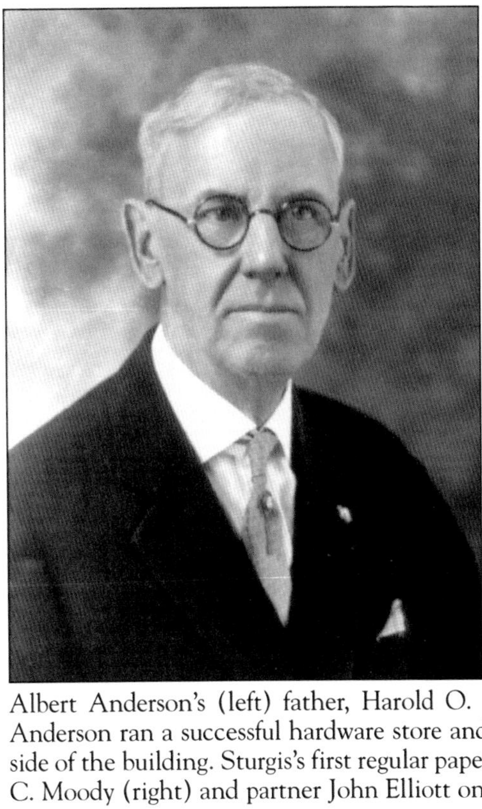

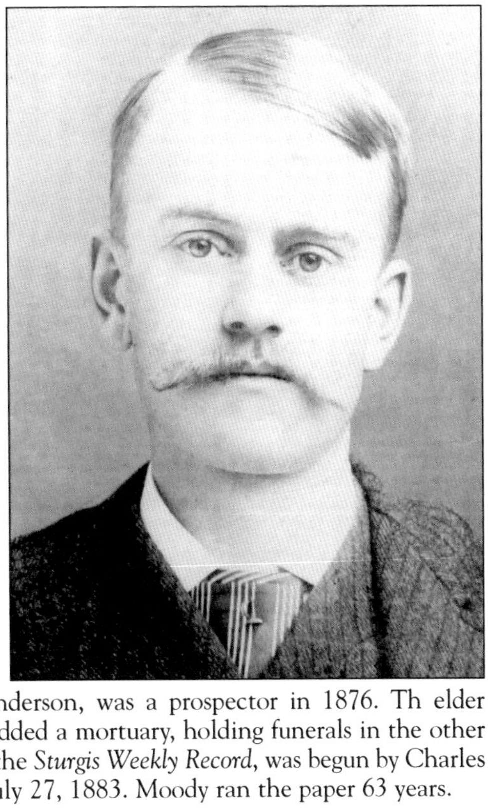

Albert Anderson's (left) father, Harold O. Anderson, was a prospector in 1876. Th elder Anderson ran a successful hardware store and added a mortuary, holding funerals in the other side of the building. Sturgis's first regular paper, the *Sturgis Weekly Record*, was begun by Charles C. Moody (right) and partner John Elliott on July 27, 1883. Moody ran the paper 63 years.

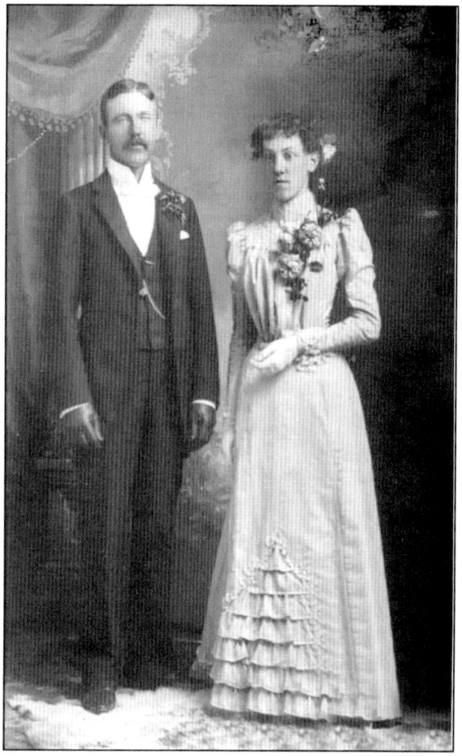

John and Ivy Hoel pose for their wedding portrait in 1899. The elder Hoel came to the Black Hills as a teamster and "wood hawk." He held the wood contract for Fort Meade and began his own ice company.

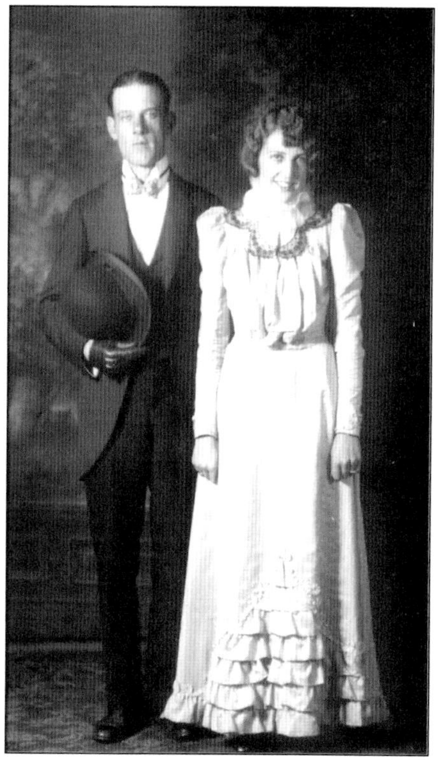

J.C. "Pappy" Hoel and wife, Pearl, are wearing the same wedding clothing for their marriage in 1929. J.C. helped in the family business and is credited with being the founder of one of the world's largest "spectator" sports—the Sturgis Motor Classic—rated the best of all motorcycle events.

Little Esther Fruth is in a captivating pose at 17 months. Henry Fruth of Saxony and his wife, Ann Keffeler, worked at and were wed in the Charles Hotel, which Fruth bought January 22, 1908. Esther had a sister, Alyce (Hale).

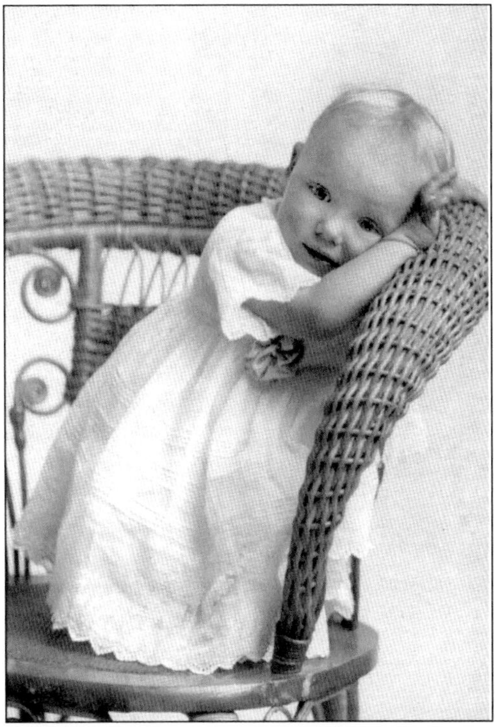

The Cooper family is pictured in 1921. The family ranch was located six miles northeast of Sturgis. When the Meade County Bank collapsed, Otto Cooper was wiped out—the family survived with only "an old black milk cow, a very large garden—and assistance from Miles Cooper." Pictured are, from left to right: (front row) Jefferson, Miles, Mary, and Bryan; (back row) Edith (Waldman), Otto, Allen, Harold, Lawrence, and Edna.

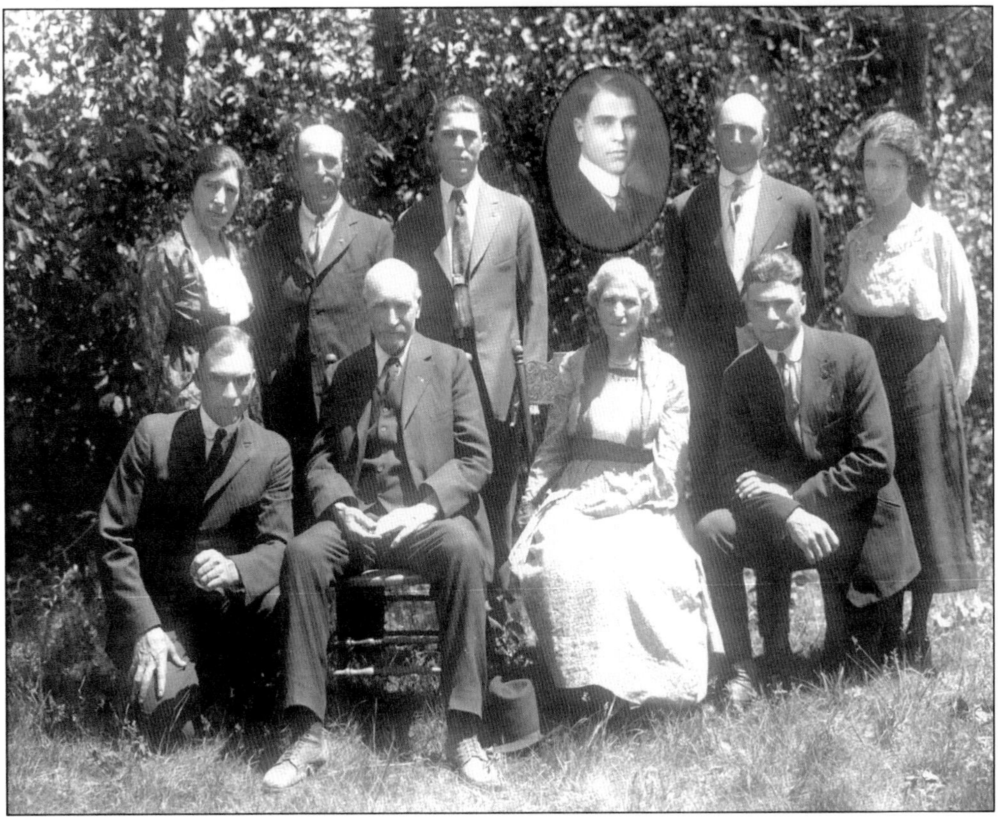

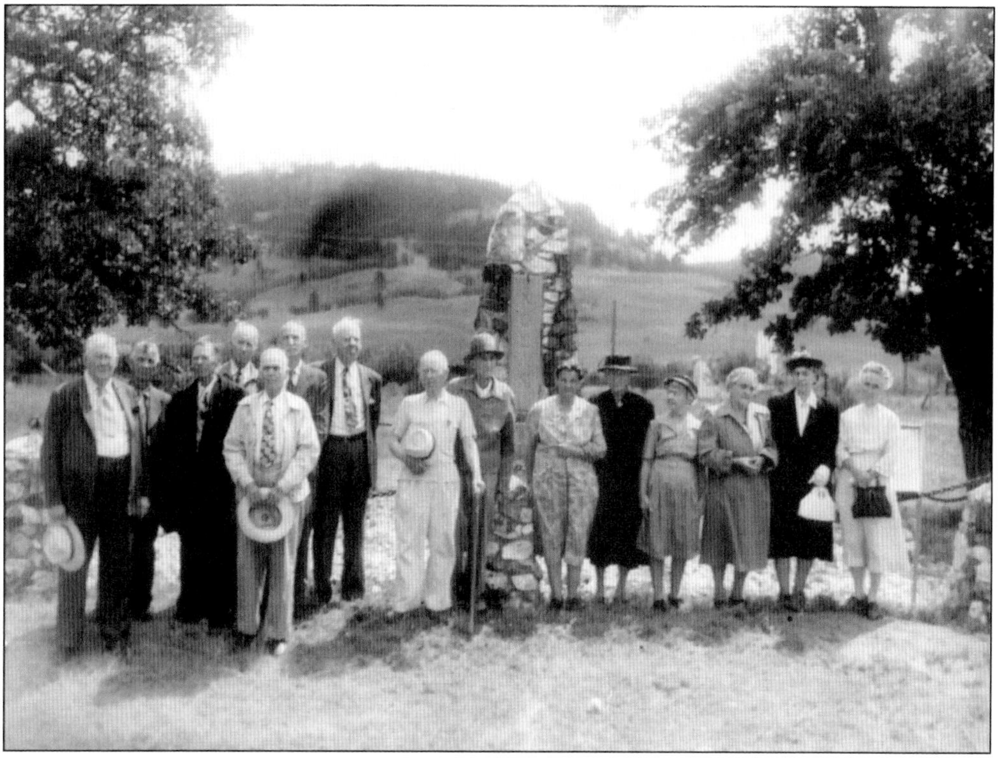

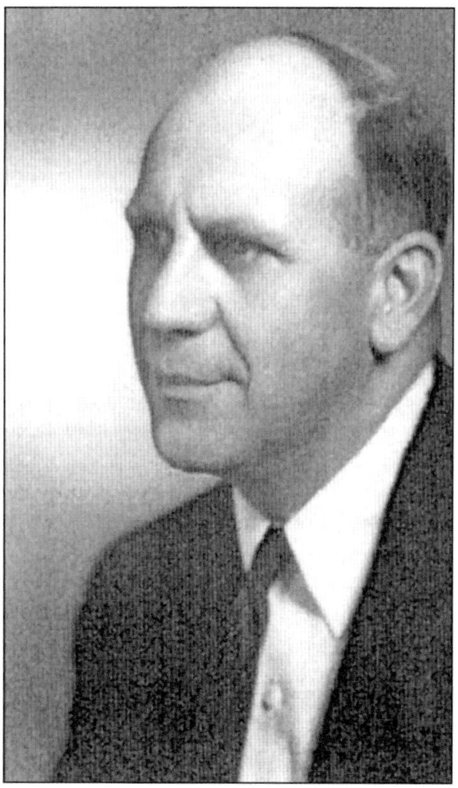

The monument was dedicated to Charles Nolin. In the photo are Freeman Steele Sr., Claude Schnell, Charlie Merritt, Mr. and Mrs. Bob Sparks, Howdy Jenks, Sim Welch, Albert Anderson, George Biesman, Mr. and Mrs. Hamilton, Mame Johnson, and Anna Poss. The others in the upper left are unidentified, but Jesse Brown and Scott Davis could be two of them.

Dr. Joseph N. Hamm, a Naval physician in the Pacific Theater during World War II, had a busy medical practice in Sturgis and Deadwood from 1948 until 1976 when he became West River Dean of the University of South Dakota's School of Medicine. He helped develop the school's four-year program and was instrumental in getting many of its graduates to provide health services to rural South dakota communities.

Katherine (Kate) Raskob Kilker was a charming young lady when she posed for Sturgis photographer Ole A. Vik in the early 1900s. She grew up in the big stone house on Highway 34, east of Sturgis.

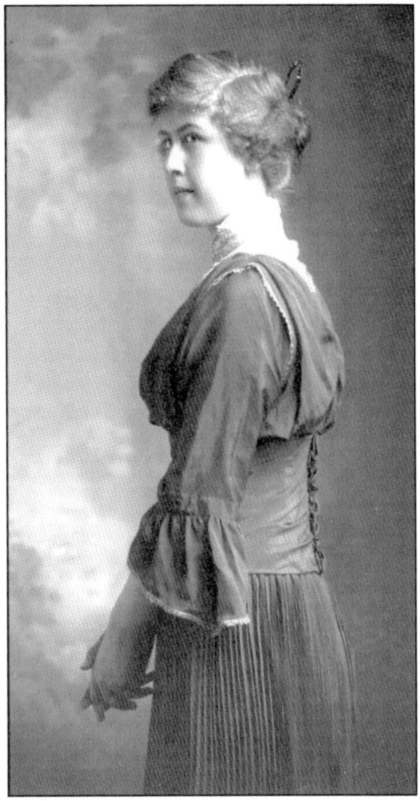

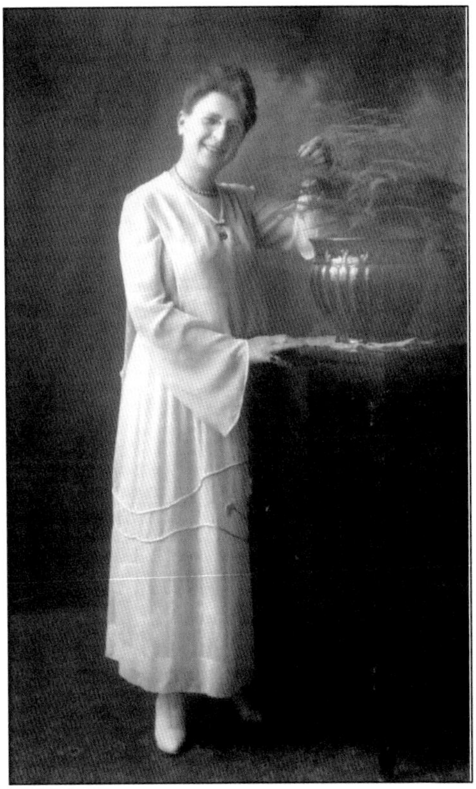

Jessie Keene, Worthy Matron of Mato Paha Order of the Eastern Star (OES) chapter #22, looks pensive in this 1917 study. Jessie was the aunt of Edna Long.

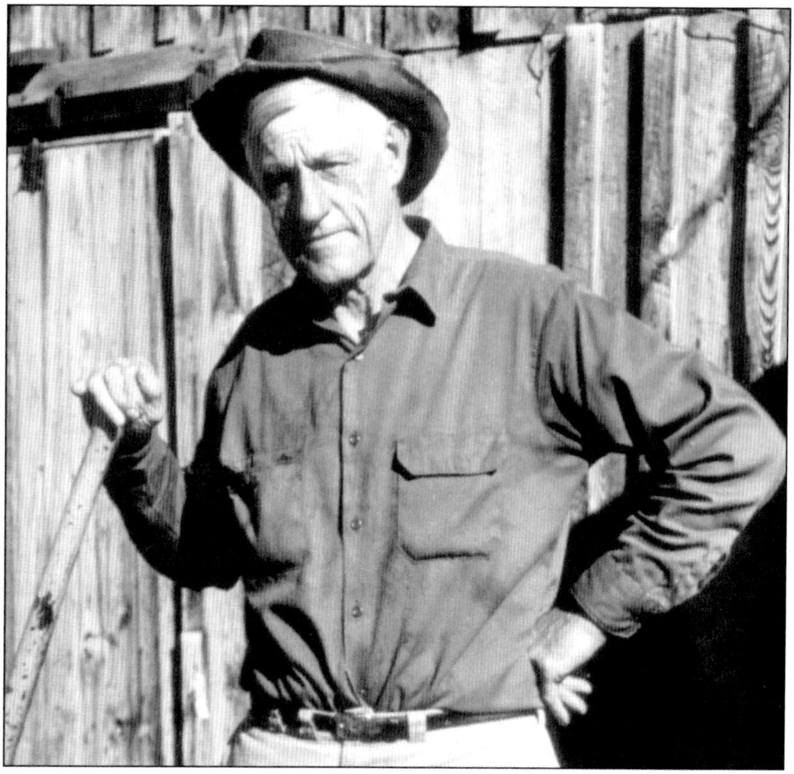

Bill Grams, son of Harry and grandson of William, was Meade County senator from 1946–1977. Senator Grams represented the third generation to continue the family's sawmill operation. The Grams' did their own logging and wood hauling until 1967, when they began to contract for more help to meet the demand for lumber.

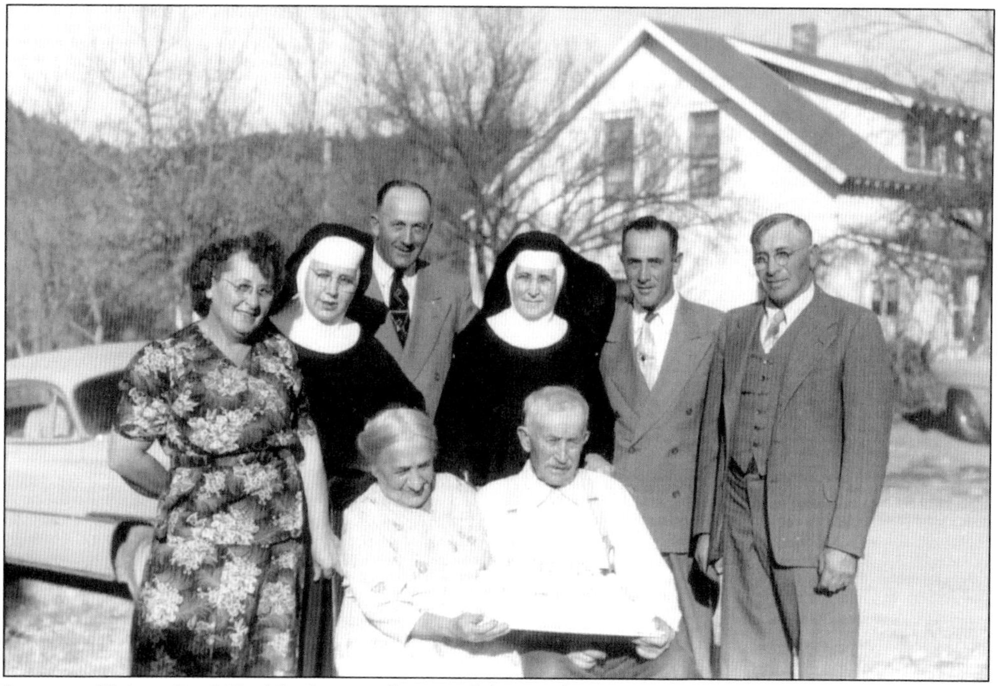

Louis and Mary Grubl hold a large cake to celebrate their 50th wedding anniversary, while the rest wonder where the ice cream is. The Grubls donated the altar for Saint Aloysius Catholic Church. There was no date on the picture—the cars are from the early 1950s.

One of Sturgis's best loved citizens, Lucille Poznansky was responsible for many positive improvements to the area—yet she died a pauper and a recluse. Born January 23, 1887, in Nebraska, she grew up in Deadwood and wrote numerous articles about the historical characters she had come to know and love. Lucille was active in fraternal orders, St. Thomas Episcopal Church, Meade County Sunday School, and the Meade County Fair.

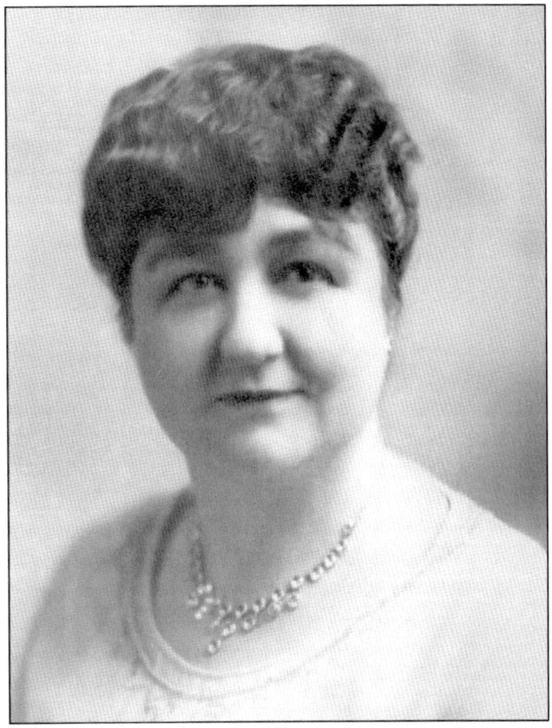

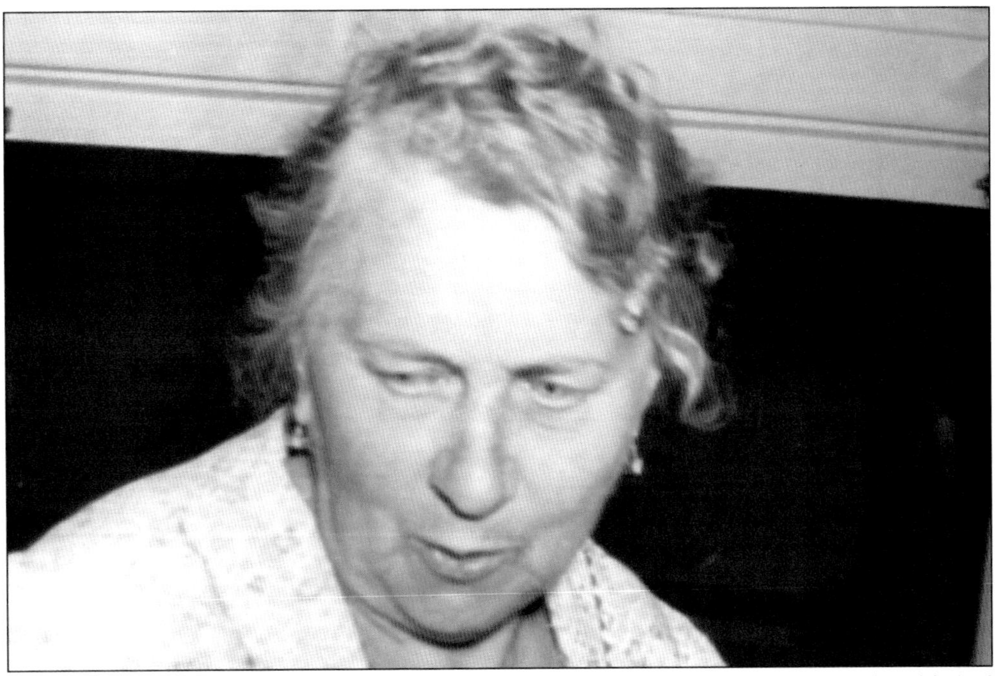

This lady must have been born with a skillet in her hands. Martha Brown cooked and baked for nearly every public function for miles around following her husband's death in the flu pandemic. In 1900, Martha came to Sturgis to work as a servant for five dollars a month. She raised her family by catering meals for large groups. In 1938, she did a realistic portrayal of Poker Alice for the town's 60th Anniversary celebration.

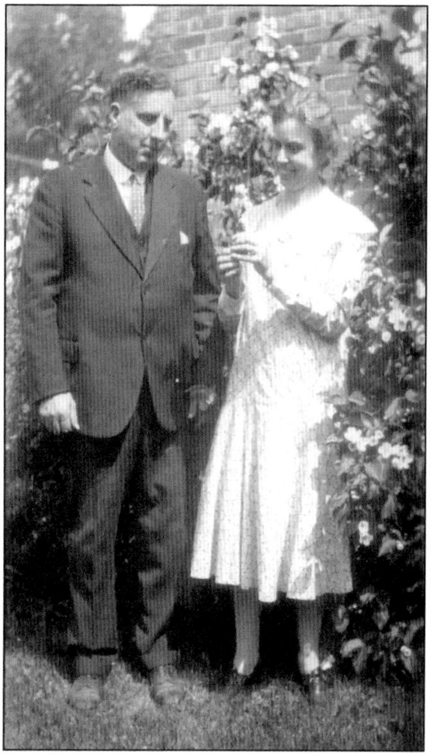

The Rev. C.D. Erskine and Madge Erskine are seen here. The Erskines came to Sturgis in 1906, where Reverend Erskine became the minister at First Presbyterian Church. Active in political and civic causes, Reverend Erskine and his friend Father Columban wielded a lot of influence in the community.

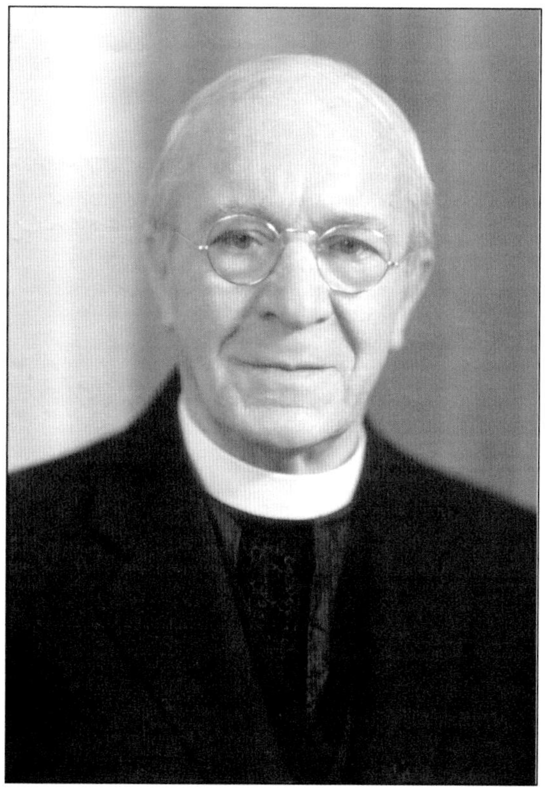

Kindly-looking Rev. Father Columban Bregenzer also arrived in Sturgis in 1906, and perhaps this is why he and the Erskines formed such a strong friendship. Born in Switzerland, the priest was a familiar sight as he drove around the countryside with horse and top buggy, stopping to visit and providing services at outlying parishes. Father Columban remained in Sturgis the longest of any clergymen—43 years.

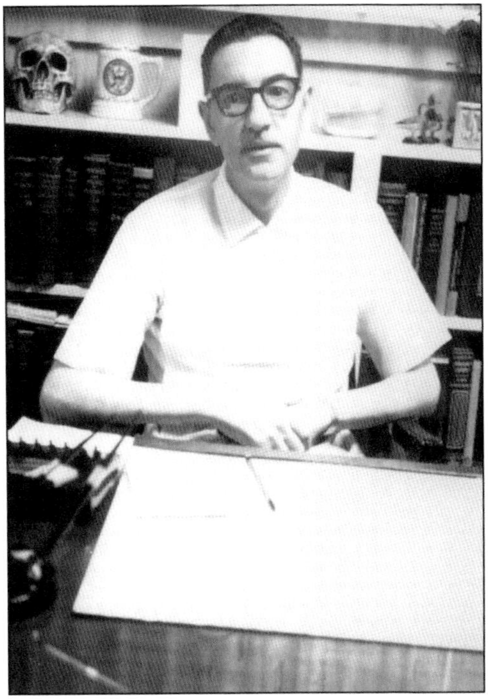
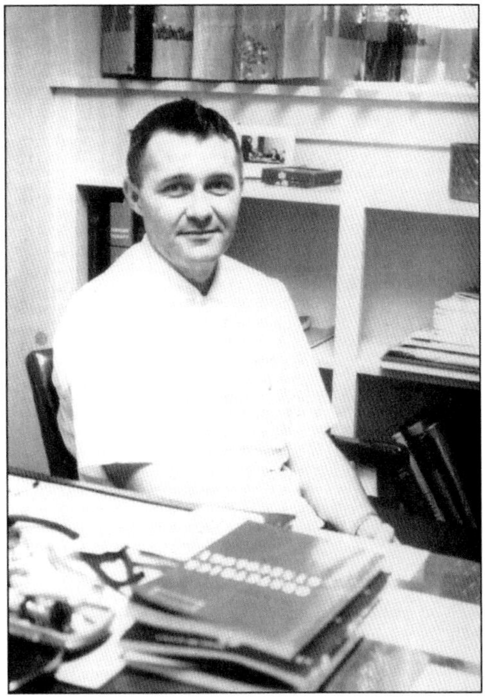

Doctors L.L. Massa and Duane Berry were synonymous with the best of medical care in Sturgis. The Massa-Berry Clinic was well known throughout the Black Hills in the 1950s and is still operating today.

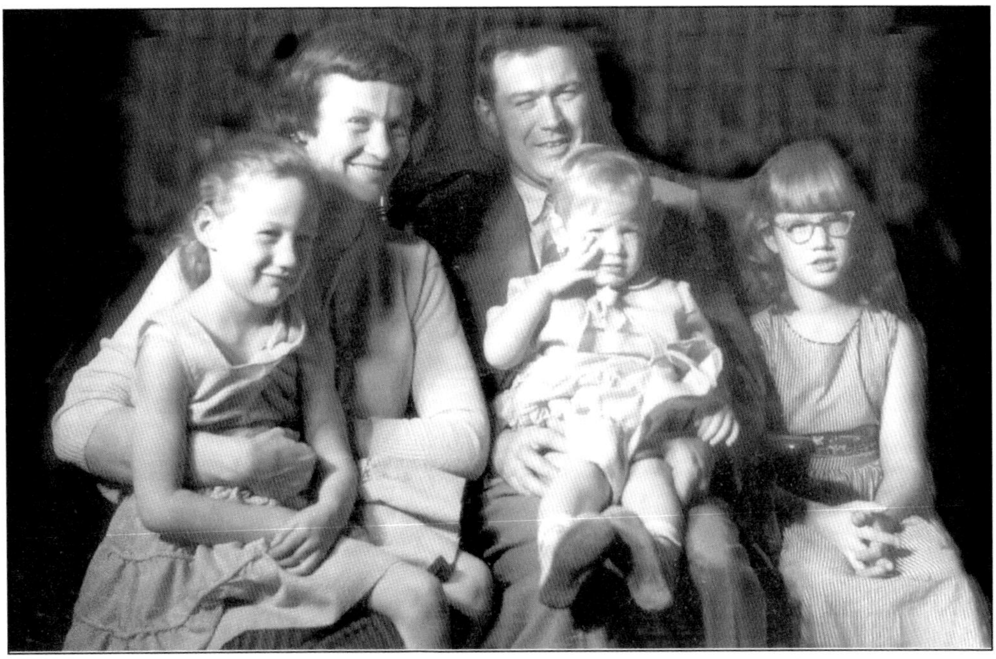

Sturgis had another favorite physician in the person of handsome Dr. Bill Jones. The Jones' family portrait from 1949–1950 shows, from left to right, Judy, Zinita (Mrs. Jones), Dr. Jones holding Margie, and Ginny. Margie Jones currently has a veterinary practice in Sturgis.

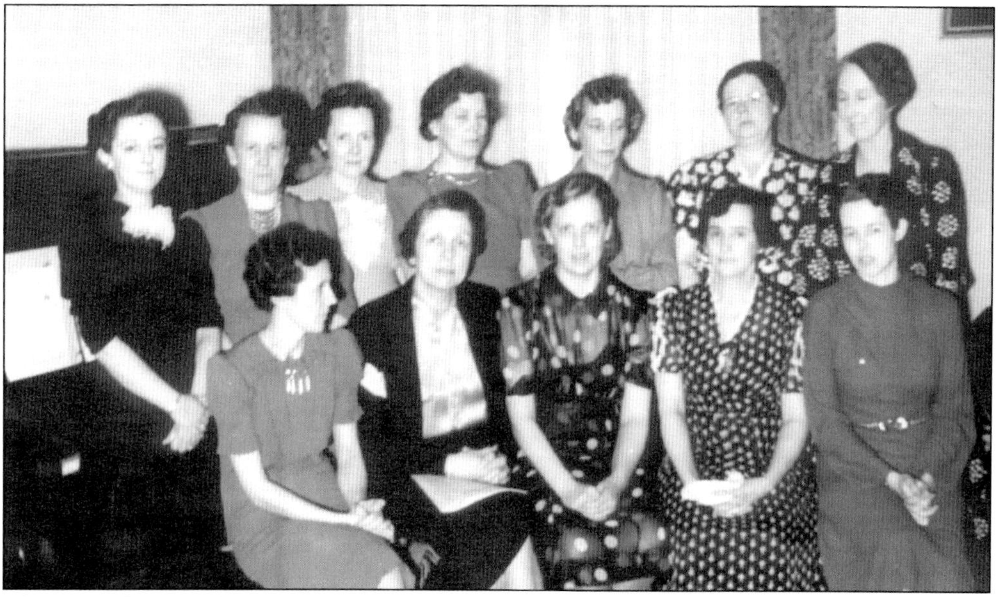

The PEO Chapter of AY was organized April 17, 1939. Pictured are the original members, from left to right: (front row) Reba Richards, Eula Farnsworth, Lillian Lushbough, Blanche Hardy, and Marian Sherman; (back row) Lenore Milne, Norma Cole, Carolyn McGibney, Hildur Carlson, Georgia Riedesel, Elizabeth Steele, and Blanche Barber.

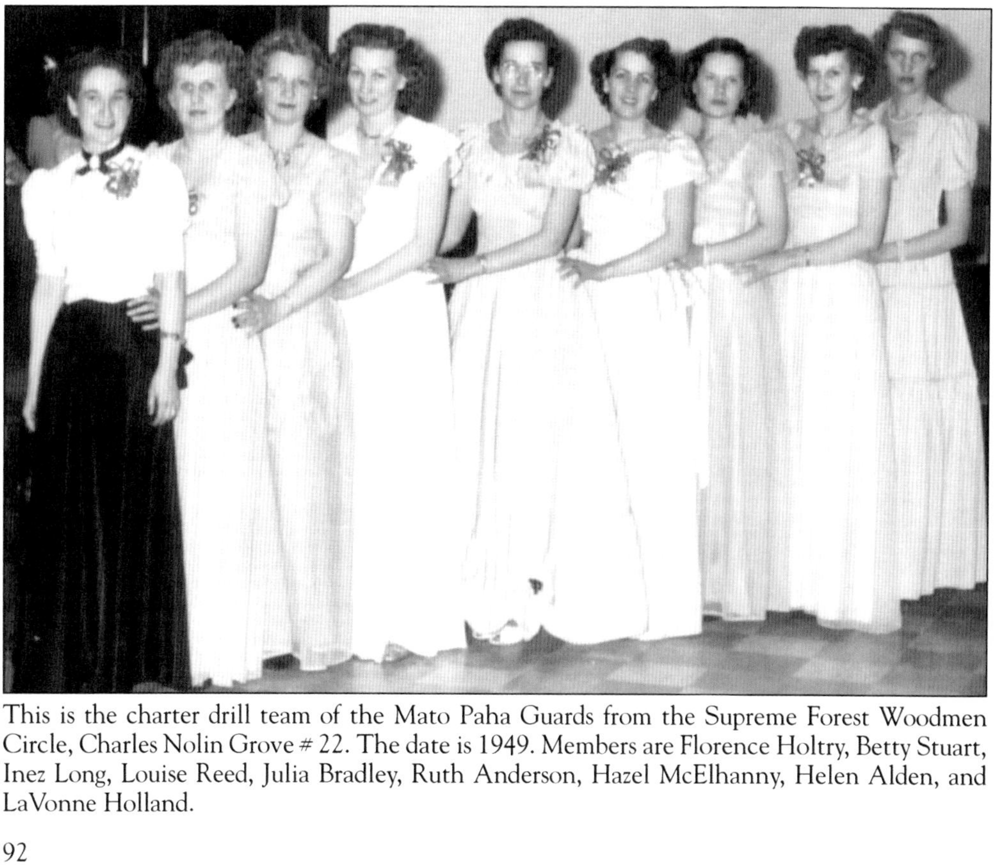

This is the charter drill team of the Mato Paha Guards from the Supreme Forest Woodmen Circle, Charles Nolin Grove # 22. The date is 1949. Members are Florence Holtry, Betty Stuart, Inez Long, Louise Reed, Julia Bradley, Ruth Anderson, Hazel McElhanny, Helen Alden, and LaVonne Holland.

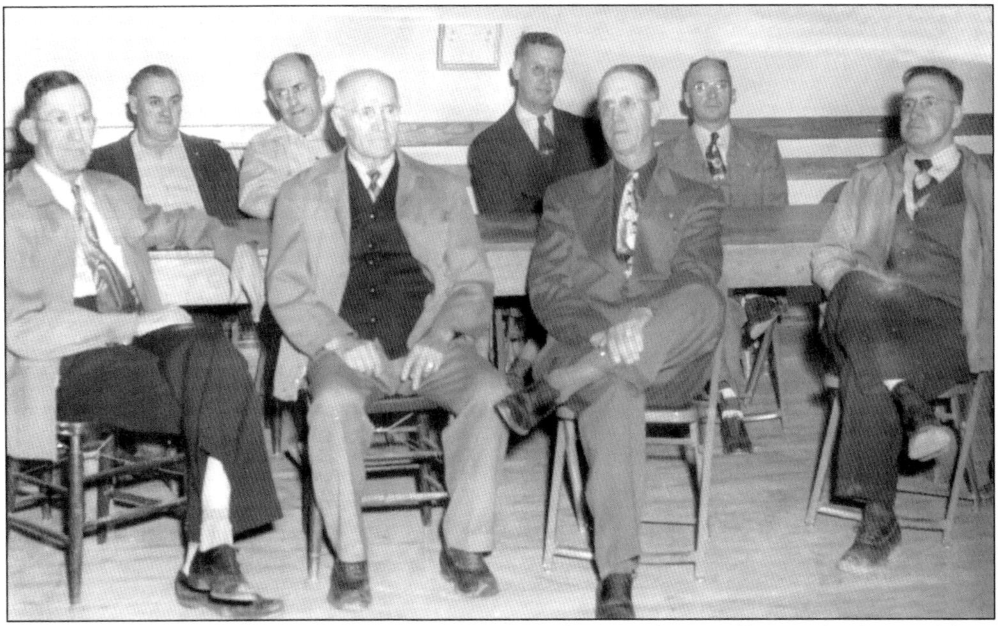

These distinguished gentlemen were the Directors of Benevolent Hall in 1950. Pictured here are, from left to right: (front row) Leonard Schryvers, W.A. Thurston, G.E. Williams, and W.E. Owens; (back row) William J. Plunkett, Sid Voorhees, Harold Anderson, and J.W. Sweeney.

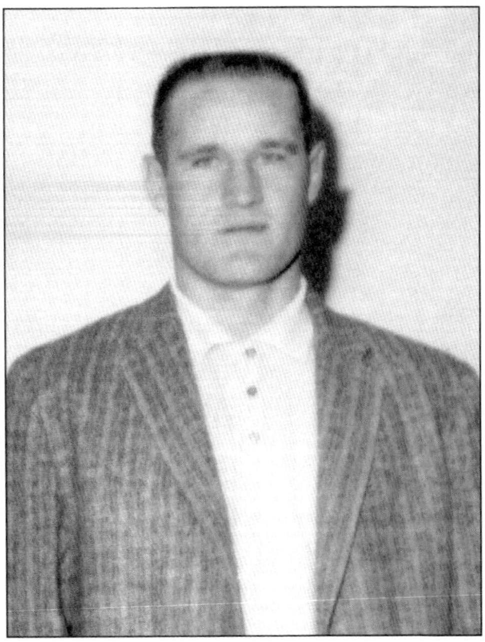

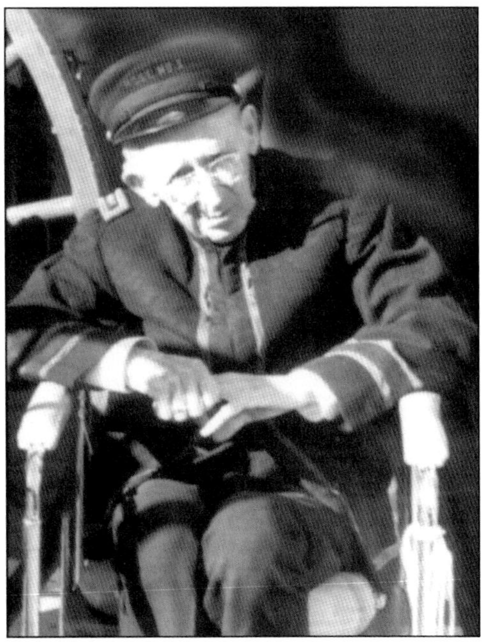

Carroll Hardy, left, led Sturgis to the state basketball championship in 1951, starred in football at the University of Colorado and for the San Francisco 49'ers. He played major league baseball for the Boston Red Sox (once pinch-hitting for Ted Williams), the Cleveland Indians, and Minnesota Twins; and scouted for the Denver Broncos. George Biesman, right, an early member of Hose Company No. 1, is pictured here in his old fireman's uniform on his 100th birthday in 1968.

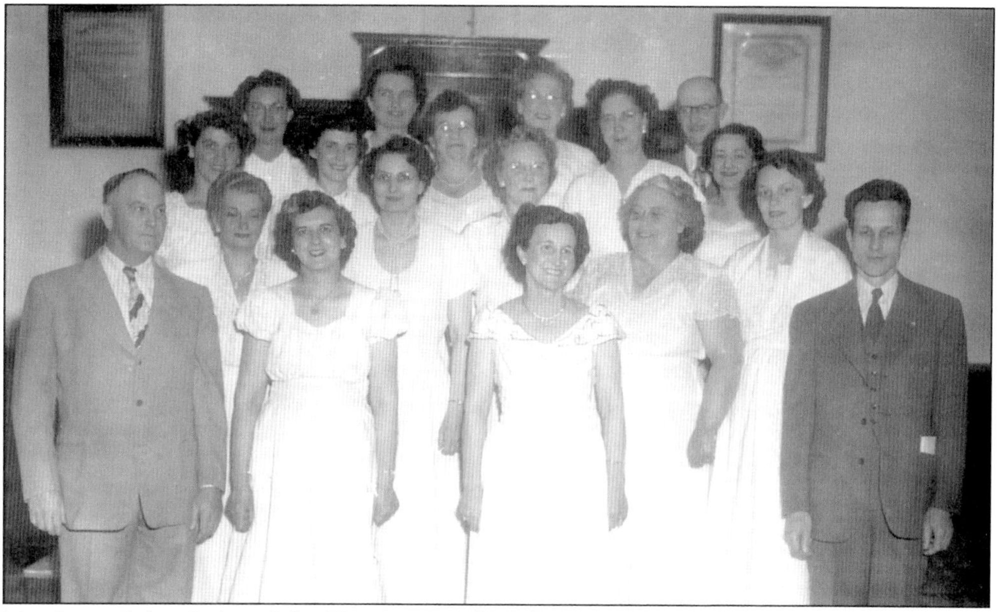

Members of the Order of the Eastern Star (OES) in 1951 are Gerry Hardy, Eunice Orem, Jackie Johnson, Gail Roudt, Beryl Heckert, Van Fossen, Peggy Thompson, Florence Williams, Lois Thompson, Margaret Morrell, Vernon Officer, Evelyn Brow, Charles Williams (Associate Patron), Adelaide Donaldson (Associate Matron), Doris Forbes, Worthy Matron, Jim Forbes, and Worthy Patron.

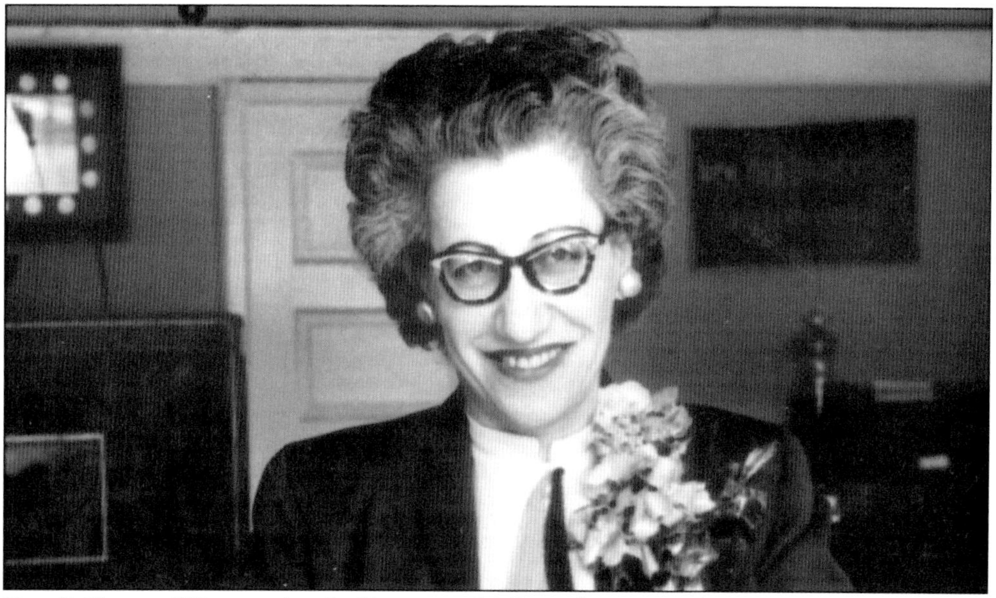

Kate Soldat was "30 years ahead of her times," folks said. In 1937, she began the Sturgis Credit Bureau and a shopper's newspaper. She was an *Associated Press* reporter, a court reporter, real estate broker, member of the Sturgis City Council, and the first female president of the League of Municipalities. In 1950, Kate became South Dakota's first woman mayor and the second female mayor in the United States. To top it off, Kate (Dorothy Allison's mother) was a charter member in and longtime secretary for the Black Hills Motor Classic.

Seven

A Day at the Races

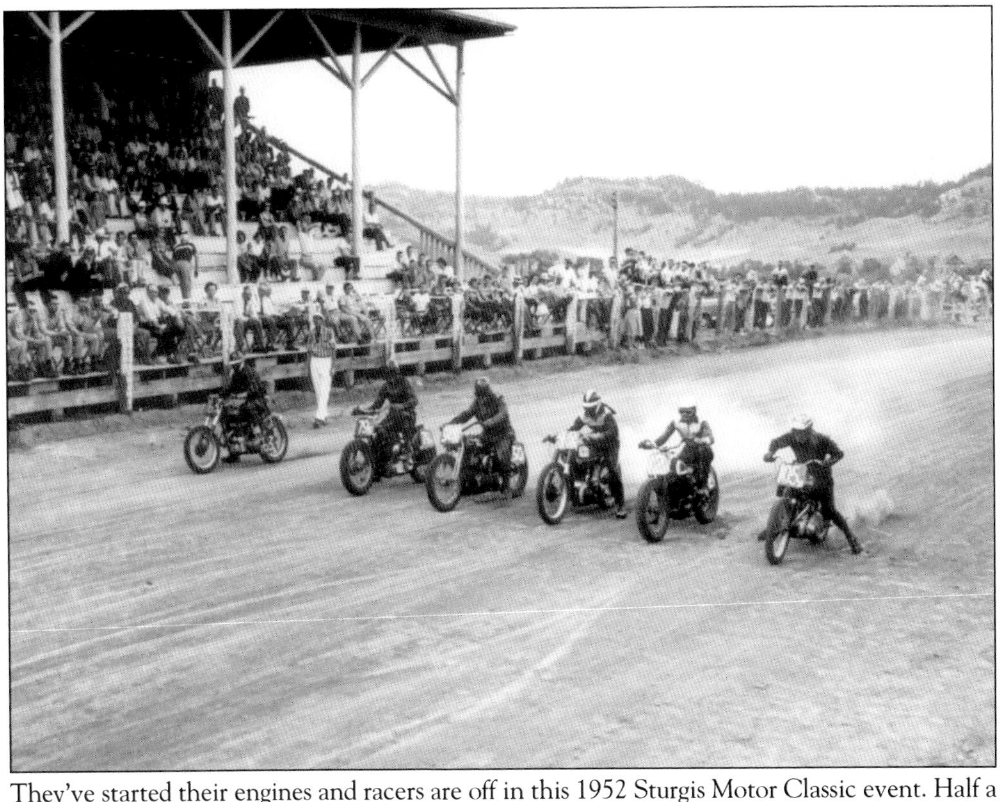

They've started their engines and racers are off in this 1952 Sturgis Motor Classic event. Half a century ago, spectators paid more attention to the participants than to the sidewalk crowds.

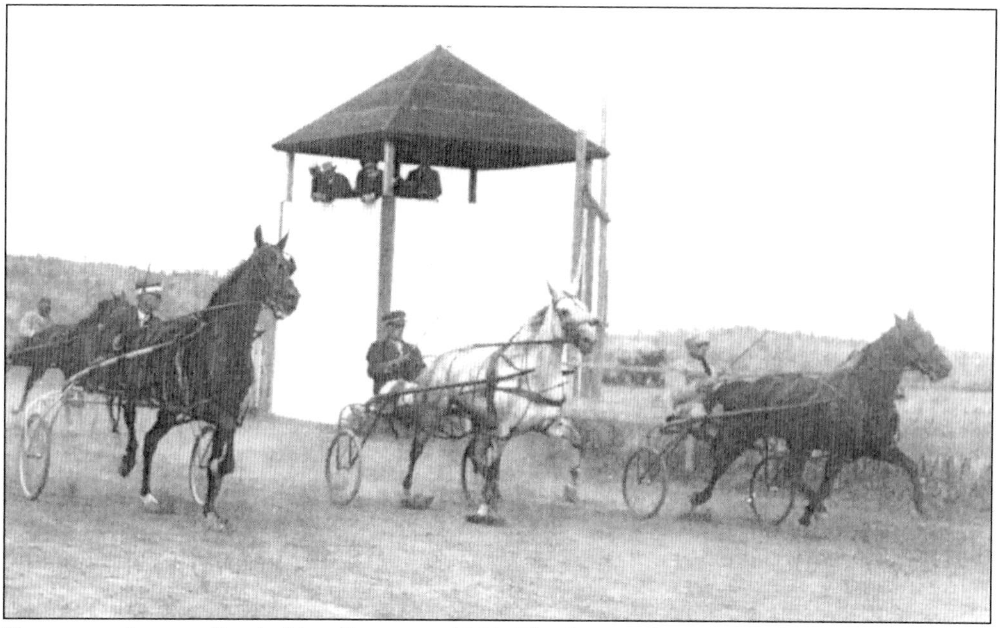

Harness racing was first held in Sturgis in 1904. This heat is for pacers, who are moving both legs on the same side at the same time. Some early owners of these Standard-bred horses were Ed J. Garlick, Horace Farnsworth, Burt Hamblet, J. Lee Forbes, Jack Kelly, and Matt Flavin. Ed Garlick won a huge trophy in 1913 for his stallion Sturgis Boy. It is on display at Old Fort Meade Museum.

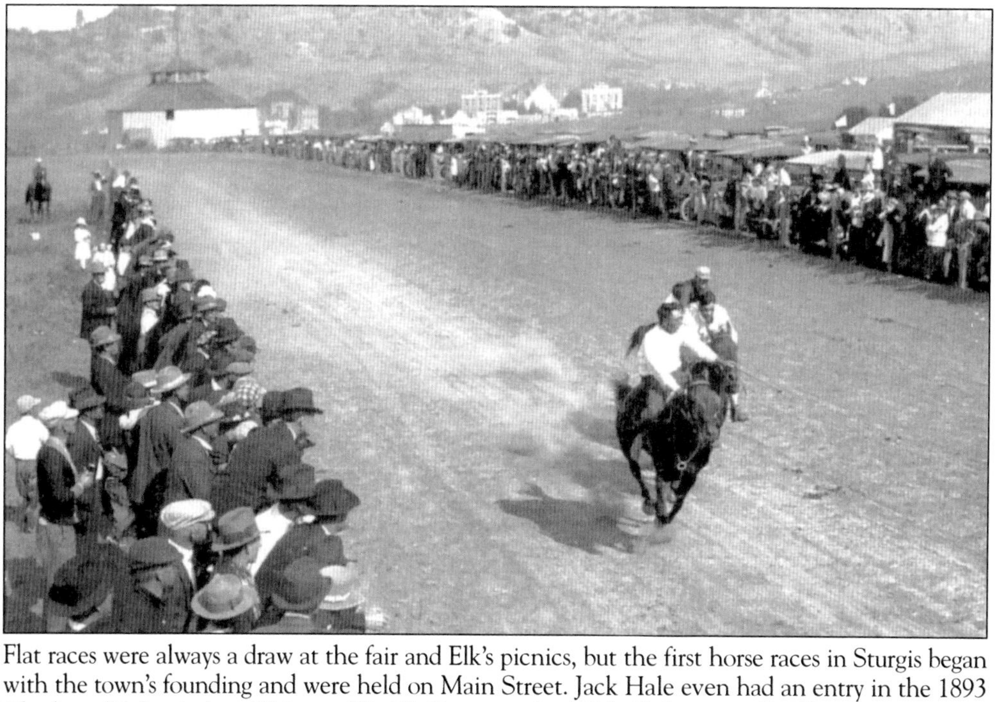

Flat races were always a draw at the fair and Elk's picnics, but the first horse races in Sturgis began with the town's founding and were held on Main Street. Jack Hale even had an entry in the 1893 Chadron (Nebraska) to Chicago World's Fair race. In 1905, Hale was still selling horses to the army. Popular relay racers in 1920 were George McFarland Jr., Veo Gale, and Bobby Kleven.

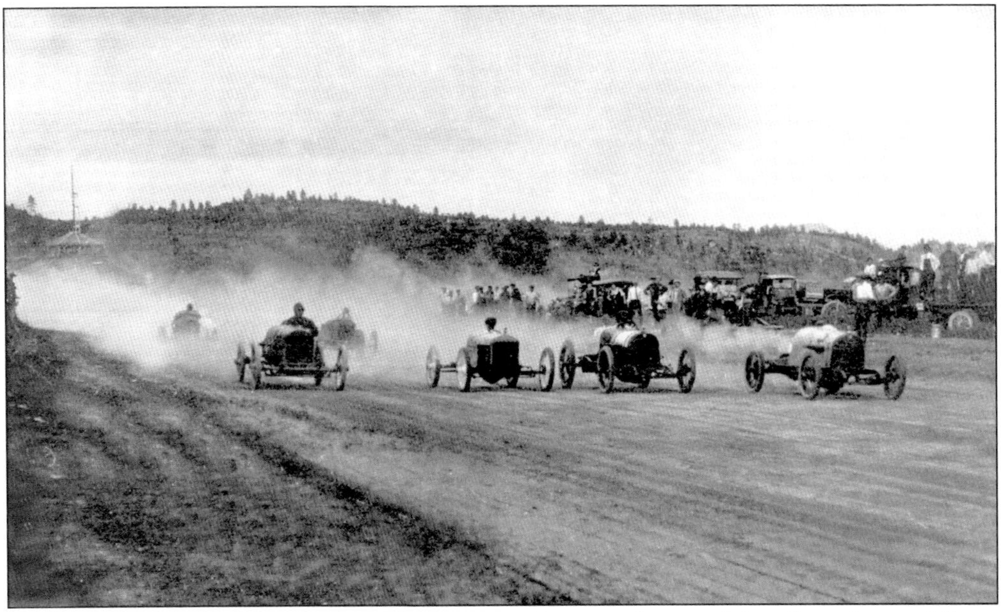

Auto racing became a popular sport until mass production of automobiles allowed more folks to own one. The first race cars were modified Model T Fords with a top speed of 50 miles per hour. Frank Aukerman entered Elmer Arnett's car in the first Sturgis race at the fairgrounds. The photo is dated 1922.

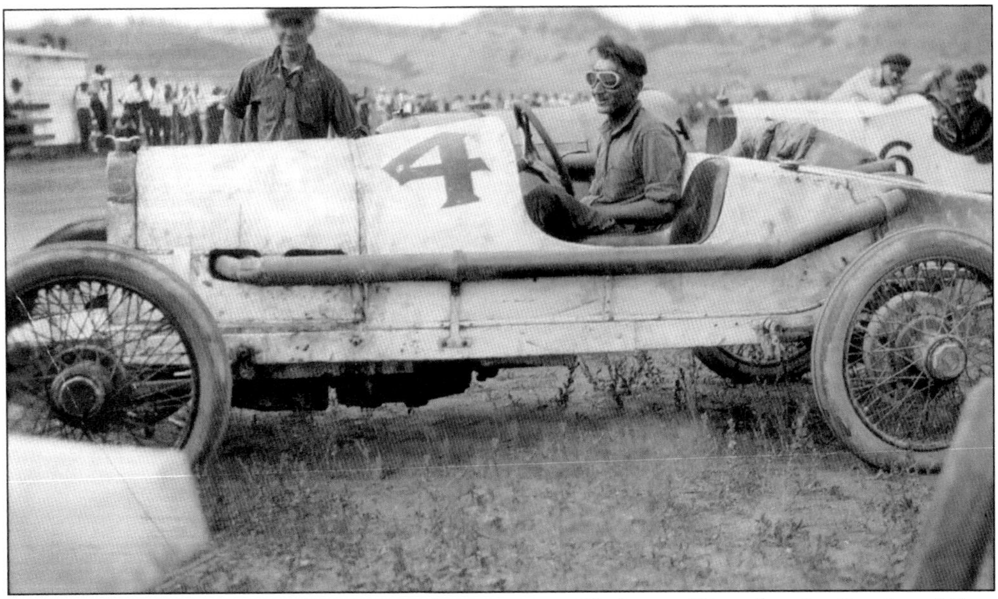

No information is given on this driver, whose name is Chalmers. Those besides Frank and Burt Aukerman who promoted local auto racing back then were Ed Miller, Hugh Jones, Walt Miller, and Frank (Skinny) Cornwell.

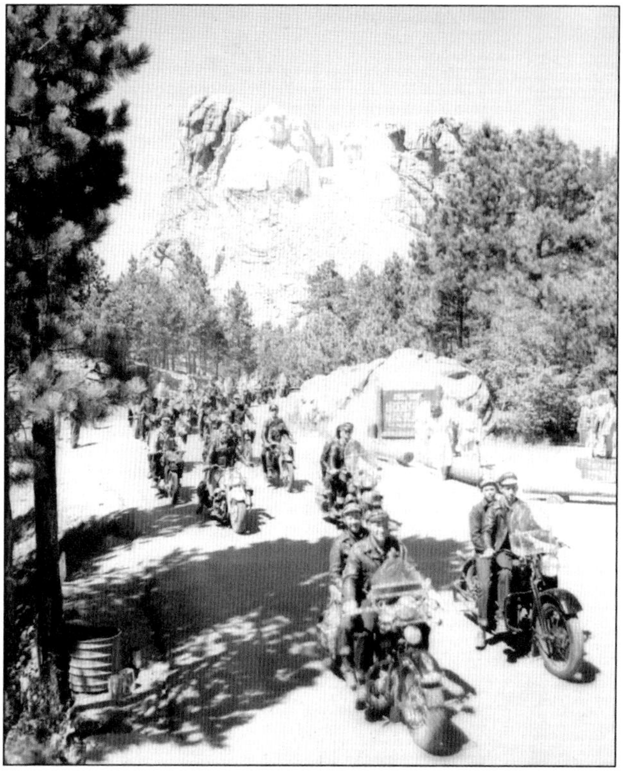

The Jackpine Gypsies Motorcycle Club prepares to leave Mount Rushmore National Memorial in 1949. "Gypsy tours" of the Black Hills were a much anticipated part of the early Sturgis Motor Classic rally. Bikers today still rate the area as a favorite destination.

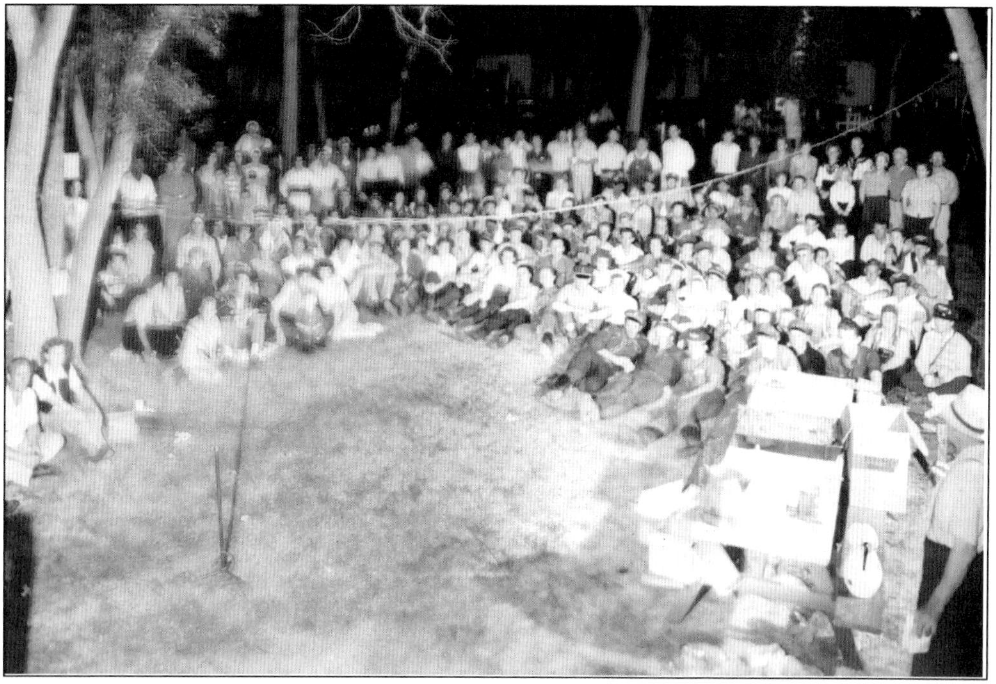

In 1947, rally partying looked like this and was a family event. The coffee pot's on at the Gypsy camp. J.C. "Pappy" Hoel and Neil Hultman were the originators of the Jackpine Gypsies club. Pearl Hoel fed the group—two dollar dues got you a lifetime membership.

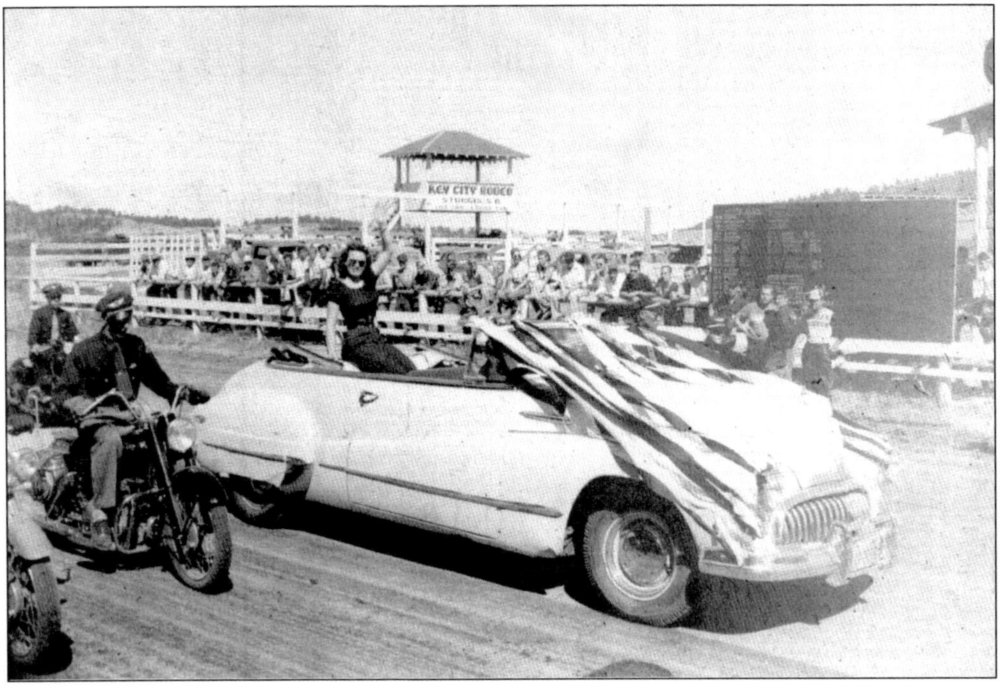

Queen of the Rally in 1949 was pretty Daisy Rundle from Anamosa, Iowa. Queens were chosen from female attendees and reigned over the biker festivities. The title was changed to "Queen of the Classics" in 1954.

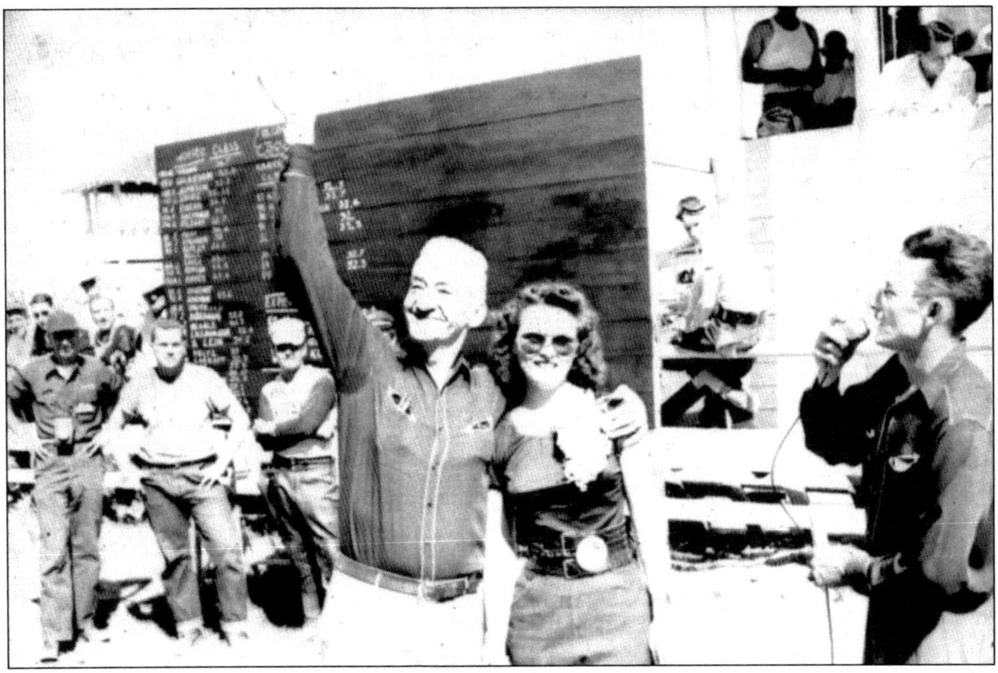

Dick Williams presents queen Daisy Rundle to the crowd. Who is that "other guy," anyway? The first rally in 1938 offered $500 in prize money that the group "didn't have," prior to the event, and according to Pappy Hoel, the club had to charge everything and hope for the best in gate returns.

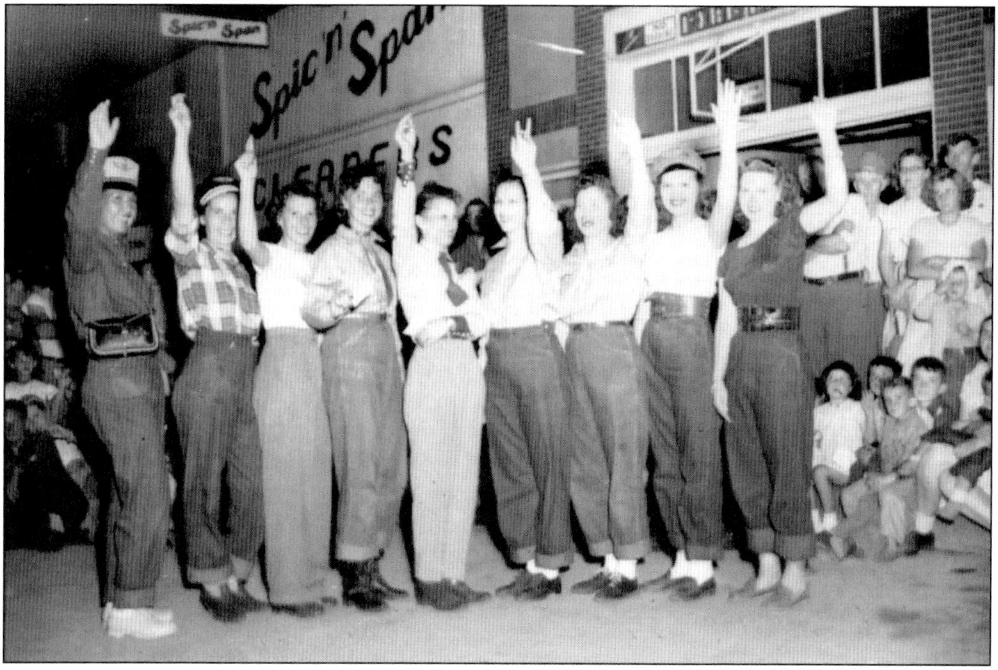

Here are the biker babes of 1949. These queen candidates are fully clothed, but look every bit as appealing as their successors. Wave to the crowd, girls!

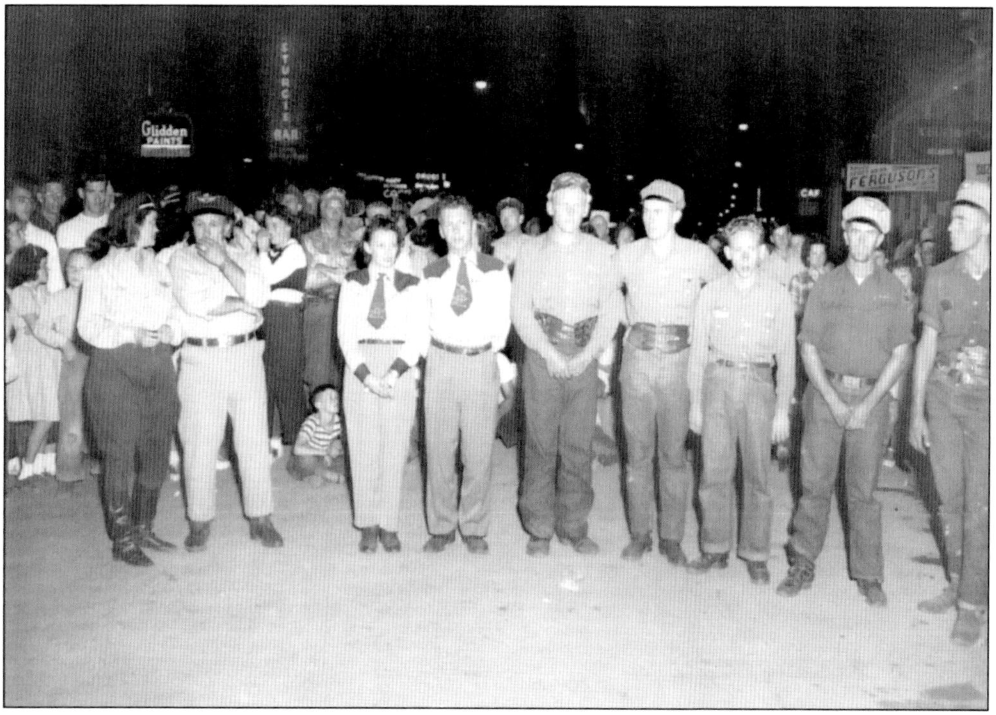

This is how the biker crowd dressed when representing their respective motorcycle clubs. Prizes were given for a number of categories—the best entries received tanned deer hides with hand-painted Black Hills scenes on them.

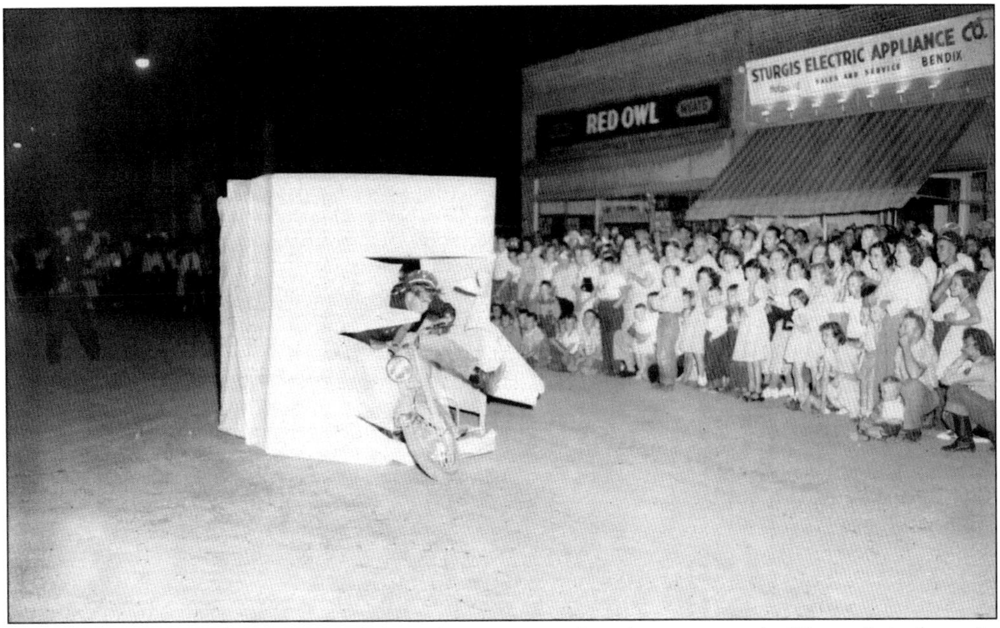

Whoa! This stunt rider appears to be nearly separating from his motorcycle. He made it through, though. There were lots of daredevil things a fella might try in '49. No doubt that he got the attention of the ladies for being a brave man, and it was probably a lot trickier than it looks here.

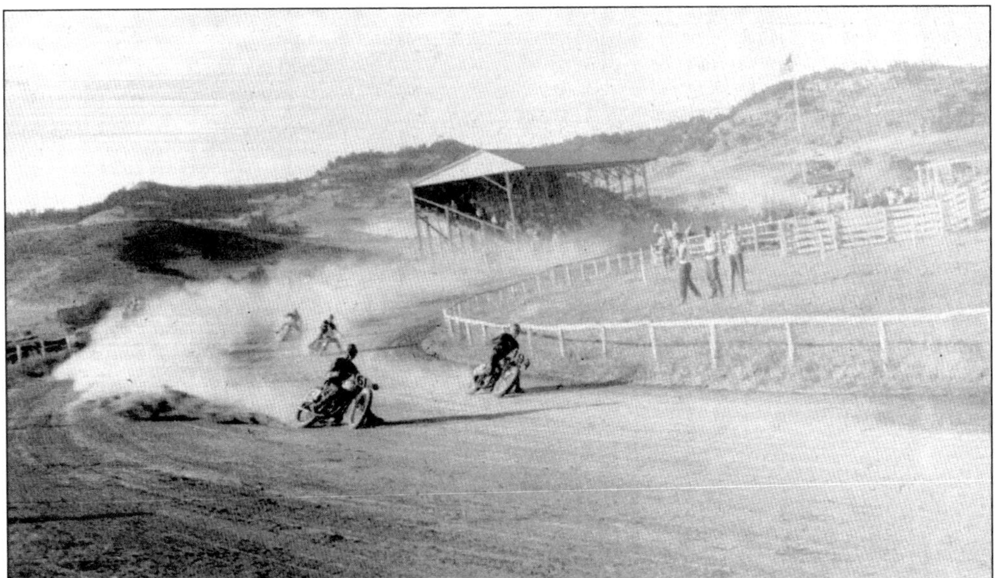

Racers careen around the track during the 1949 Sturgis Rally. No races were held during World War II, but later events included a national five-mile championship on the half-mile track, which was sanctioned by the American Motorcycle Association (the only such race in the United States). Bruce Barnes managed the races for the motor classic in the early days.

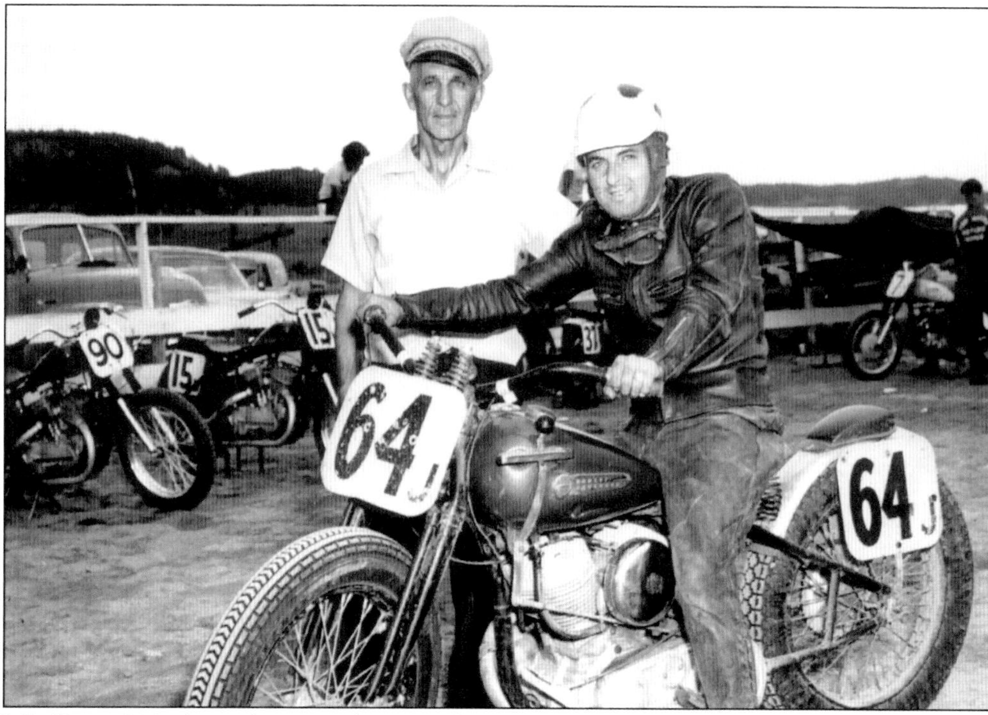

J.C. "Pappy" Hoel was the man who started it all. From ice man to motorcycle enthusiast, the Sturgis native proved over and over the value of a good idea. Pappy is standing next to an unidentified racer in 1952.

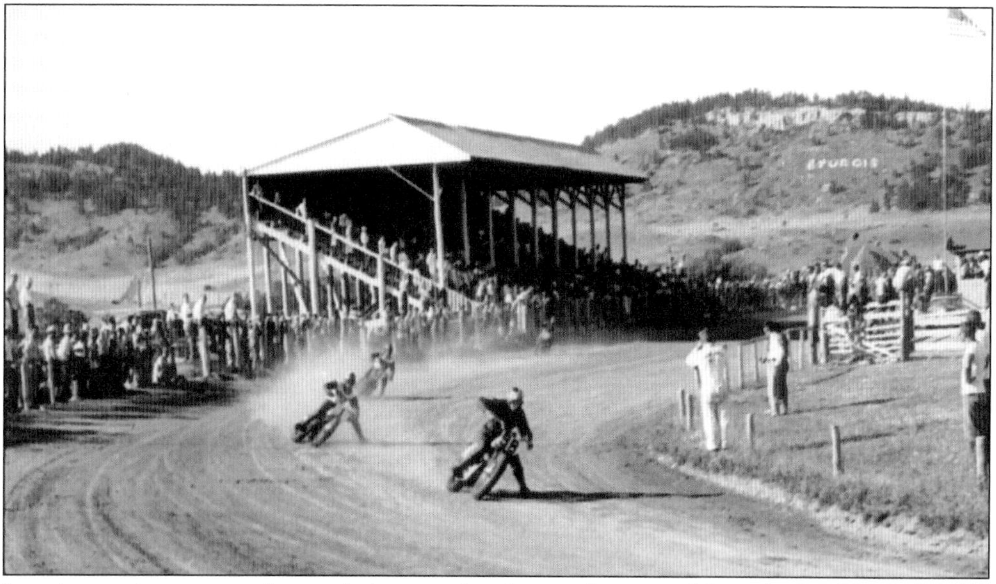

Just about spinning out of control, the outside rider may be in trouble in this 1952 event. Biker fans come from 50 states and approximately 60 countries to be a part of today's spectacle. In 1995, South Dakota's Sen. Larry Pressler introduced legislation allowing temporary suspension of duty on American-made motorcycles shipped back into the country "for participation in the Sturgis Motorcycle Rally and Races."

Eight

What's a Fella to Do?

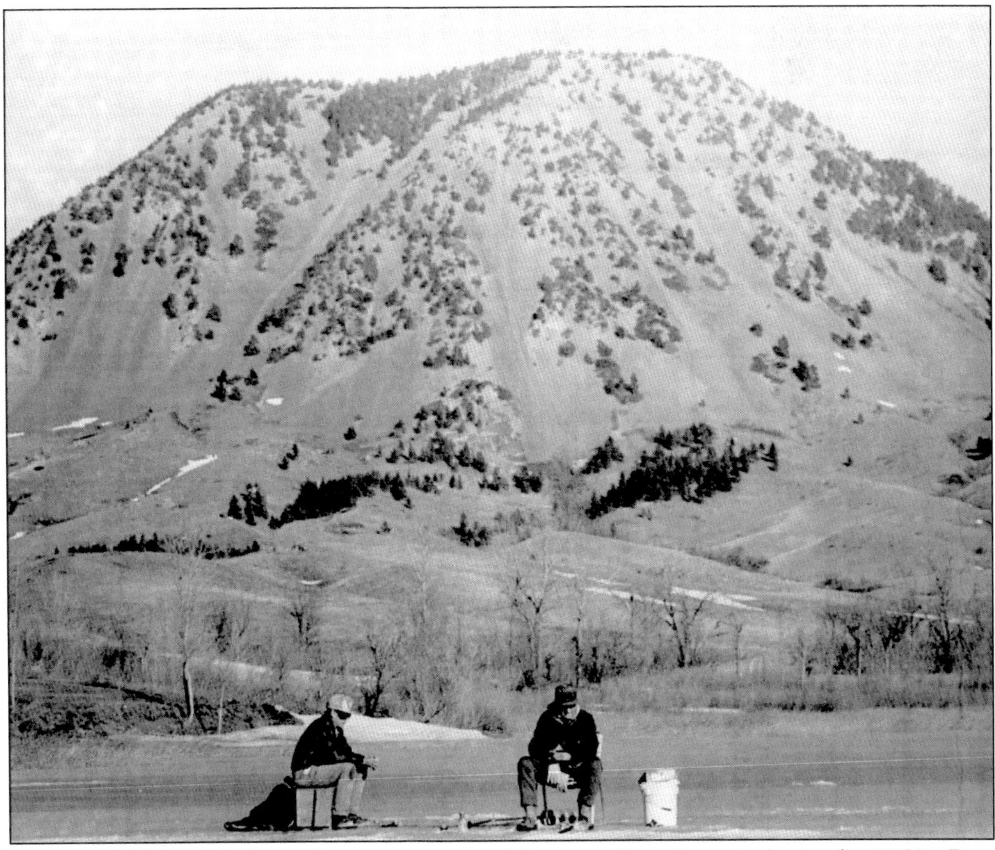

Kelly Donaldson and Ernie Conway were ice fishing on Bear Butte Lake in the 1950s. Bear Butte was a mapping landmark for early explorers and a place of worship for Indian peoples. Ezra and Lois Bovee settled near the butte in 1888. In 1940, the Bovee family offered burro rides to the top, and worked with historian Thomas Odell to establish Bear Butte State Park, dedicated August 8, 1965. Bear Butte Lake, a WPA project, was created in 1938.

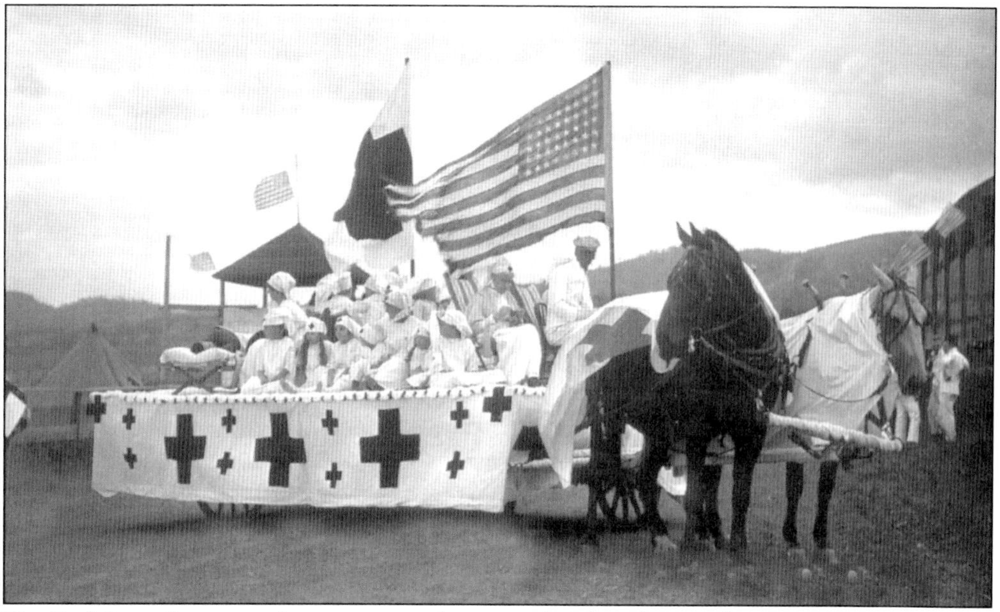

The Red Cross float is ready to move out for a parade. This photo is dated September 26, 1917 and is part of a World War I observance that included seeing area recruits off to battle.

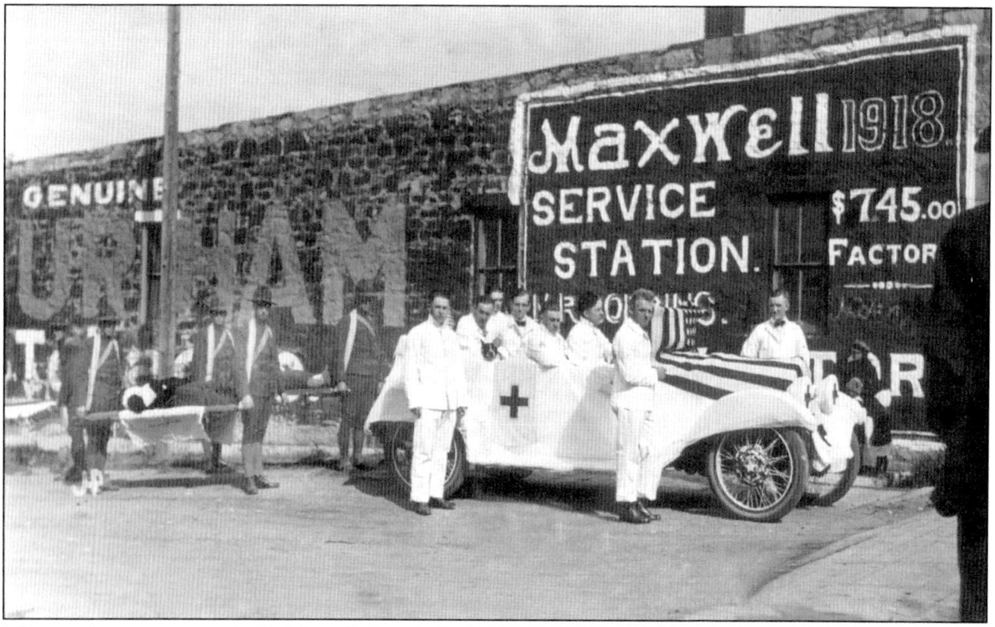

This is the same parade. Soldiers behind the car have "wounded" victims on the stretcher and have won second prize for their entry. That fall, one could order a 1918 Maxwell car for $745 from the factory, says a painted billboard on the side of the garage building.

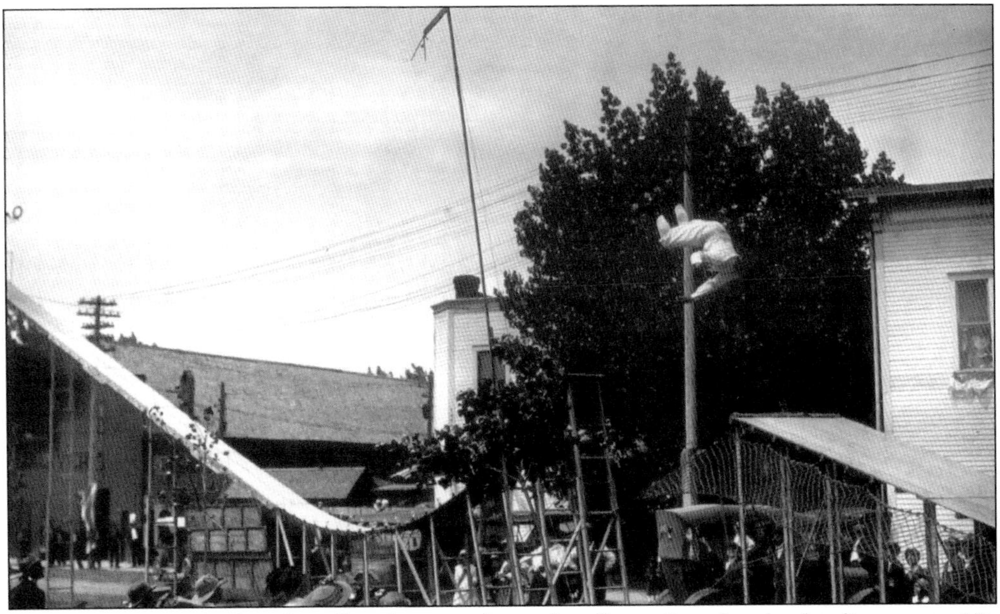

A human cannonball with roller skates makes a headlong dive for the landing ramp. His somersault looks a little short of the mark. Did he make it?

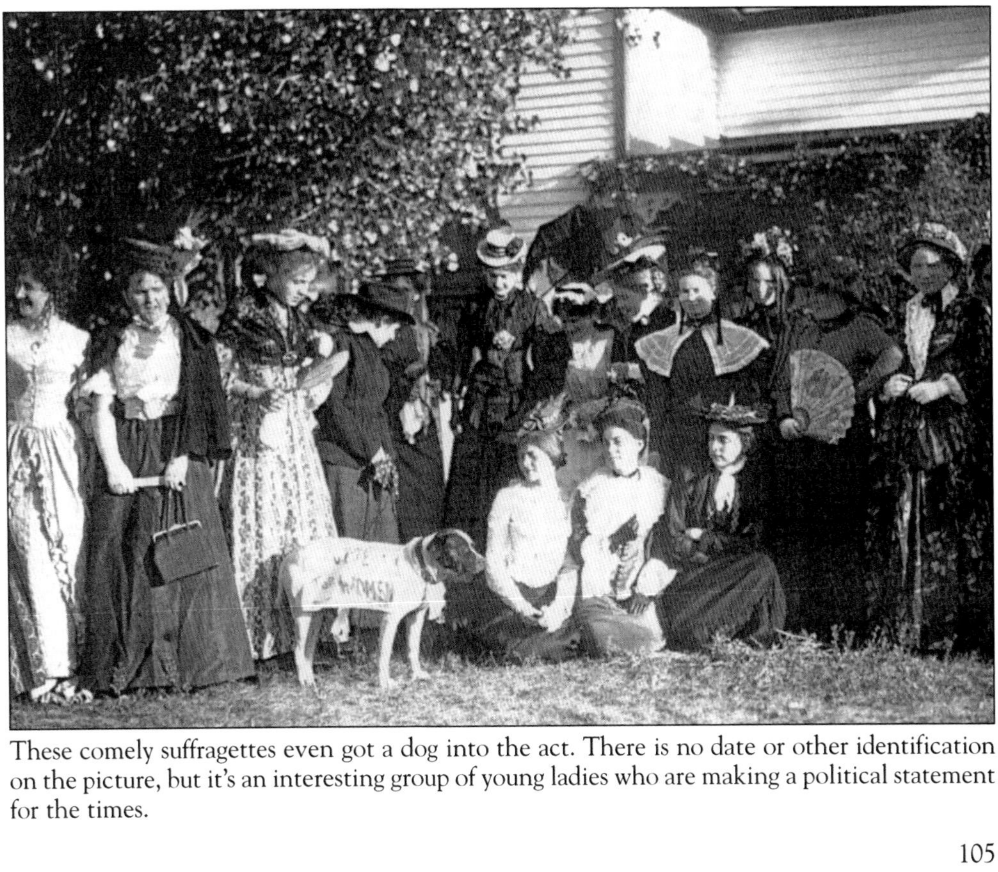

These comely suffragettes even got a dog into the act. There is no date or other identification on the picture, but it's an interesting group of young ladies who are making a political statement for the times.

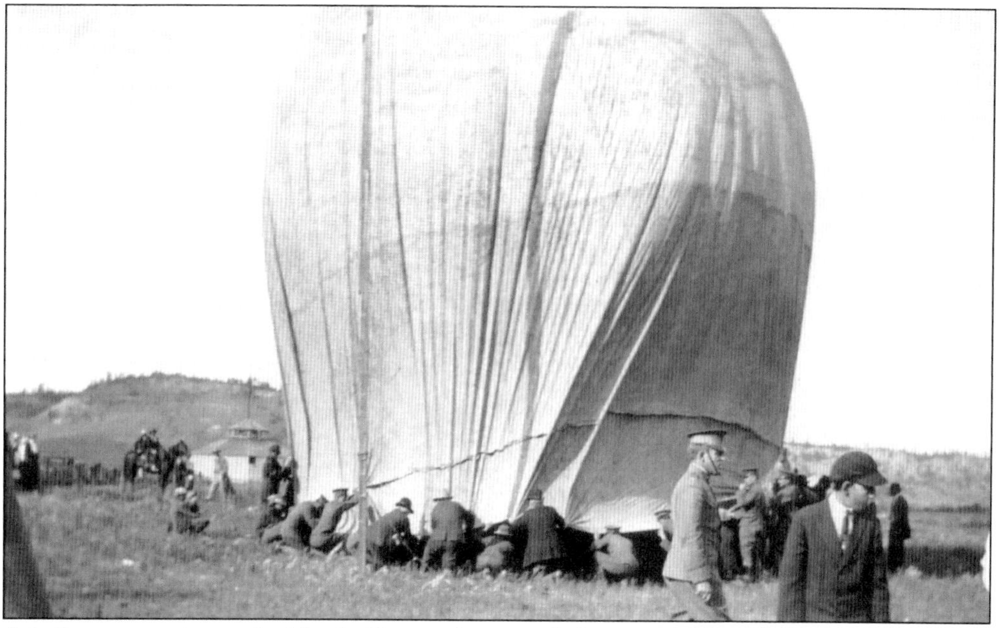

A balloon ascension at the Meade County fairgrounds fascinated folks of all ages with the idea of flight in the early 20th century. Traveling aeronauts, who ballyhooed their feats of going aloft in a balloon, drew huge crowds to see these performances and swelled entrance admissions. Some balloonists even took animals as large as horses along in their gondolas.

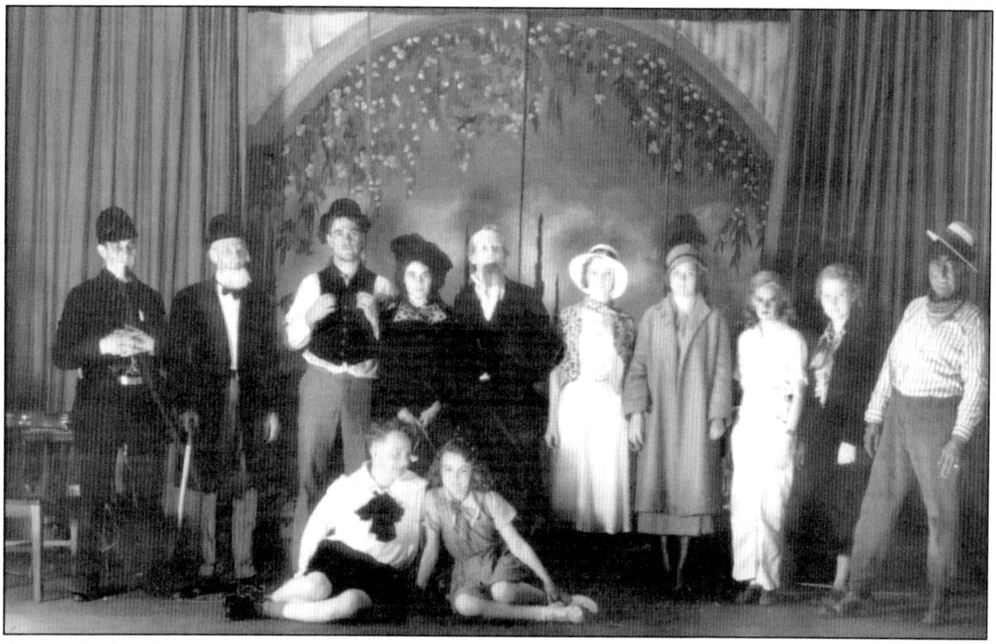

Sturgis had a theater company as early as 1899, performing *Cinderella* at the Jones Opera House, east of city hall. Seen here is the cast of a talent show presented at the Crook Theater and directed by Bob Cruickshank. Pictured, from left to right, are James Forbes, A.W. Devers, Jack Caton, Mary Wright, Vernon Officer, B.J. Cruickshank, Veronica Cotterill, Margaret Whitlock, Barbara Cruickshank, and Bob Cruickshank. In front are Billy Jurvis (Jarvis?) and Estelline Foverty.

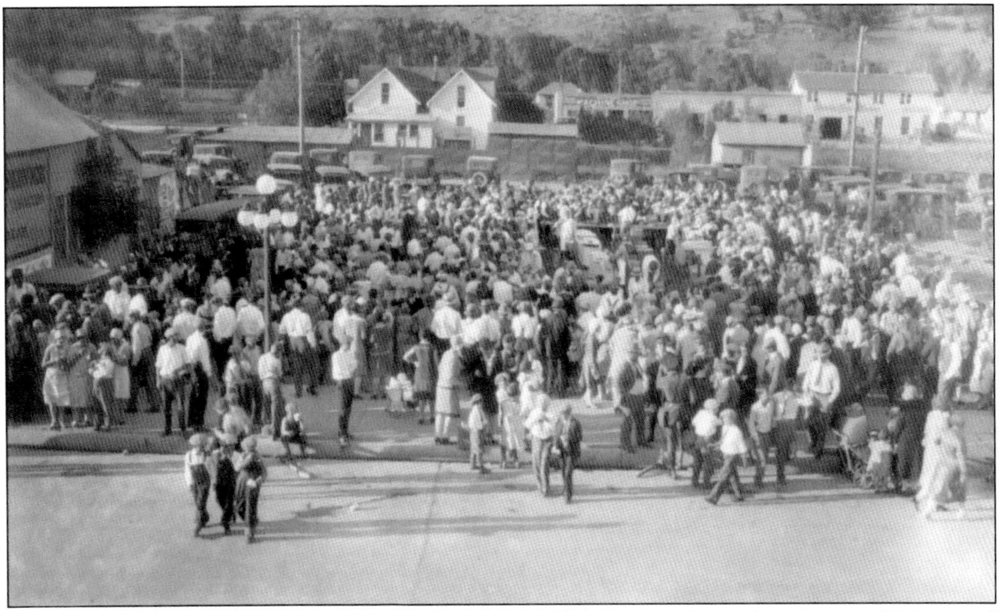

Progress Days were held downtown in the 1920s. This view is from the corner of Main and Junction looking north at where the auditorium was later located. The white house belonged to the Brodskys. Booths display the latest innovations for the modern consumer.

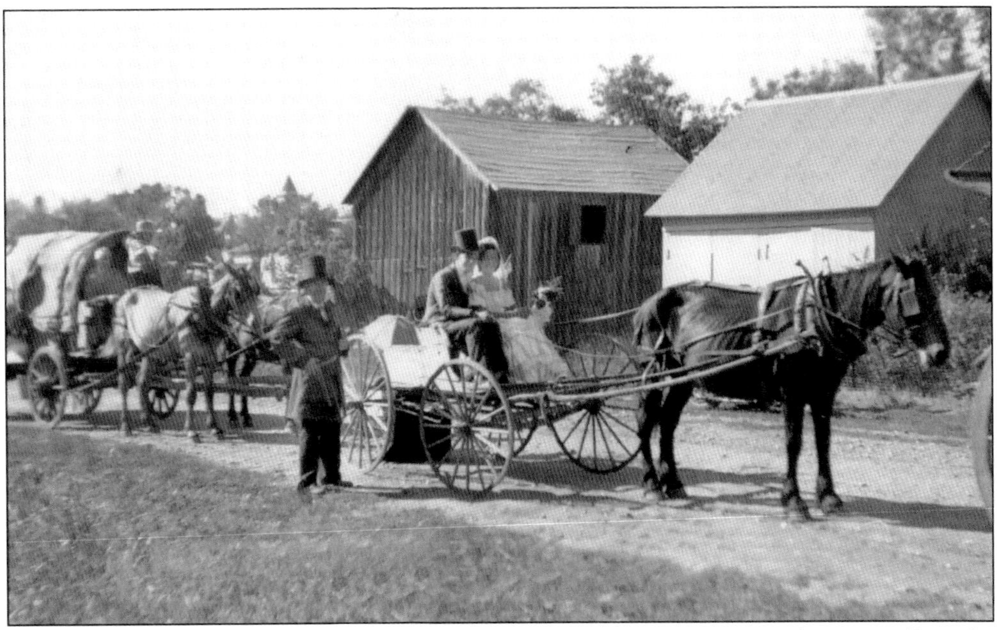

Emerging from the Great Depression, Sturgis townspeople had little money, but went all out for the 60th anniversary celebration of the town's founding held September 2–4, 1938. The Sturgis Commerical Club, Rev. C.D. Erskine, president, sponsored a historical pageant of America's past. The high school band concert band drew 1,000 to the new auditorium.

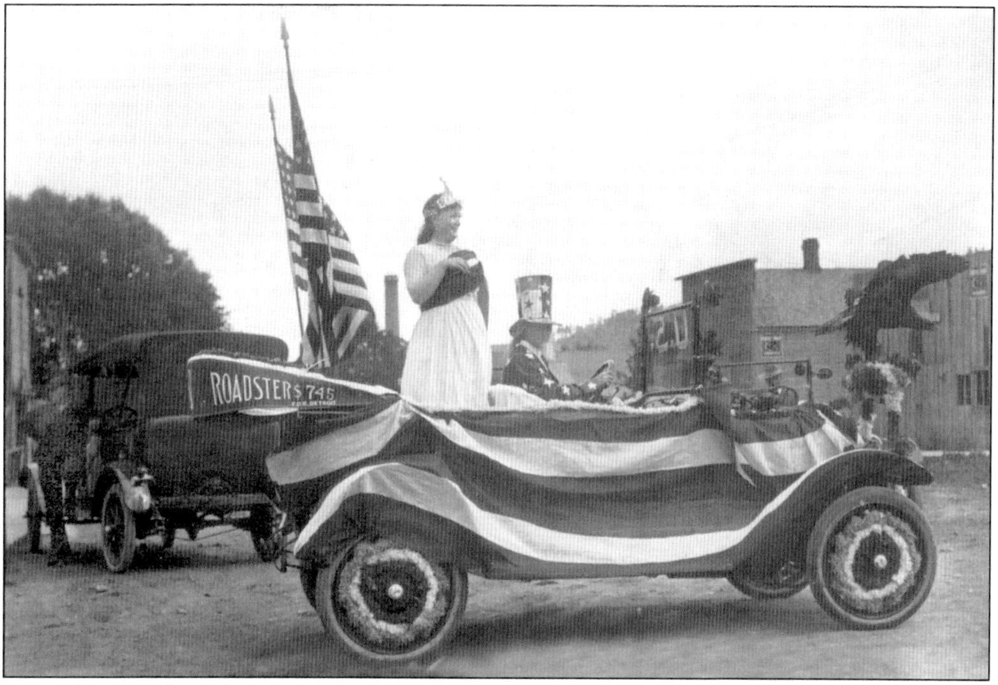

Miss Liberty and Uncle Sam were good for third place in the auto parade category on September 26, 1917. Patriotism was certainly evident at this event.

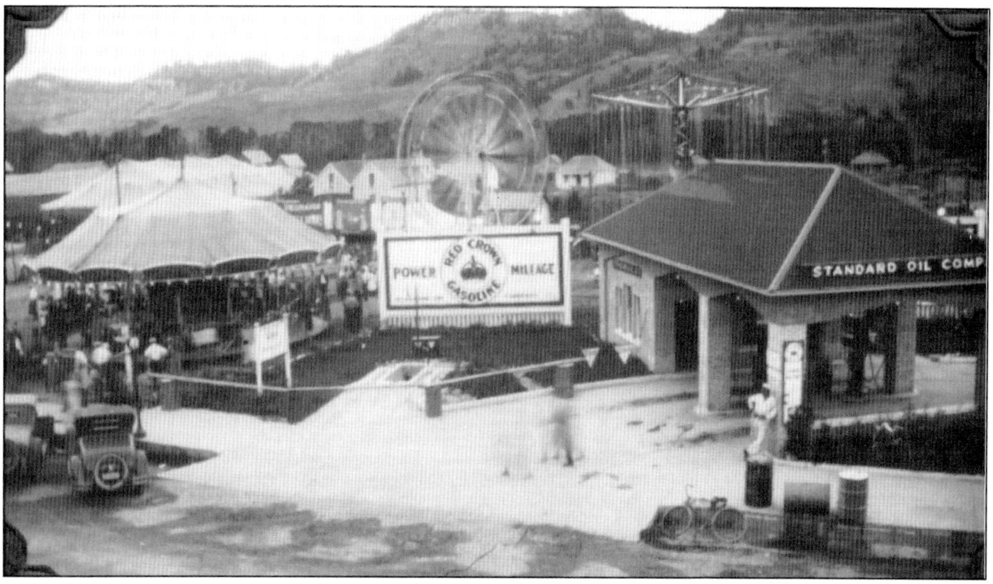

This 1932 carnival attracts the crowd, while the station attendant waits for a customer. Carnivals often ran afoul of the law. Sheriff Barnes arrived in town, said a news source, and found " . . . a couple of their games were pure gambling." The "girlie" shows were illegal, too.

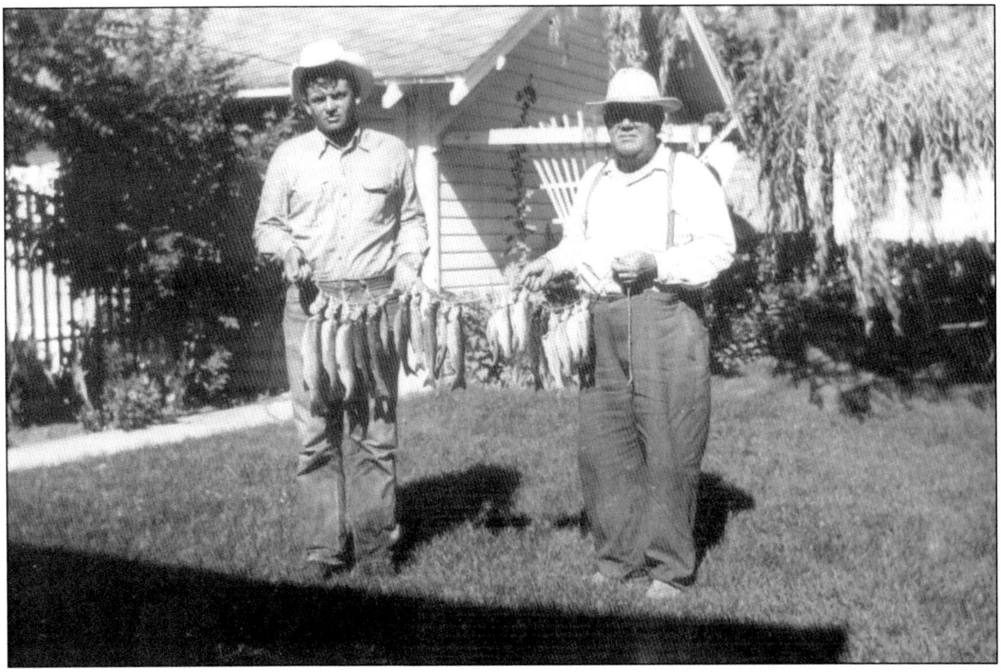

Bruce Walker, left, and Harold Walker, right, are seen here with a mess of good eatin' for a couple of bankers. Harold and his uncle, J.B. Jennings, purchased Bear Butte Valley Bank in 1924. Bruce joined the banking firm in 1951. Father and son had a combined 78 years in banking and were active in community affairs.

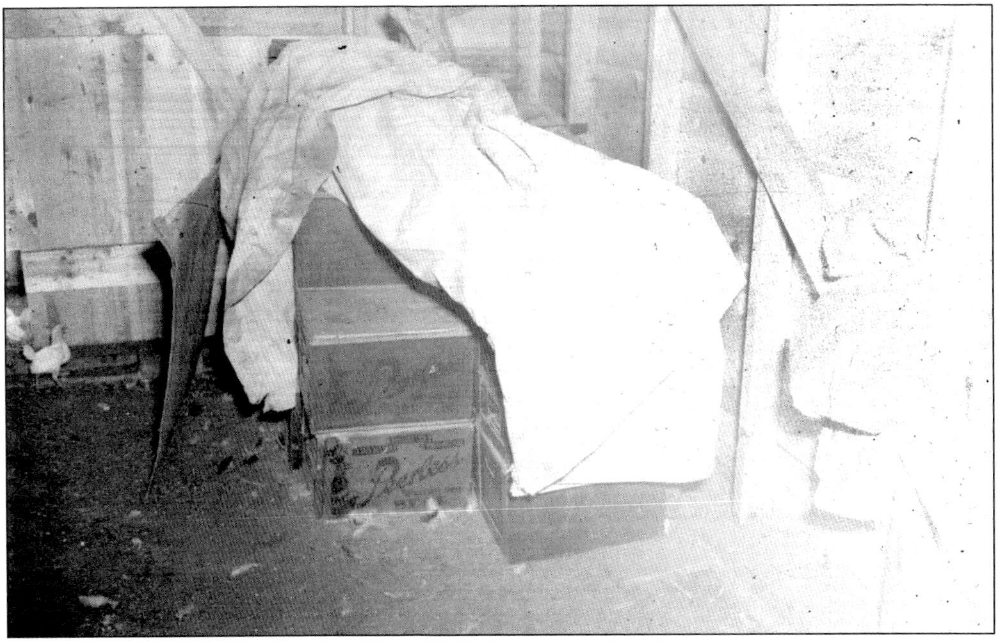

This cache of bootleg Peerless beer was found in Meade County during prohibition. Moonshining was practiced by many during the 1920s and 1930s—not only to quench thirst, but to add a little money to household incomes.

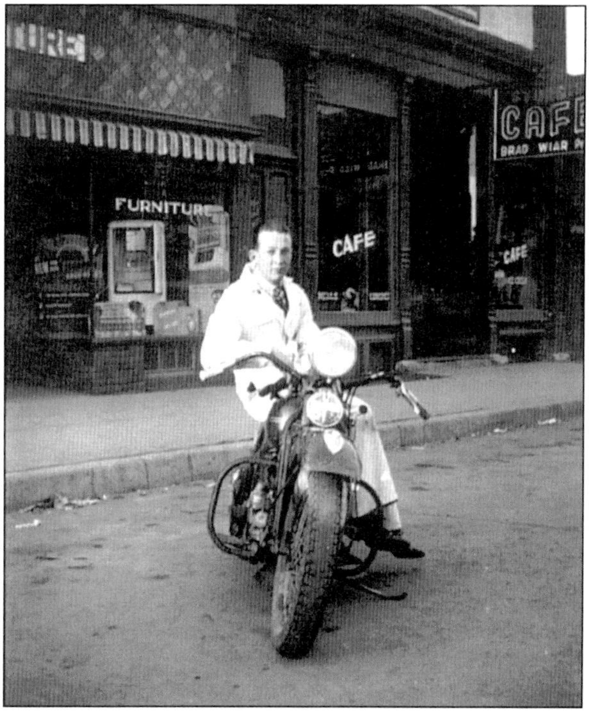

Rex Jerde sits on his motorcycle in front of the Sturgis Cafe, Brad Wiar, proprietor, and the H.O. Anderson furniture store at 1053 Main in 1939. At the time, two-wheeled transportation was beginning to be a popular trend in the Key City of Sturgis.

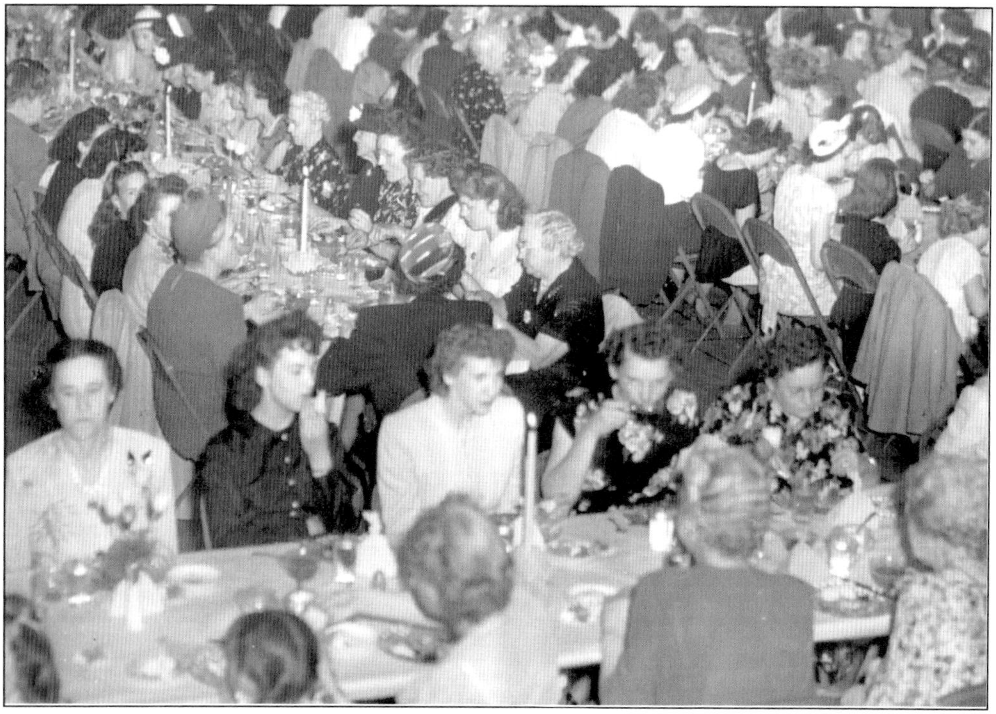

The Methodist church held its Mother-Daughter banquet at the city auditorium on May 24, 1949. Identified at the first table are: (back row) Doris Schryvers, unidentified, Marjorie Morrison Todd, Rebecca Morrison Buchanan, and Marie Morrison; (front row) Marianne Braden, Donna Braden, Marvell Braden Means, Mrs. Schweppe, and Mrs. O.H. Braden.

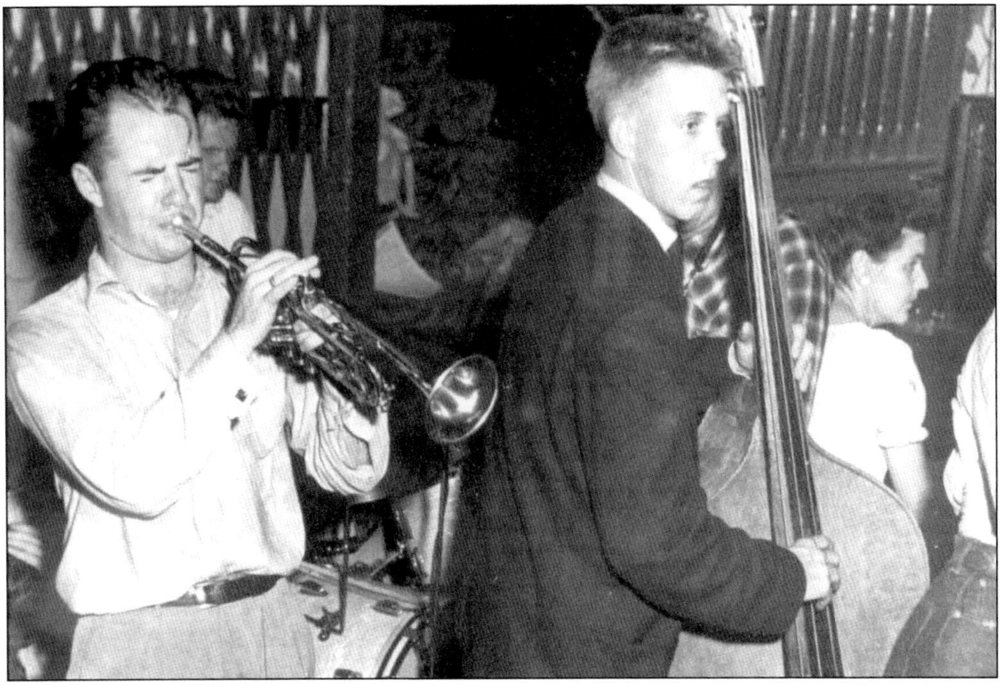

A local dance combo plays out in the late 1940s or early 1950s. That's young Bill Plunkett on the horn. Who are the others?

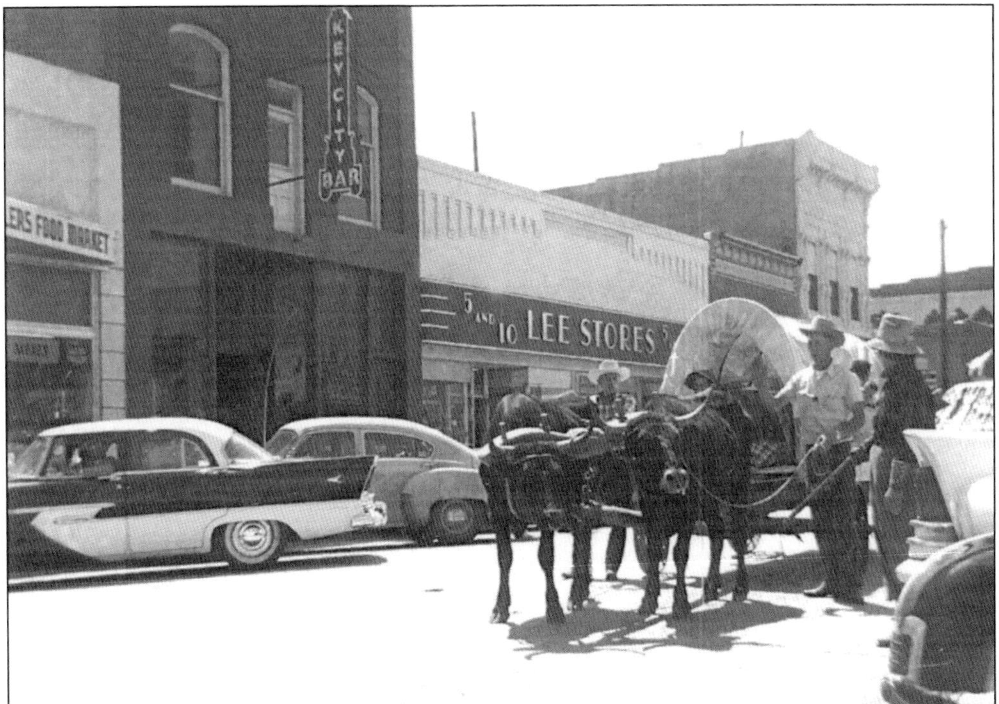

Heading down Main Street nearly a century after the first ox teams made their appearance, this group is drawing a lot of interest from onlookers.

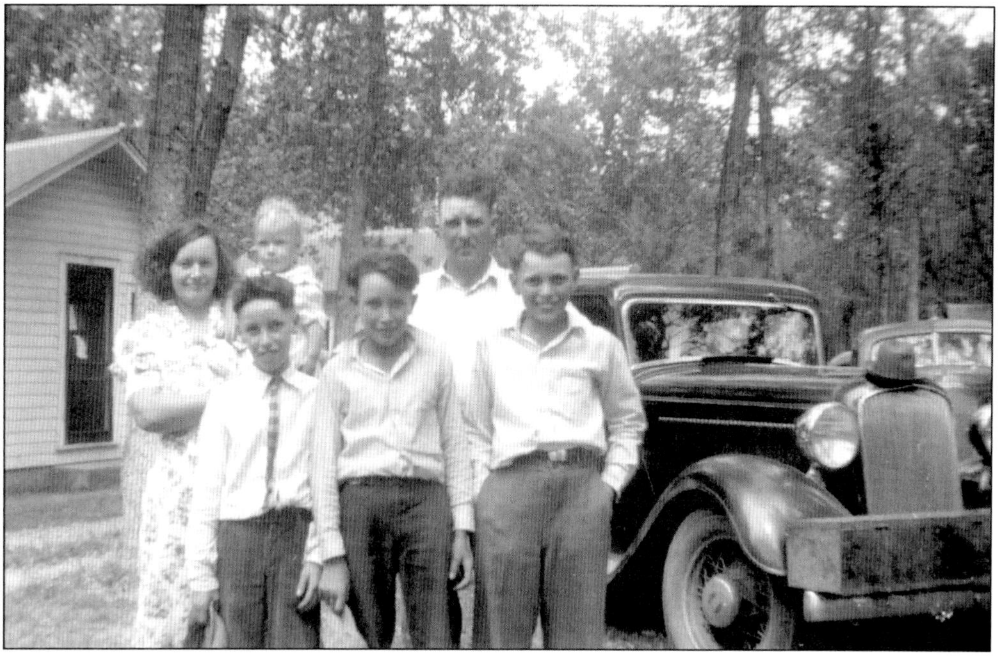

Ray and Fern Casteel and family are at Sturgis's city park in 1939. Vivian is the baby, and Clayton, Kenneth, and Eugene are standing in front.

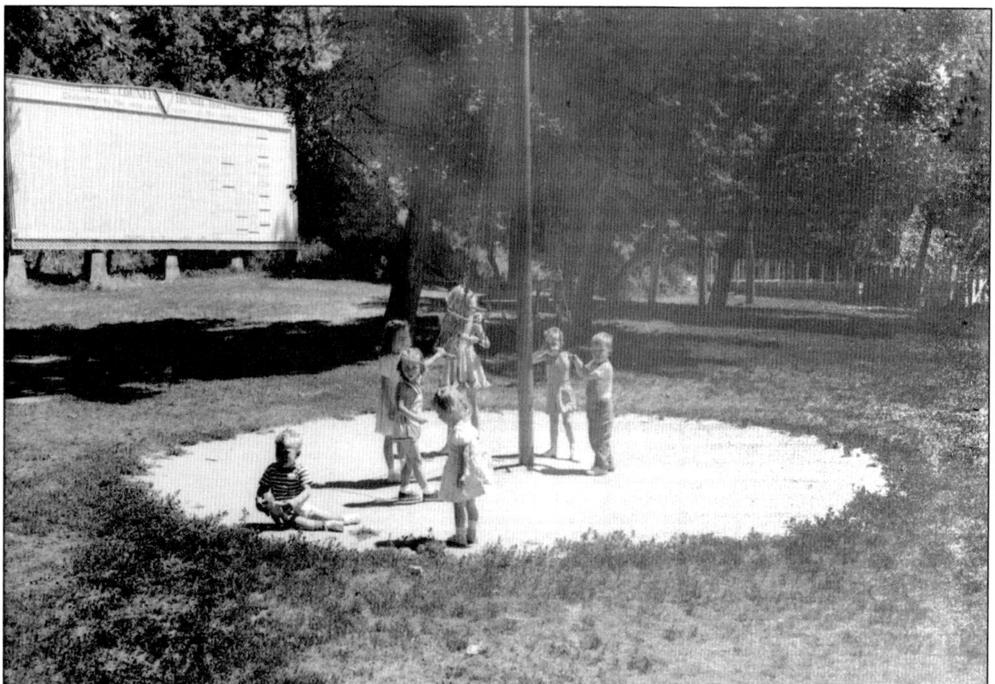

Children here are playing at the city park. It was known as Beatty Park and Bear Butte City Park in the early days, and it was here that Bob Cruickshank won medals for dancing the Highland fling at early Scottish festivals. The Meade County Honor Roll, in the background, is dedicated "to the men and women of the armed forces."

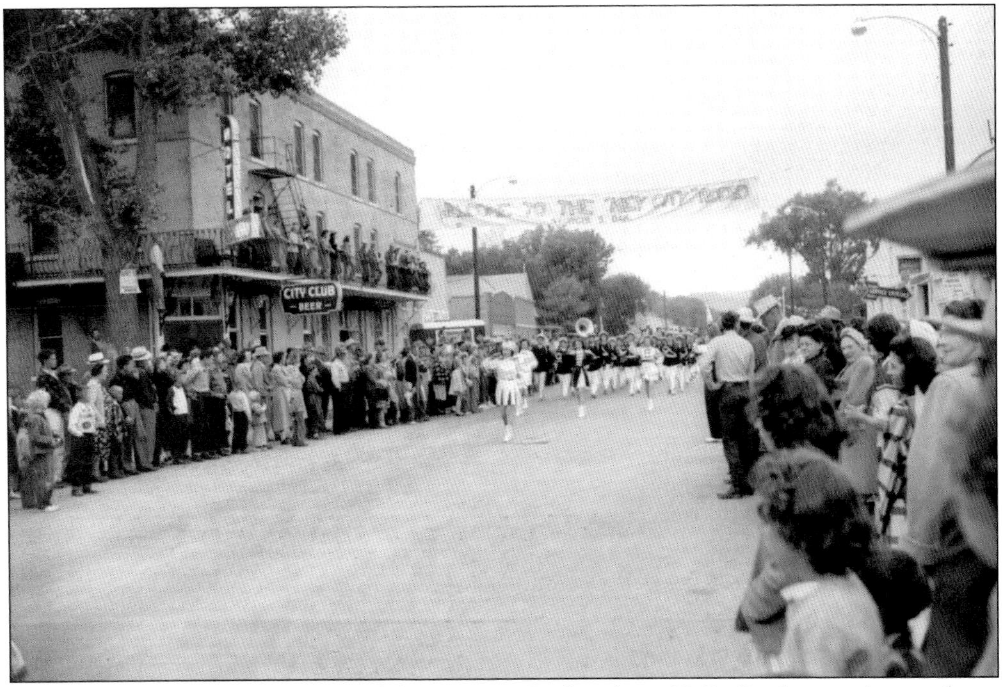

Another parade—this one is part of the Key City Rodeo about 1949. Cowboys and cowgirls are even on the balcony of the Fruth Hotel. The Tribby Chevrolet garage is at the right.

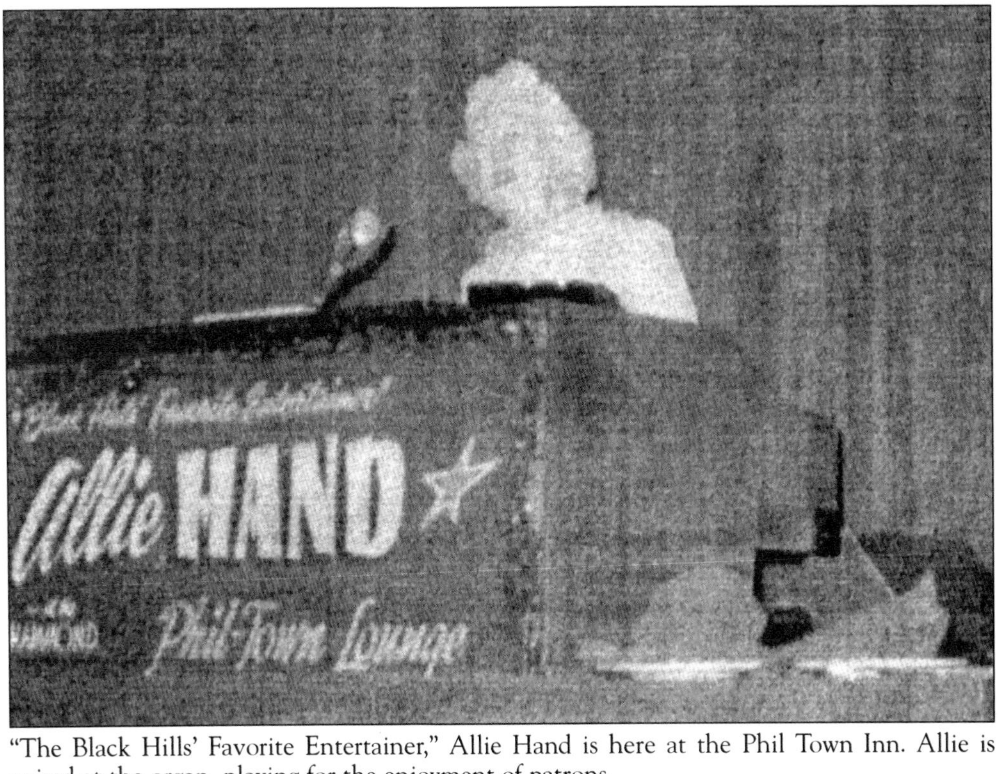

"The Black Hills' Favorite Entertainer," Allie Hand is here at the Phil Town Inn. Allie is poised at the organ, playing for the enjoyment of patrons.

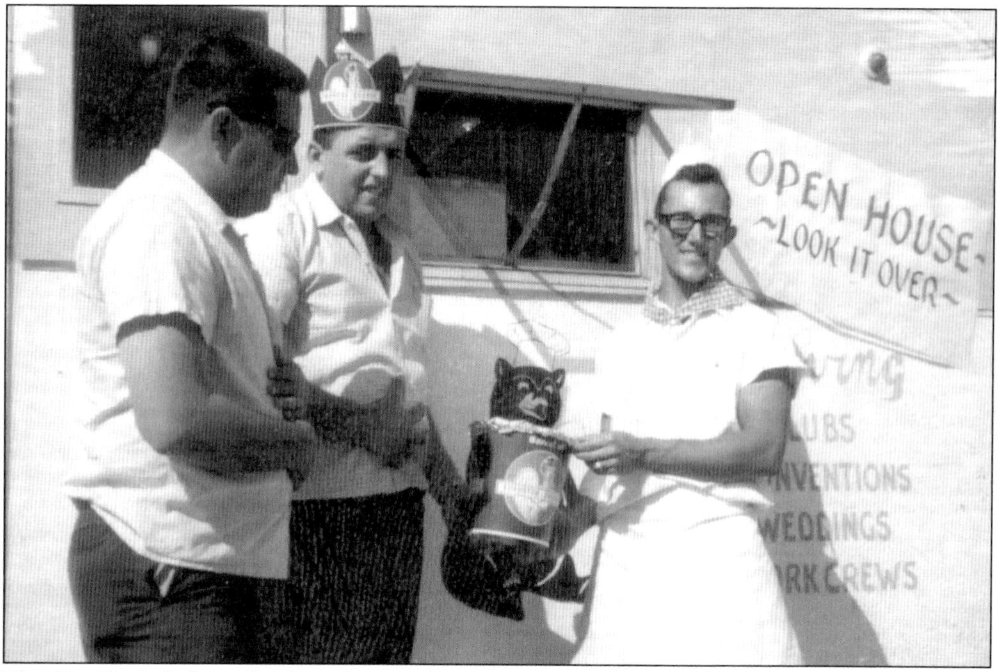

The Big Bear Cafe in Boulder Canyon has its open house. At left is Jerry McGovern, Ray Puckey—the "Sturgis Chicken King"— is wearing the hat, and Jim Forbes holds a bucket of fried chicken. Long before, "Chicken Thief Louie" St. Croix lived in a dugout outside of town and carried on the business of selling chickens to restaurants—but he never owned any chickens.

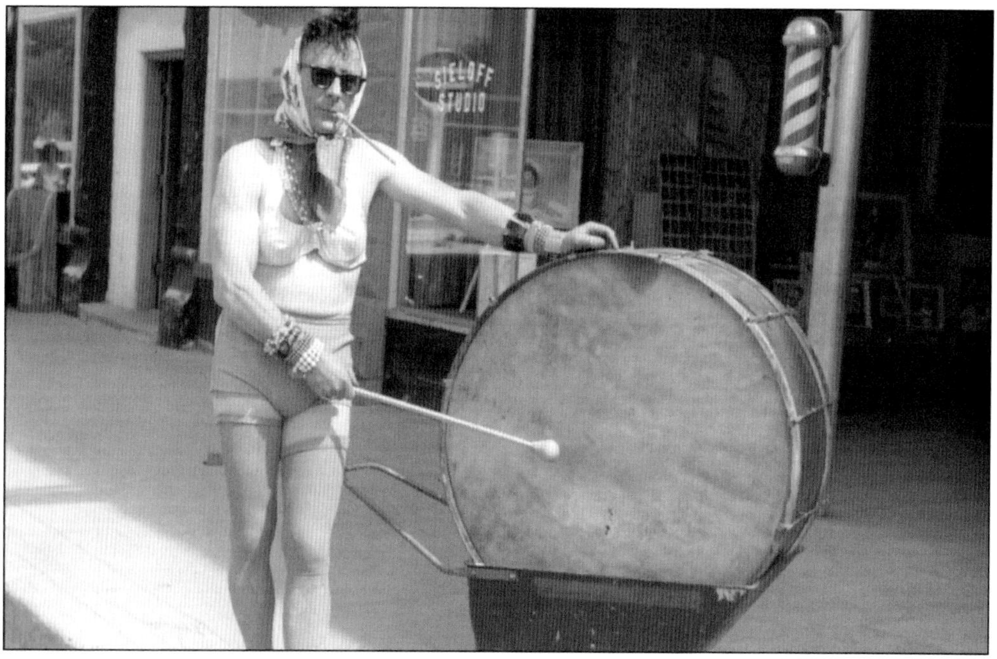

Bob Williams draws a little attention to himself and to the Crazy Days parade in 1954. The wardrobe is quite provocative—even by today's rally standards. Sieloff Studio is visible in the background.

Nine

Back at the Ranch

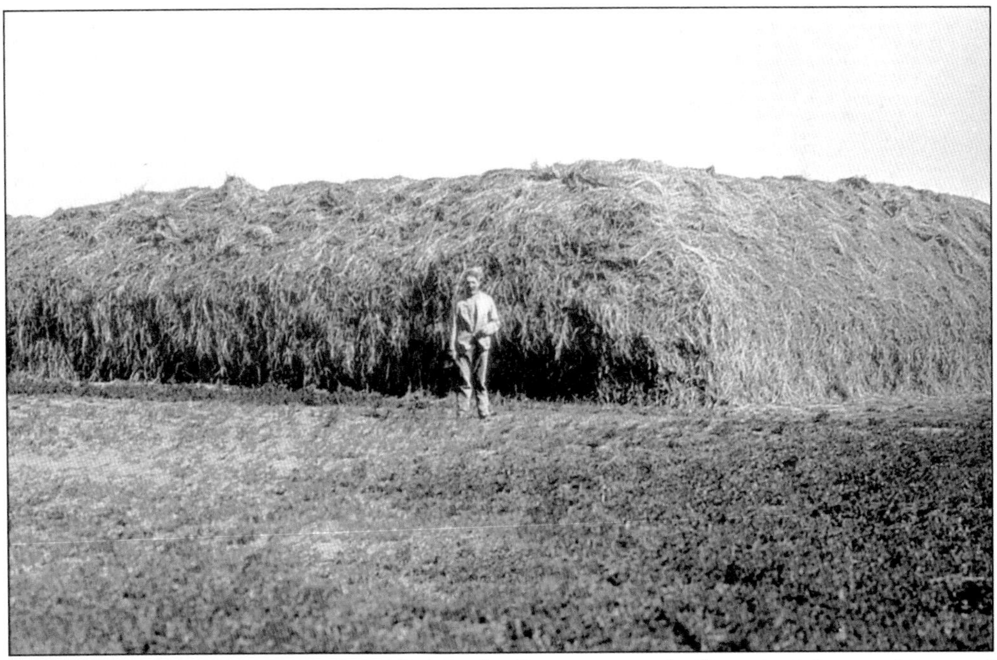

This hay stack photo is dated 1917. Meade County was ideally suited for ranching and agricultural pursuits, with Sturgis as the trade center. An early newspaper said on November 29, 1879 . . . " freighters have been flocking in for hay—sold for 75¢ per cwt."

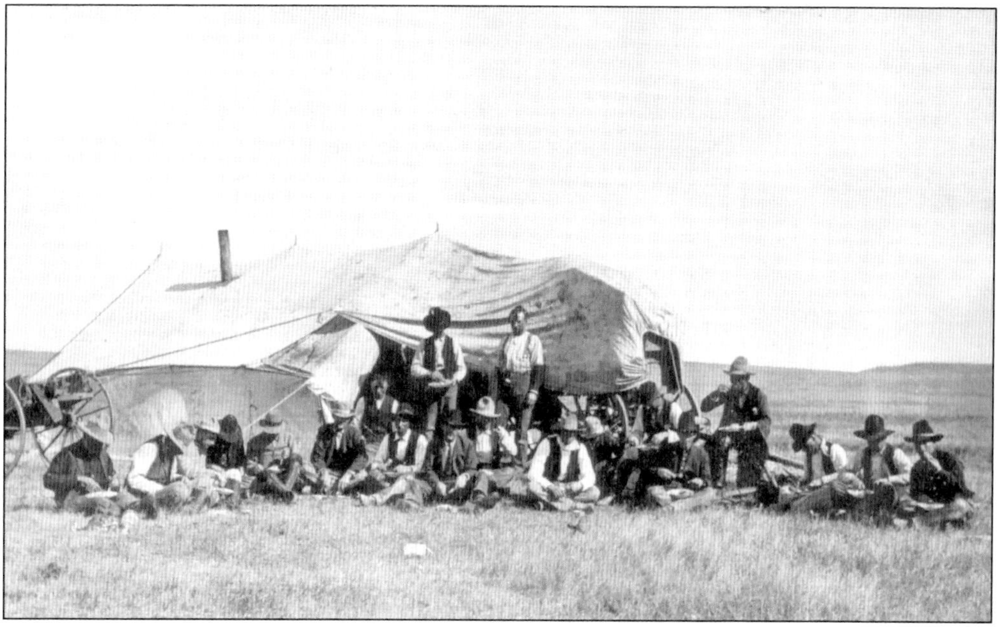

Roundups were an important part of a cattleman's operation. Stock was sorted, branded, and culled for market. The roundup wagon was a store on wheels that supplied the outfit with hardware, blacksmithing needs, feed, and extra clothing. The chuck wagon was a portable kitchen. This 1908 view says it is "the last Pool wagon."

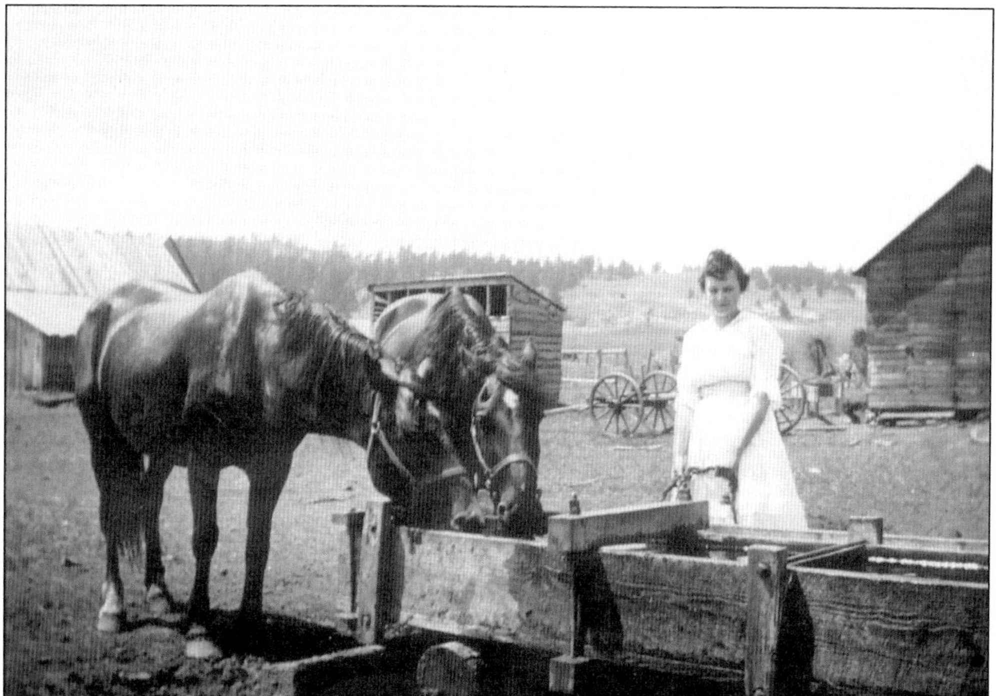

Fern Murray Casteel waters a sleek, matched team on the home place, located one mile west of town in 1918.

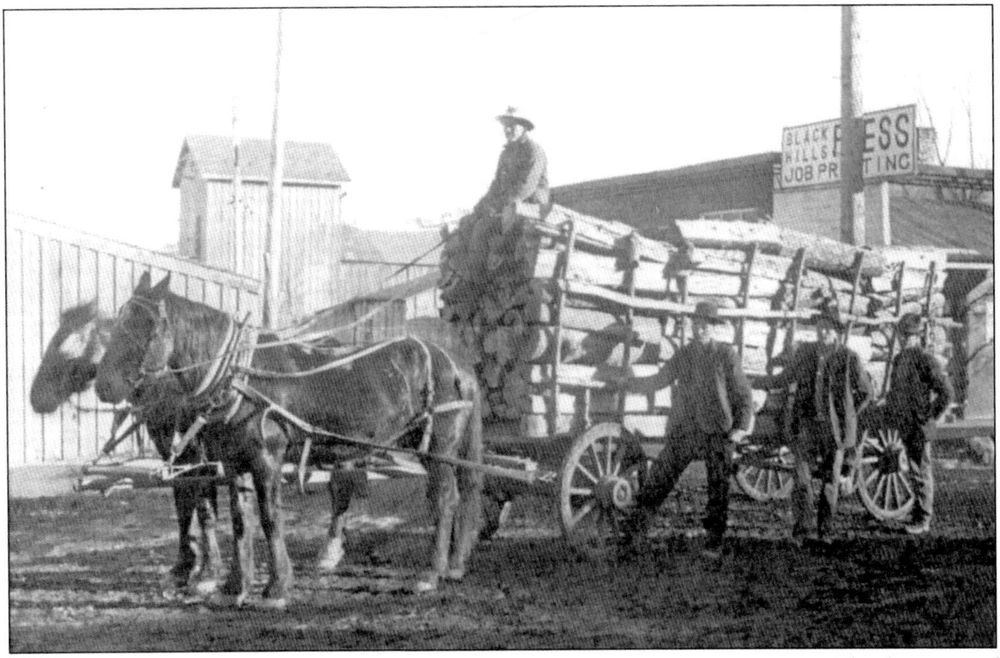

A lumber wagon is heading for the sawmill, probably in the 1880s–1890s. The logs are of different shapes and sizes, and were probably gathered from various sources rather than cut down. This photo was taken on First Street, between Main and Sherman. The *Black Hills Press* building is at right.

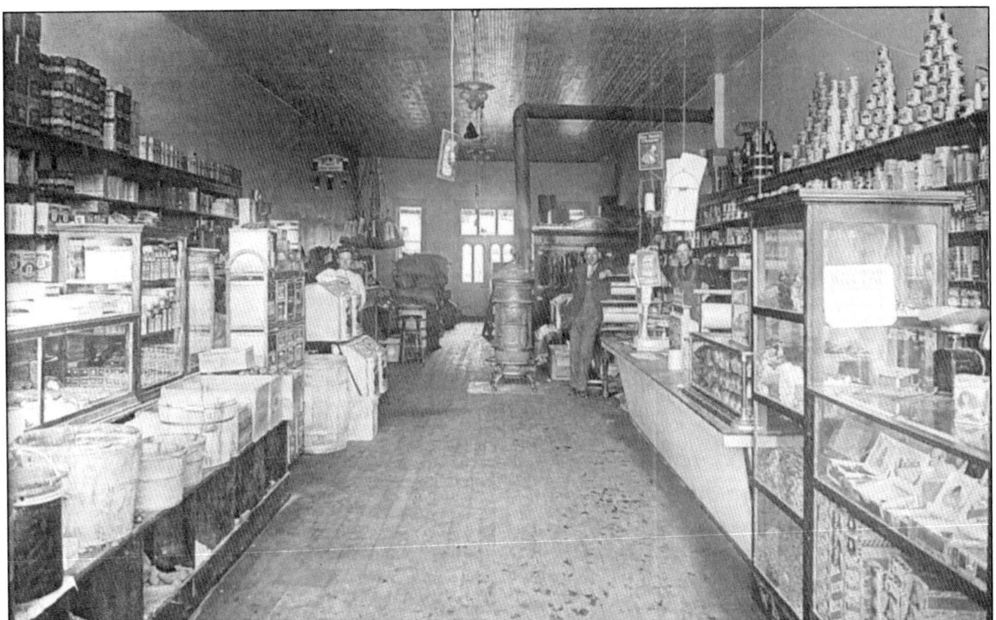
The general store was the forerunner of today's chain discount store. Shopping was done in bulk a few times a year by rural families and ranchers, necessitating large stocks to be kept on hand. Area farmers found a ready market here and took merchandise out in trade. Goods shipped from the East included stoves, beds, chairs, lamps, cloth, and tobacco. Note broom display at rear of store.

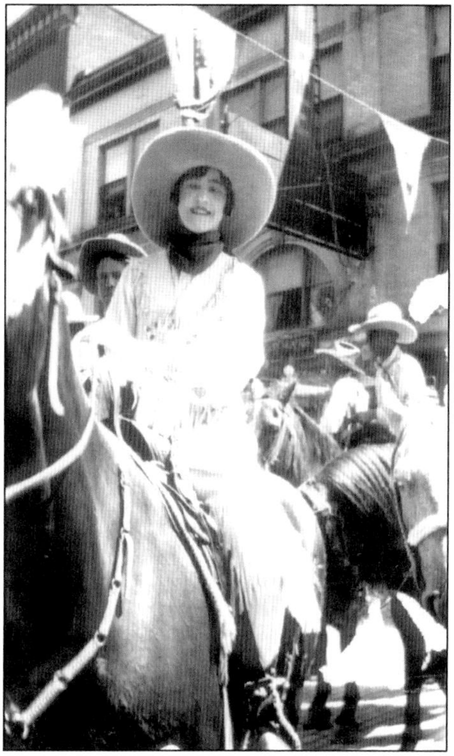

Mattie Goff Newcombe was a trick riding champion and darling of the rodeos over 80 years ago. As a girl she rode over the prairie like the wind and trained her own horses. With her husband, Maynard Newcombe, the couple ranched nearby for many years. Mattie still has her old cowgirl wardrobe, and it still fits her.

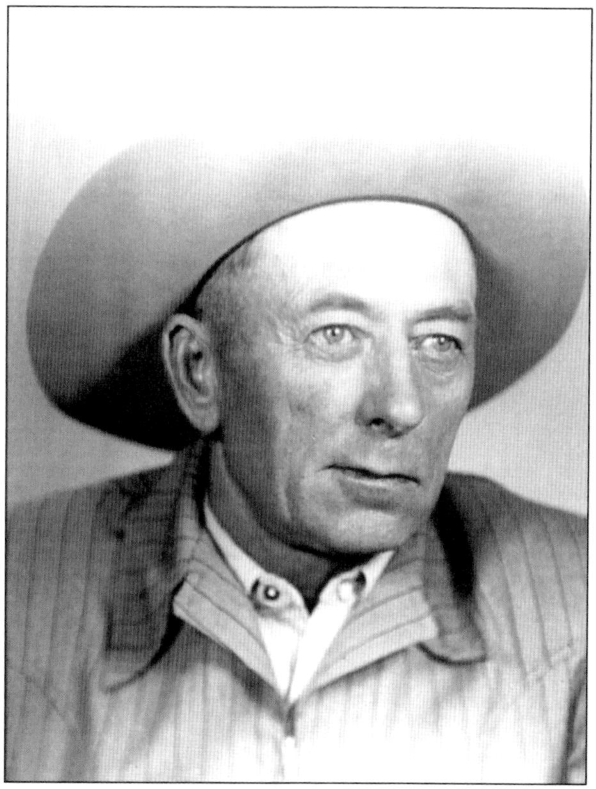

Candidate for sheriff E.M. Bowen looks like a determined fellow who could do the job, all right.

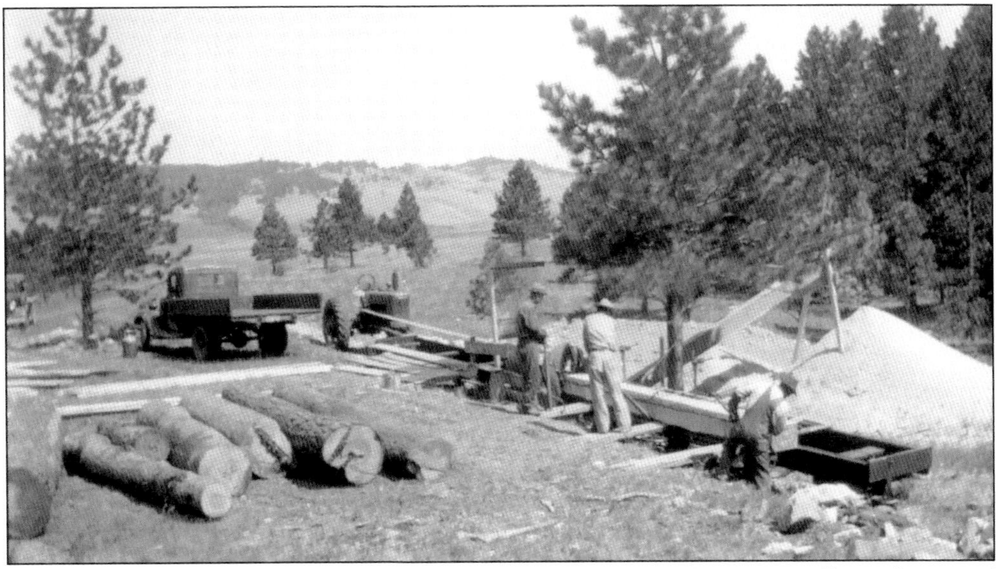

Many types of home-grown businesses flourished, like this sawmill. Sturgis Roller Mills, owned by George F. Earley, took first place and the gold medal at the 1893 Chicago World's Fair with his "Dewey's Best" flour. "Earley buys 40,000–50,000 bushels of wheat annually from Meade, Pennington, Lawrence, and Butte County ranchers," said the press. Earley's mill produced 75 barrels a day of his prize flour.

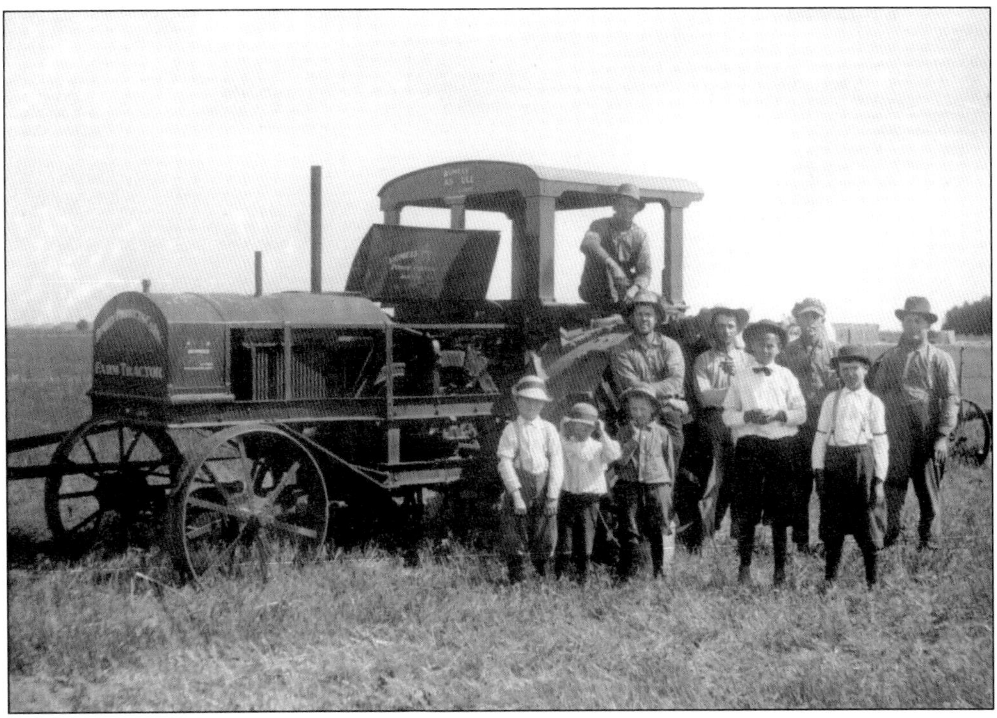

A Rumley farm tractor is seen here. The subjects aren't identified, but this is obviously a proud new purchase by a family or group of neighbors who plan to share the use of it for some time to come.

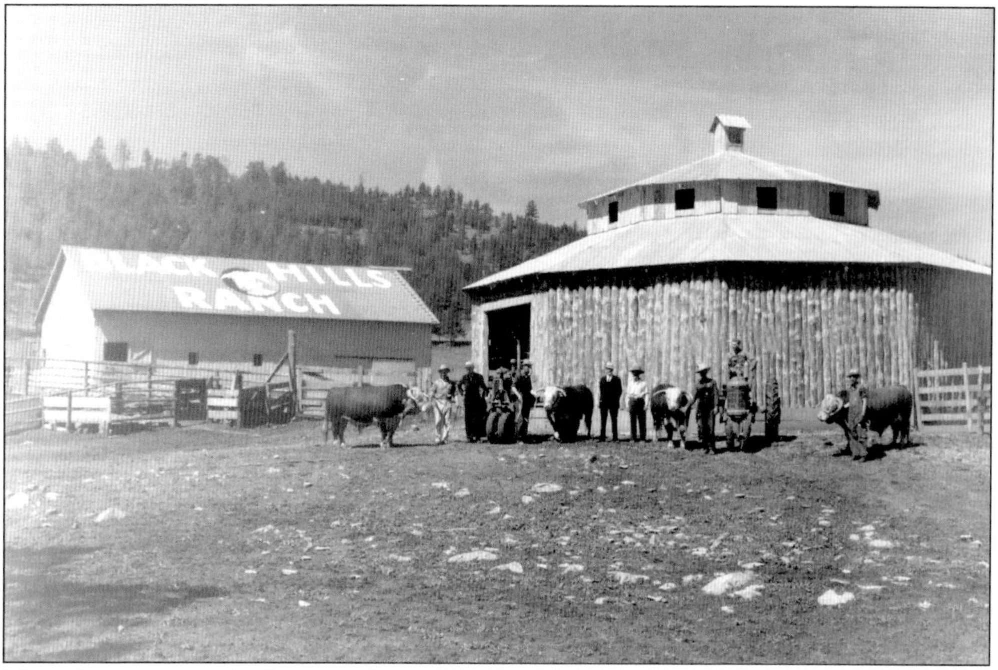

The information on this historic photo identifies "Blair Bros. round sales barn at Black Hills Hereford Ranch 1939." The unusual barn is constructed of vertical logs.

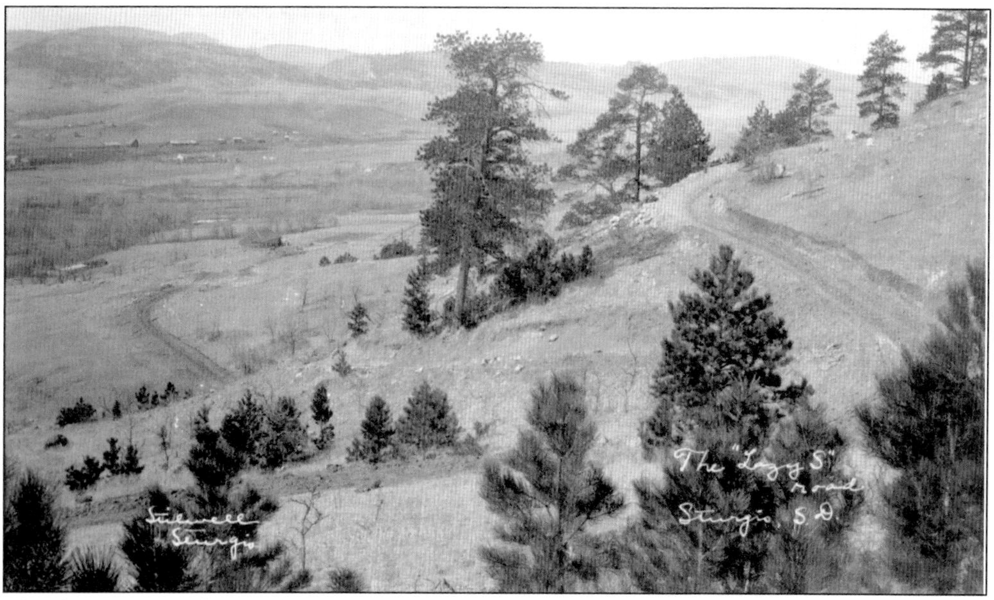

"On the Lazy S road," says this post card published by Stillwell cards of Sturgis. The road—even with its log-lined embankment—doesn't look like a fun place for a buggy ride after a rain.

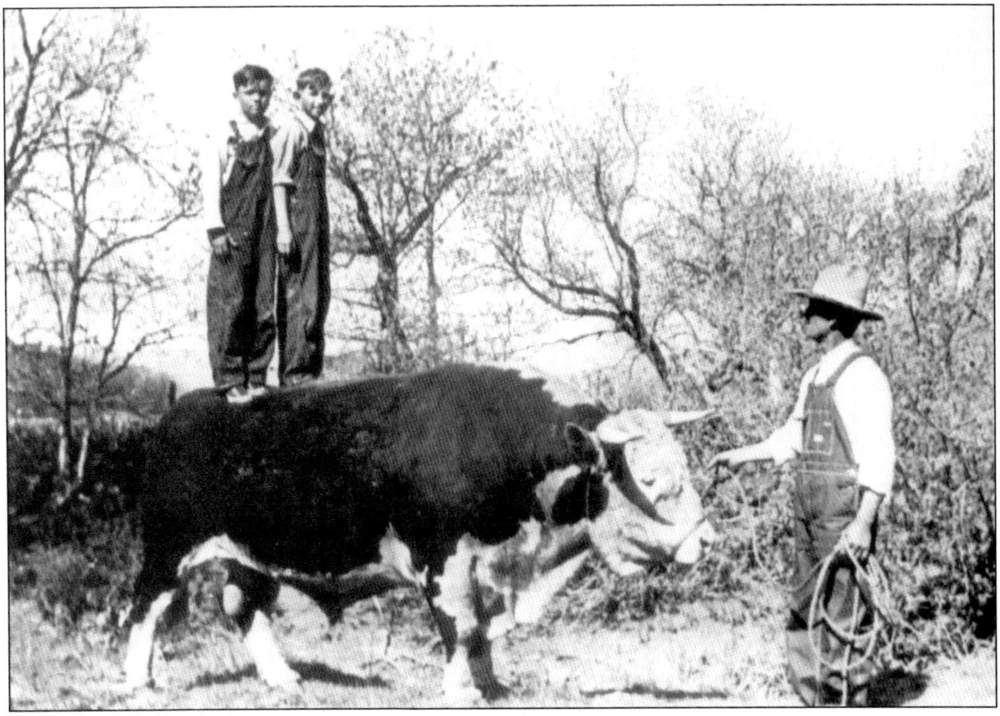

George and Veldon Blair on a prize Hereford bull held by Enos Blair. The bull is four years old in the picture and weighs 2,700 pounds.

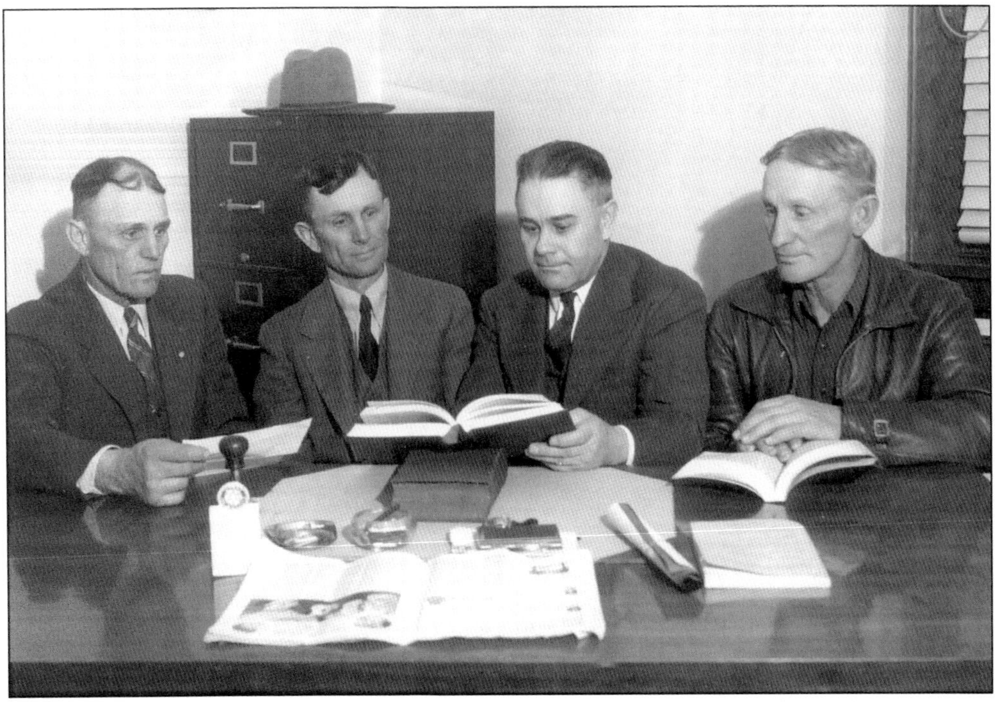

The Blair families were part of a ranching dynasty in the region. Shown left to right in 1942 are John, Henry, Strauther, and Enos. The portrait is by Taylor Studio, Sturgis.

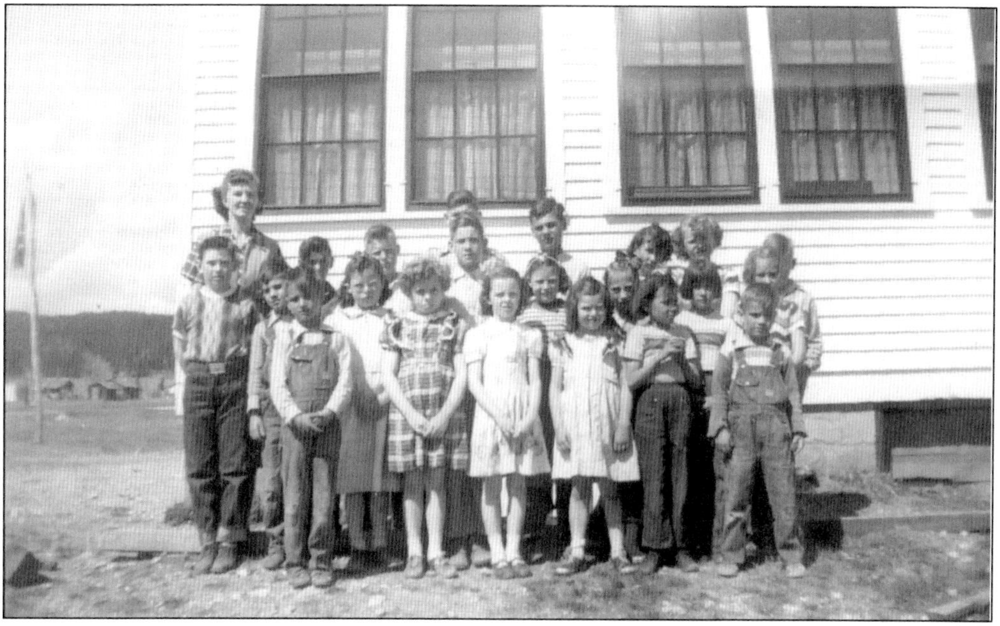

Tilford school is seen here in 1950–1951. Pictured are, from left to right: (back row) teacher Amy Hanks, Bob Pawlowski, Frank Goff, Sharon Haas, Darlene Crowser, and Jim Pawlowski; (middle row) Dale Snyder, Jack Crowser, Lloyd Dawkins, Tom Goff, Irene Weiers, Loretta Stetler, Dixie Crowser, and Betty Ann Haas; (front row) Wayne Goff, Fred Goff, Betty Weiers, Linda Blair, Ruth Dawkins, Angenette Snyder, Bonnie Crowser, and Gene Goff.

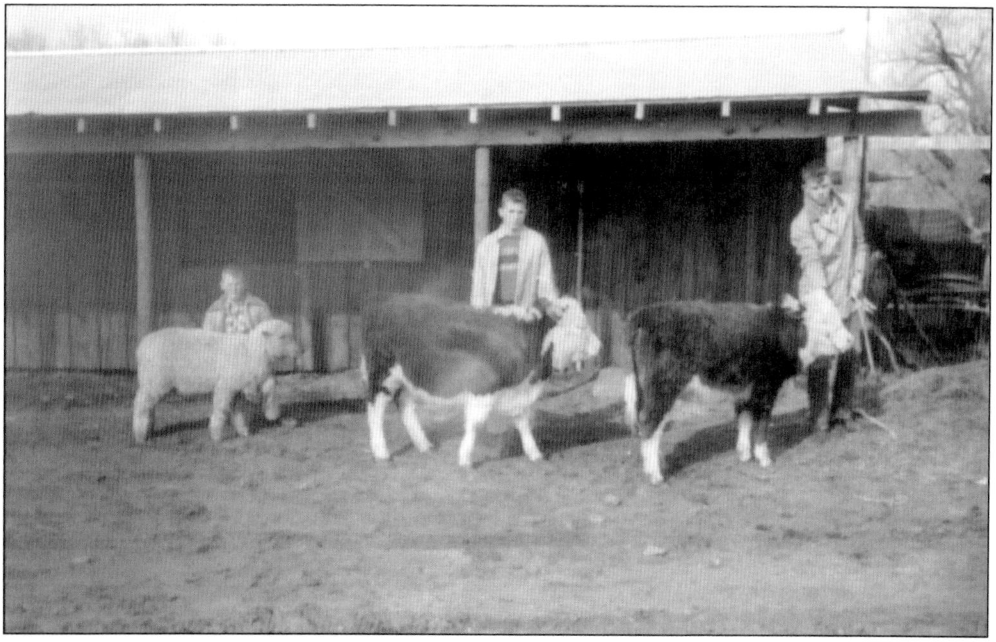

Pictured getting ready for the fair 1959–1960, Ross Lamphere has the sheep, and Dale (center) and Marc (right) are shown with their Hereford calves. Dale Lamphere has since gained world recognition for his bronze sculptures.

This photo shows Dean Snyder and Hereford "number 337," taken in 1955. A 1,000 pound steer at the time yielded about 342 pounds of meat, with the rest utilized in dozens of by-products. In pioneer days, the cattle market was strong for hides and tallow—the latter being used in candles before electricity.

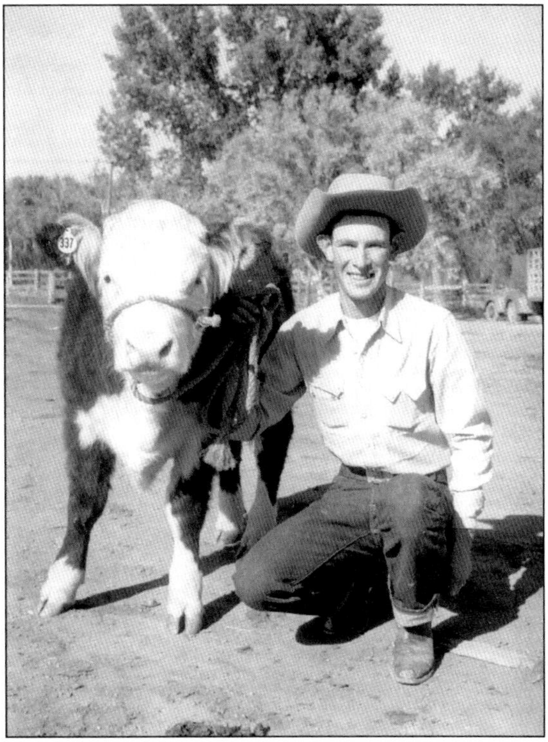

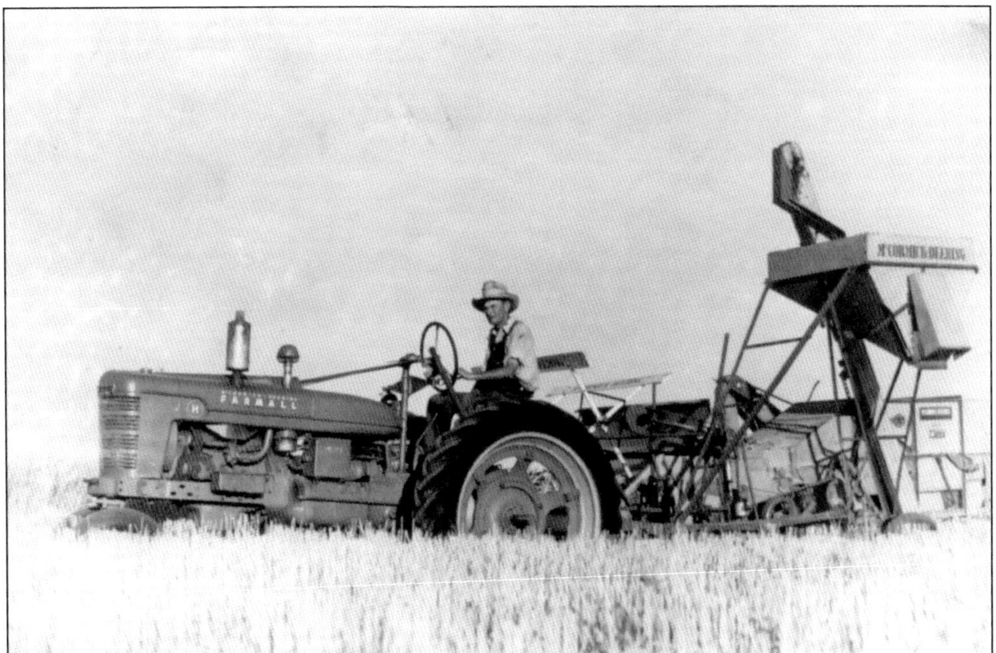

Clifford Snyder on his Farmall tractor, is here doing a day's work. In 1932, farmers organized to hold their wheat crops "until prices reached one dollar per bushel." "Present prices do not give the farmers the price of production," they said. The Farmer's Feed and Seed Company built a grain elevator in Sturgis in 1936, which remains a landmark to this day on South Junction Avenue.

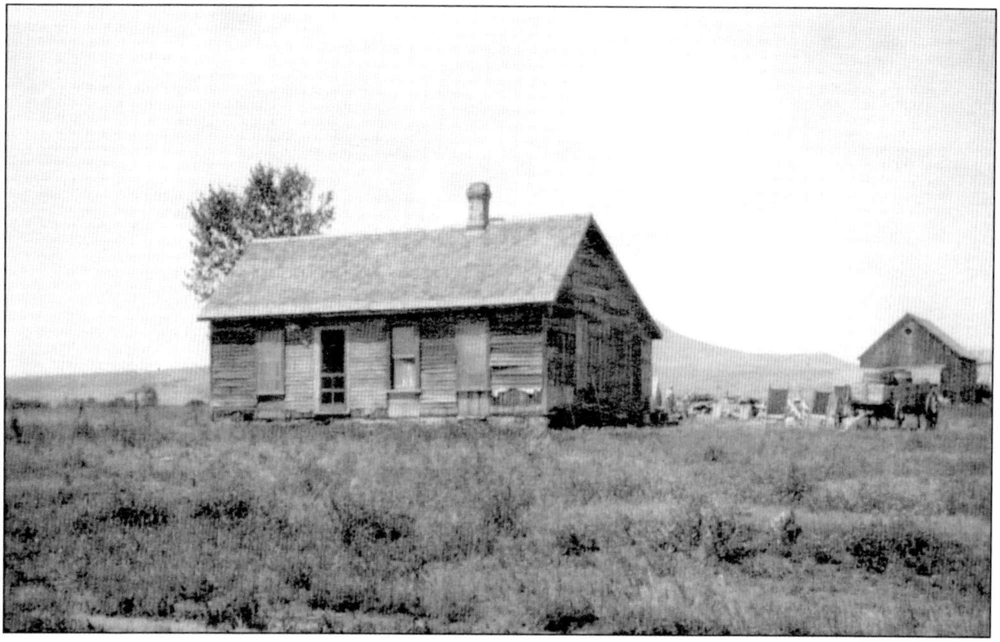

The Patton place was a typical homestead around early Sturgis and Meade County. The home was later remodeled by Hank and Helen Karrels, turning it into a modern and comfortable residence for many more years of use.

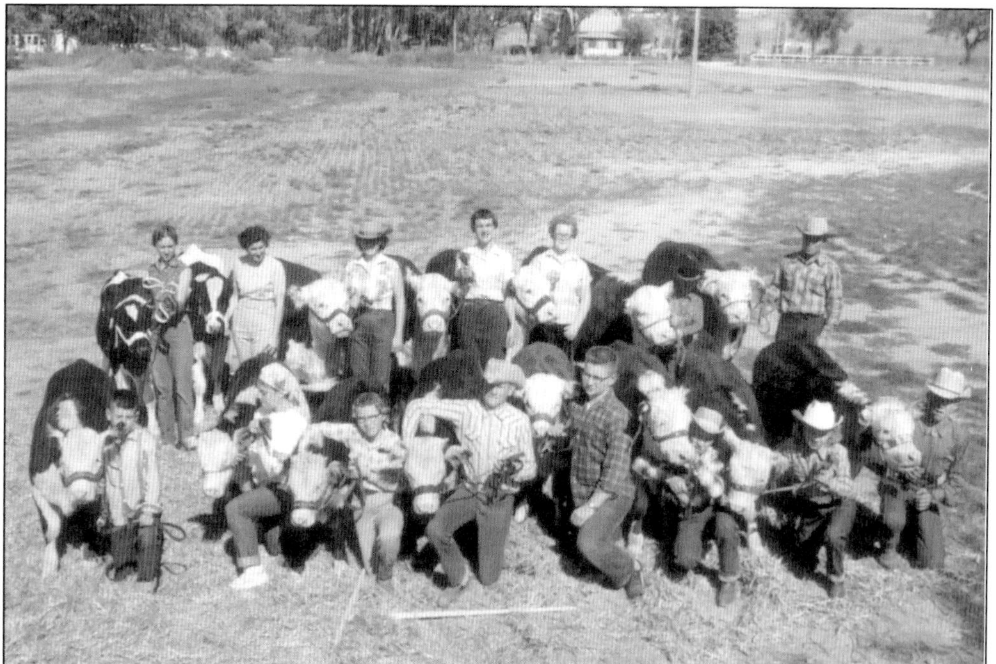

Preparing for the big 1958 calf show are these members of the Pleasant Valley 4-H Club. In the back row are Nancy Thompson, unidentified, Angenette Snyder, Jean Jordan, Joan Jordan, and unidentified. In the front row are unidentified, Linda Blair, Mary Bryant, Bob Jorenson, Dale Jordan, unidentified, Tootie Jorenson, and Gene Jorenson.

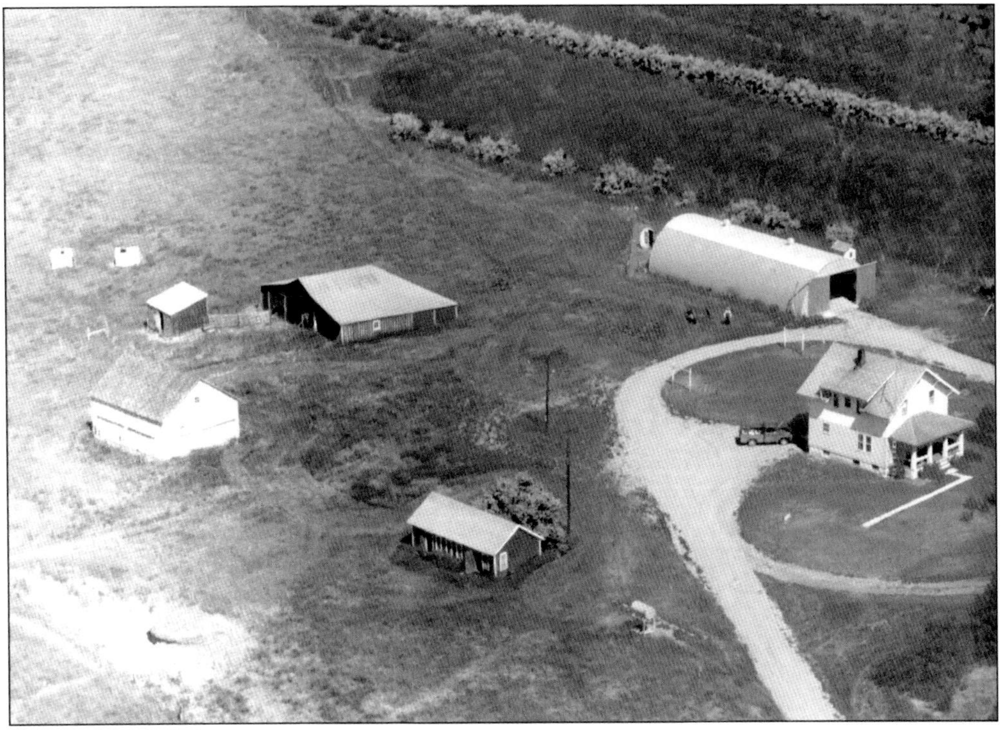

Howard and Thelma Mayer's ranch north of Sturgis on old Highway 79 in 1952. Oldtimers often blamed the end of cattle empires on barbed wire. In 1884, the *Sturgis Weekly Record* noted that "Thousands of dollars of stock are now being annually ruined by barbed wire." True, but it was also the loss of freedom that they missed.

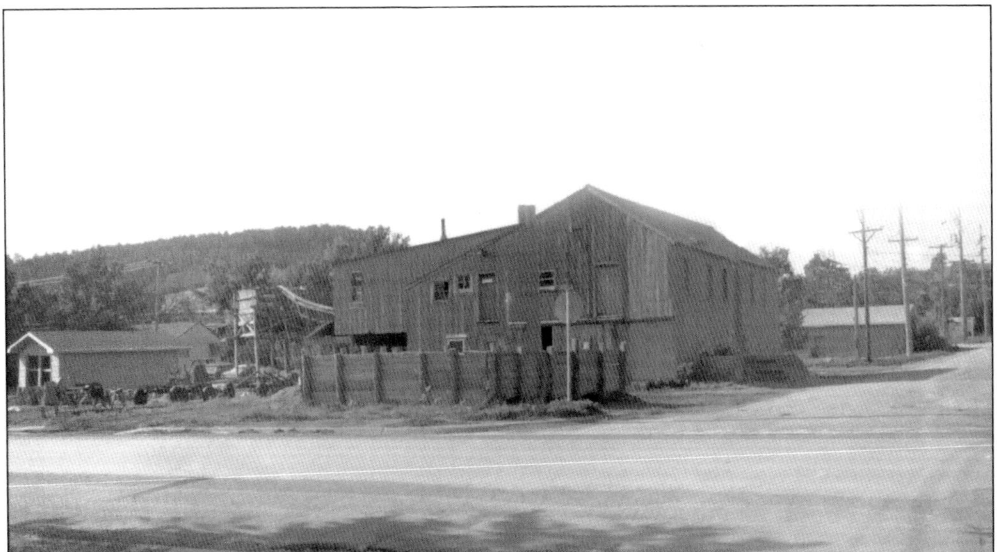

Grams' sawmill served several generations of customers and saw the town grow up around it. Founded by William Grams in 1883, the large building shown was erected at 898 Lazelle in 1938. The Grams did their own logging and hauling until 1967, when they began contracting this work to others.

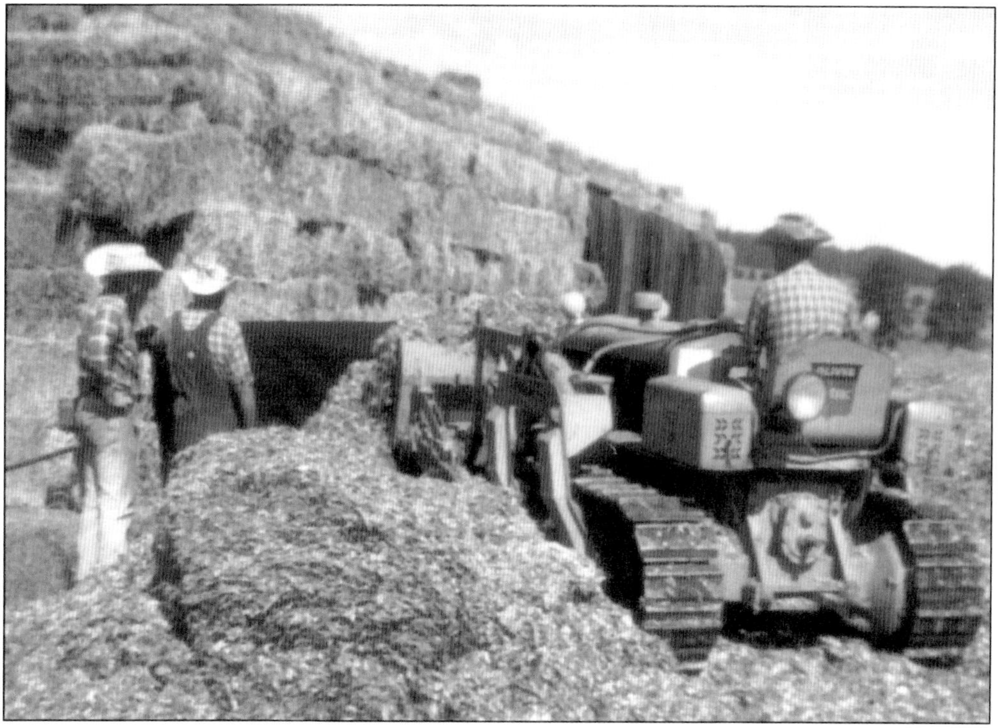

Making silage on the Snyder ranch is seen here around the mid 1950s. Bales stacked high will soon be converted to other uses. Grasshoppers caused havoc over the years in the county. Lottie Weihe Hooper noted that the hoppers "devoured everything including the horse" and then "pitched the horse's shoes to see who won the right to eat the collar."

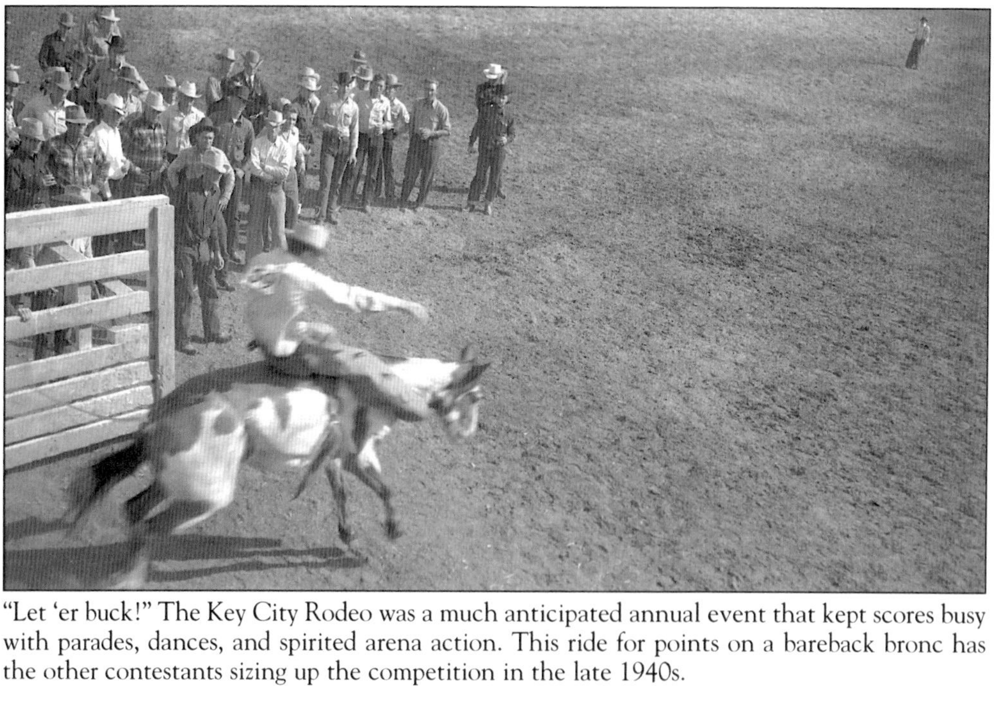

"Let 'er buck!" The Key City Rodeo was a much anticipated annual event that kept scores busy with parades, dances, and spirited arena action. This ride for points on a bareback bronc has the other contestants sizing up the competition in the late 1940s.

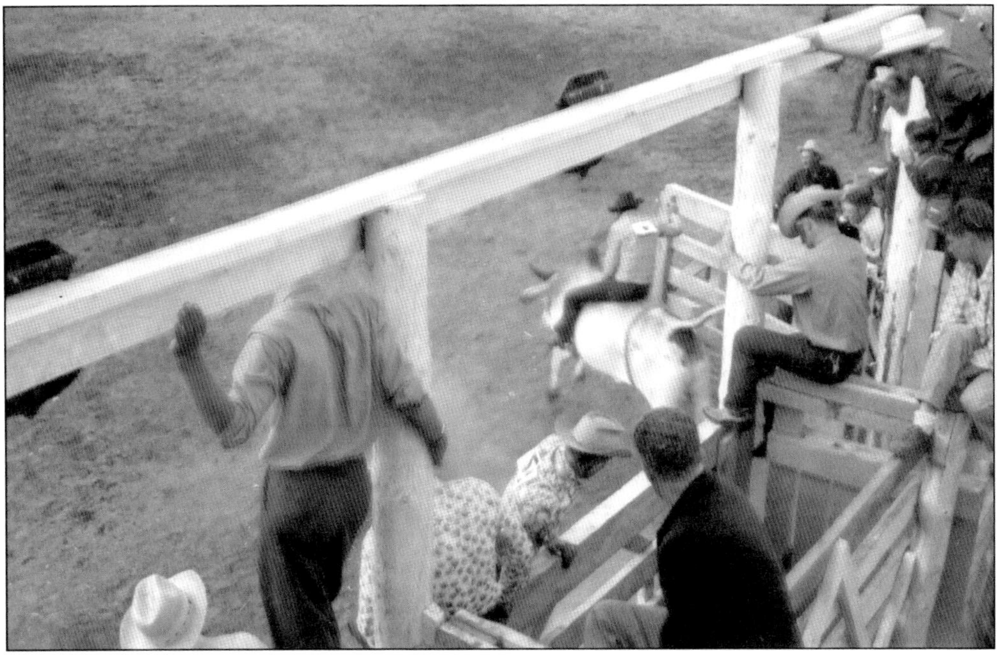

In rodeo, fence sitters are called "chute roosters." Riding a hump-backed Brahma bull is a very dangerous sport. Bullfighters, dressed as clowns, are deadly serious as they cavort around barrels to distract an angry bull that has dislodged his rider, allowing the latter to reach safety.

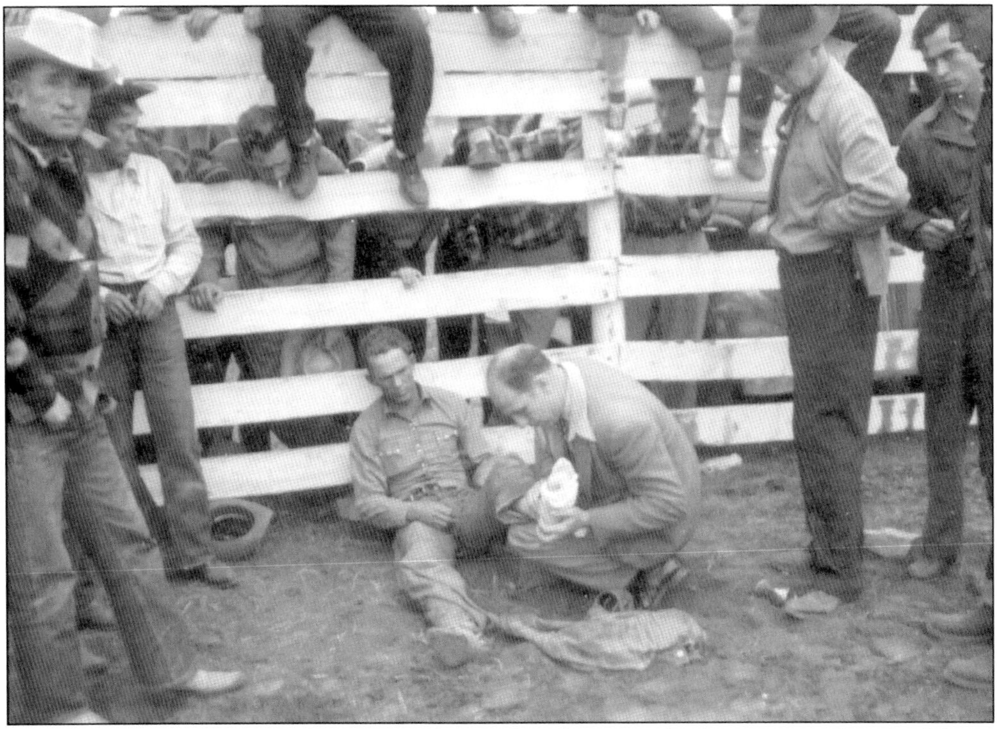

"Golly, that hurts!" The cowboy won't admit it, but those wrecks that come with rodeo life are just as painful for him as for any city dude who might have received the same injury.

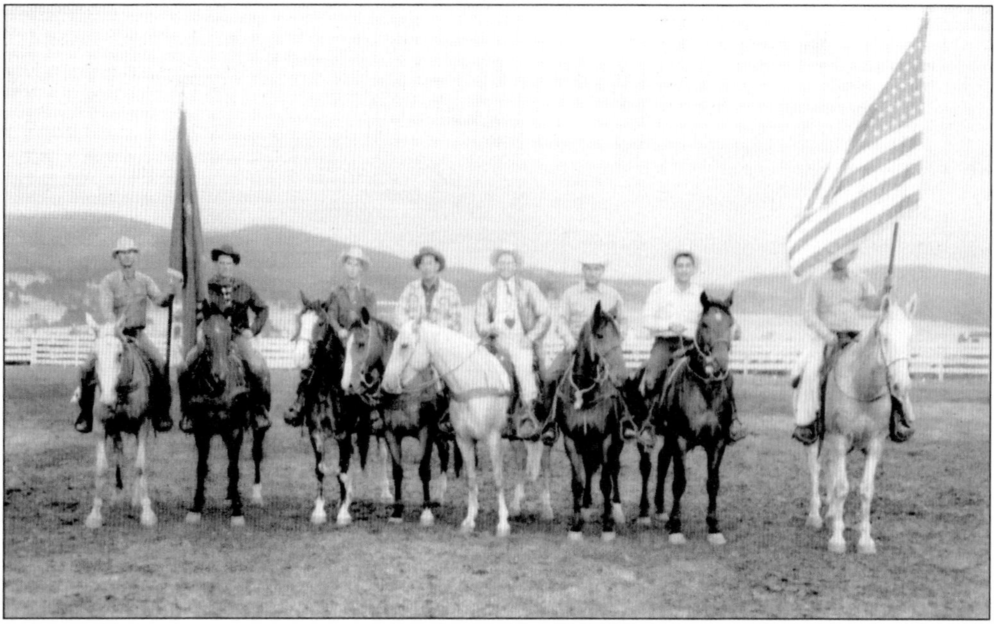

A good start for any rodeo is its grand entry of participants, and the presenting of the colors to the crowd. We wish we had an identification lineup for this great photo from the late 1940s or early 1950s. Perhaps someone you know is pictured here.

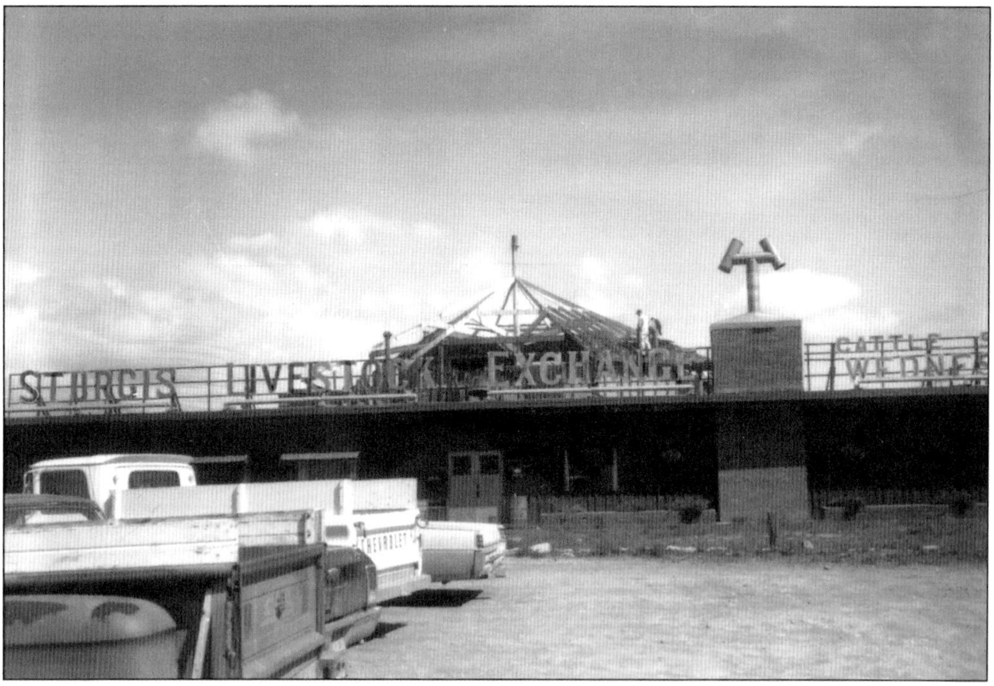

The Sturgis Livestock Exchange pavillion is seen here in 1959, owned by Harley and Jim Roth. Until recently, the sales barn held regular sales of cattle and horses, which drew buyers and sellers from a large area. A sign on the building advertises Wednesday cattle sales. The building has been razed and the property converted to other uses.